Japan and the European Union

Japan and the European Union

Domestic Politics and Transnational Relations

ATSUKO ABE

THE ATHLONE PRESS
LONDON & NEW BRUNSWICK, NJ

First published in 1999 by
THE ATHLONE PRESS
1 Park Drive, London NW11 7SG
and New Brunswick, New Jersey

British Library Cataloguing in Publication Data
*A catalogue record for this book is available
from the British Library*

ISBN 0 485 11556 5 HB

Library of Congress Cataloging in Publication Data
Abe, Atsuko, 1968-
    Japan and the European union : domestic politics and transnational relations / Atsuko Abe.
        p. cm.
    Based on the author's doctoral thesis, presented to Cambridge University.
    Includes bibliographical references and index.
    ISBN 0-485-11556-5 (hb)
    1. Japan--Foreign economic relations--European Union countries.   2. European Union
countries--Foreign economic relations--Japan.   3. Japan--Politics and
government--1945---Decision making.   I. Title.
HF1602.15.E9   A23   1999
337.5204'09'048--dc21
                                                                                                99-046722

Distributed in The United States, Canada and South America by
Transaction Publishers
390 Campus Drive
Somerset, New Jersey 08873

Typeset by Bibloset
Printed and bound in Great Britain by
Cambridge University Press

Table of Contents

List of Figures and Tables

Abbreviations

ACEA	Association of European Automobile Manufacturers
CCMC	Committee of Common Market Automobile Constructors
CEPS	Confédération Européenne des Producteurs de Spiritueux
CFSP	Common Foreign and Security Policy of the European Union
DG	Directorate General, European Commission
DTI	Department of Trade and Industry, UK
EBC	European Business Community
EC	European Community
EPA	Economic Planning Agency, Japan
EPC	European Political Cooperation
EU	European Union
FDI	foreign direct investment
FIVS	International Federation of Wines and Spirits
GATT	General Agreement on Tariffs and Trade
IPE	International Political Economy
IR	International Relations
JAMA	Japan Automobile Manufacturers Association
JETRO	Japan External Trade Research Organization
KK I	First Division of International Economic Affairs, the International Economic Affairs Bureau, Ministry of Foreign Affairs, Japan
LDP	Liberal Democratic Party, Japan
MAFF	Ministry of Agriculture, Forestry and Fishery, Japan
MFA	Ministry of Foreign Affairs, Japan
MITI	Ministry of International Trade and Industry, Japan
MOF	Ministry of Finance, Japan
MOT	Ministry of Transport, Japan
NCC	National Consumers Council, UK
NMUK	Nissan Motors UK
NTB	non-tariff barrier
OTO	Office of the Trade and Investment Ombudsman, Japan
SEA	Single European Act

SMMT	Society of Motor Manufacturers and Traders, UK
SWA	Scotch Whisky Association
TRC	Tax Research Council of Liberal Democratic Party, or of the government, Japan
VER	voluntary export restraint
WE I	First Division of Western Europe, the Asia and Europe Bureau, Ministry of Foreign Affairs, Japan
WTO	World Trade Organization

Japanese Terms

amakudari	'descent from heaven'; a custom of former bureaucrats to be recruited after their retirement from the Japanese government
anken-shugi	'single-issue-ism', or 'policy-making by improvisation'
gaiatsu	foreign pressure
gyokai	industrial sector(s)
jidosha zoku	automobile tribe
joryushu kumiai	Japan Distillers Association
Keidanren	Federation of Economic Organizations
keiretsu	group of firms that have close business relations via financing, personnel, technology, etc.
Nikkei	*Nippon Keizai Shimbun*, a Japanese economic newspaper
ohbeya-shugi	collective office mentality
sake	fermented rice liquor
shaken	Japanese MOT tests
shochu	spirits made of rice, wheat or sweet potatoes. They are divided into two categories, *kou-rui* (group A) and *otsu-rui* (group B)
shoko zoku	industry and commerce tribe
shuzo kumiai	Japan Central Association for *Sake* Producers
yoshu kumiai	Association of Wine and Spirits Producers of Japan
zaikai	big business circles
zeisei zoku	tax 'tribe' politicians, who are tax specialists
zoku giin	'tribe' politicians who are specialists in a specific policy issue

Preface

Nearly ten years ago when I first began studying Japan–EC relations, people were courteous to say that the topic was very interesting, but some more honest people, including my advisors, demanded a better reason to study. In their eyes, Japan and the EC were very important, but their relationship mattered little compared with the individual significance of either economy in the world political economy. Japan a decade ago was experiencing robust economic success, threatening US hegemony in some people's eyes. The EC, for its part, attracted much attention due to accelerated movement towards further integration. Economic transactions between Japan and the EC grew steadily. However, there were practically no important political relations or events that connected these two economic giants.

One of the benefits provided by international relations (IR) perspectives in analysing Japan–EC/EU relations is to conceptualize a bilateral relationship in the broader context of the world system. Bilateral relations cannot be totally independent of the development of the international political economy. A decade on since the end of the Cold War, a new framework, other than the traditional realism of IR, may be useful to see the multi-layered relations and transactions among actors of different levels.

Micro-level analyses on Japan–EC relations may reveal the limitations of traditional realism, which focuses solely on nation-state actors. The role of multinational corporations (MNCs) is, for example, an important aspect of Japan–EU relations, which the international political economy (IPE) emphasizes in viewing international affairs. The involvement of international organizations is also a significant factor in the trade conflicts that strongly characterize Japan's relations with the EU. In other words, the roles and implications of international organizations and other non-state actors need to be accounted for in order to see the whole picture of this bilateral relationship. For this purpose, a cross-level study that encompasses state and non-state actors would represent a solid framework for the understanding of relations between Japan and the EU.

Furthermore, the United States is a very important factor in Japan–EU relations, as structural IR would stress. Not only the United States' position in the international political economy, but also its special relationships with both Japan and the EU make it inevitable that Japanese and European decision-makers weigh the influence of the United States in dealing with each other. Including the US factor clearly makes sense from the perspectives of hegemonic stability theory and other systemic theories of IR.

The time frame of the following analysis is between 1985 and 1995, including the period when European strategy towards Japan changed. During this decade, the relationship between Japan and the EC developed from one of misunderstanding and relative indifference to one of greater cooperation. The development is particularly manifest in the business arena, supported by governmental endeavours to nurture Japan–EU bilateral relations.

Economic as well as political conditions in Japan have dramatically changed in the 1990s and especially domestic politics since 1993. The second half of the 1990s, therefore, likely provides quite a different context for Japan's relations with the EU. However, since the transition of Japanese political economy is still ongoing, it is difficult to predict, or even to grasp, the effect of Japanese domestic transformation on Japan's foreign economic relations, although a casual glance suggests continuity in foreign policy in general. This book does not attempt to look into this area, but focuses on the earlier period to view the dynamism at work in Japan–EC relations.

Furthermore the birth of the World Trade Organization (WTO) in 1995 is another very significant event in the relationship between Japan and the EU, especially in trade matters. The importance of international organizations is much discussed, but the issue of the WTO and its impact on Japan-EU relations will be a side issue here, since the book concentrates on an earlier period.

Following Japanese practice, surnames are given first, except in cases of Japanese scholars whose English-language works are cited and/or who observe the Western practice for themselves.

This book is based on my doctoral dissertation. I would like to thank those people who helped me through the long years of reading, interviewing, and writing. Dr Geoffrey Edwards was always supportive as a supervisor and encouraged me through the years at Cambridge.

I owe much to the people who permitted me interviews. Dr Hugh Whittaker and Professor Michael Smith gave me valuable comments and advice at the viva for my dissertation. Professor John Paden was most kind and helpful, especially pointing out the large difference between writing dissertations and books. I thank Ms Hilda Baker for her checking the whole manuscript to correct the style and language as well as for her comments. Also I would like to express my gratitude to Mr Brian Southam of the Athlone Press to give me an opportunity to publish my manuscript. All the help I received made it possible to accomplish this task, although I am wholly and solely responsible for any shortcomings of the book.

Introduction

It is curious that two of the biggest economies in the world, Japan and the European Community/Union (EC/EU),[1] independently attract so much attention and interest but are hardly discussed as a pair, whether to compare them or to see the relationship between them. Undeniably, they have had relatively distant relations with each other. A prominent vacuum in the studies of, and thin interests towards their relations derive from it being the weakest link among the three major advanced economies, namely the United States, Japan and the EU. This book aims to help understand this formerly neglected relationship from an international relations (IR) perspective. By doing so, in turn, the study of the Japan–EU relations suggests some important implications that contribute to the development of IR studies.

This historical overview indicates why Japan and Europe had so little political interest in each other, while reiterating the significance of their economic relations. In considering Japan–EU economic relations, Japan's relationship with the United States is useful to review as a standard model for IR analysis of economic relations. Japan–EU relations, however, require independent scrutiny from IR perspectives.

BRIEF OVERVIEW OF JAPAN–EU RELATIONS

Japan and the European Union (EU) represent two of the biggest economic powers in the contemporary world. In 1995, Japanese GDP was 5218 billion US dollars, the second largest after the United States, whereas the total GDP of the EU was 8407 billion, surpassing the US (United Nations, 1997).[2] Because of their economic size, they represent important trade partners to each other. Total trade between Japan and the EU in the same year amounted to US $114 billion. Not only does the economic scale convey the importance of their relationship, domestic manoeuvring in Japan, multi-layered administration and interest representation in the EU, and transnational business alliances suggest very significant characteristics of the Japan–EU relations. (The liquor tax dispute, discussed in Chapter 4, is a strong example of this.)

  While economic matters have almost totally determined their relationship, political and military matters have been quite negligible in their relationship. Historically, the inception of the European Community (EC) coincided with the economic and social recovery after World War II in Europe as well as in Japan. This period of post-war reconstruction kept a considerable distance between the two, both psychologically as well as geographically. During the economic boom in the 1960s and the bust in the 1970s triggered by oil shocks, Japan and Europe remained relatively indifferent to each other. For Japan, the United States represented the whole Western world, and its special relationship with the US – most importantly in terms of security and trade – occupied a large part of Japan's foreign policy. As for Europe, it lacked any organizational bonding with Japan other than wider, multilateral frameworks such as the United Nations, and the General Agreement on Tariff and Trade (GATT). Despite sharing a common security concern – the Soviet Union – Japan and Europe did not have any security framework to tie them together.

  Trade, as the most obvious form of economic transaction, defined the relationship between Japan and the EC. Trade in goods grew steadily between the two, while the trade imbalance was a constant bone of contention. The EC in the 1970s and 1980s provided a substitute market for Japanese exports in those fields in which Japan had faced export restrictions by the United States. Japan targeted selected industrial sectors – automobiles, machine tools, ball-bearings, office equipment, and VCRs – rather than exporting a wide range of goods. Consequently, Japanese manufacturers dominated the European market in those sectors. Therefore, the most controversial feature of Japanese exports to the EC until the 1980s was not the actual amount of EC trade deficit, but the concentration levels of such Japanese exports. This issue of concentration remained one of the most significant issues between Japan and the EC until the early 1990s.[3]

  The Nakasone government (1982–87) emphasized foreign policy more than its immediate predecessors, but even so its central focus was still the US–Japanese relationship, leaving little room for European issues (Osabe, 1987; Togo *et al.*, 1983). During the Nakasone period, accelerated by a worsening trade imbalance, Japan and Europe blamed one another for making too few attempts to understand the other. Nishio Kanji, for example, criticized Europe's general indifference to Japan in a series of articles in *Chuo koron*, one of the leading journals in Japan (Nishio, 1985; 1986). Europe, for its part, perceived Japan as arrogant, citing its protectionism and reluctance to respond to European complaints (Mendl, 1986: 89).[4]

In short, misunderstanding and indifference dominated Japan–EC relations until the mid-1980s. This phenomenon was partly due to the role of the United States in the world structure. Both Japan and the EC emphasized their respective bilateral relationships with the United States in their foreign/external policies, thus obscuring the importance of each other. It is important, therefore, to include the United States in perceiving Japan–EC relations.

In the second half of the 1980s, however, the EC no longer merely provided Japan a secondary market after the US.[5] Japan's interest towards the EC/EU dramatically increased since the Single European Market (SEM) programme (or the 1992 programme) launched in 1987. Prior to the programme, Japan's attitude to the EC was ambivalent, since the credibility of the European Commission (the executive branch of the EC) as an international negotiation counterpart, was often questioned. Coordination of trade policies among EC member states was far from perfect. As a result, the Japanese government tended to prefer dealing with individual member states, giving Brussels only a secondary role (Maull, 1990: 63).

Realizing the impact of the SEM programme, however, Japan changed its attitude towards the EC. The two most important implications of the programme to Japan were: (1) the programme made the EC the biggest single market, including the automobile sector; and (2) it increased European competitiveness in the international economy. While this large single economy encouraged Japanese producers to increase business with the Europeans, the European protectionism it engendered also alarmed the Japanese.[6] Driven by both business opportunities and a fear of 'Fortress Europe', the end of 1980s and the early 1990s found a rapid increase in Japanese foreign direct investment (FDI) into the EC. At the official level, too, the Japanese government indicated its anxiety over the exclusive effect of the Single European Market.[7]

Another reason for the sharp increase in Japanese investment in Europe was the steep rise of the yen in 1985. The strength of the yen enabled Japanese firms to launch FDI in Europe where investment costs had previously been too high. Although financial services were the major area of investment, FDI in the manufacturing sector also increased rapidly (Thomsen and Nicolaides, 1991: 10). As the economic transactions developed between them in the 1980s, academic works also flourished – often by economists – investigating trade and investment between Japan and the EC (Balasubramanyam and Greenaway, 1992; Hanabusa, 1979; Heitger and Stehn, 1990; Ishikawa, 1990a; R. Strange, 1993; The Long-Term Credit Bank of Japan, 1990: 25–32; Micossi and Viesti, 1991; Shigehara, 1991; Thomsen and Nicolaides, 1991; Yoshitomi, 1991).

Europe gradually shifted its strategies in the 1980s, in response to the Japanese trade surplus. While anti-dumping procedures and other policies preventing excessive imports from Japan remained at work, the EC began to emphasize Japan's closed market to European products and services as one of the most significant problems between them.

In terms of Japanese investment, European governments actively rather than passively facilitated this inflow of Japanese capital. Rather than leaving decisions entirely to industrialists, some national and local governments in Europe played a significant role in encouraging Japanese manufacturing FDI in their regions. Such involvement was particularly visible in areas where the local economy had been struggling in industrial downturn.

In contrast to Japanese FDI in Europe, European direct investment in Japan remained relatively small. This imbalance in FDI paralleled the trade imbalance between Japan and the EC, compelling European criticism of the closed nature of Japanese markets – not only for trade but also for inward foreign investment. The Japanese domestic system greatly hindered, if not totally inhibited, foreign penetration.

In this respect, Japan–EU economic relations were highly comparable with Japan–US relations. European and American criticisms of Japanese economic practices were often similar, accusing Japan of being a mercantilist state.[8] Many Europeans and Americans agreed that the Japanese market was protected against imports to a very high extent by the structure of the Japanese economy and society as well as by the government (Nester, 1991; Prestowitz, 1988; Jackson, 1993). The Japanese government, on the other hand, disagreed, citing the lower level tariffs on most products than other industrialized countries (Tsusho sangyo sho, 1992). Since non-tariff barriers were recognized as more important than tariffs under the current environment for world trade, arguments between Japan and its trade partners shifted from formal trade barriers to non-tariff barriers and other domestic structures that determine Japanese political economy.

While each one's economic presence conveys significant meaning to policymakers, including business leaders, the lack of political ties has been a constant feature in Japan–EC/EU relations.[9] Although Japanese exports had raised suspicions among European manufacturers and governments in the 1970s, only in the 1980s did economic transactions between the two begin to concern policymakers, thus politicizing their relationship. Even then, their respective political elite and policymakers displayed relatively little interest in the other. Some suggested that this political indifference effectively made the EC's economic friction with Japan more difficult to overcome than Europe's friction with the United States (Tsoukalis, 1991: 266–7).[10]

In Japan, European issues tended to be obscured by the more prominent American presence, politically as well as economically and culturally. This is particularly clear in comparing the amount and depth of literature on this subject. Even at the height of the 1992 programme fever, European issues never totally replaced US topics in Japanese journals and newspapers.

JAPAN'S RELATIONSHIP WITH THE UNITED STATES –
AS A STANDARD MODEL FOR IR ANALYSIS
OF ECONOMIC RELATIONS

Despite increased economic transactions in the last two decades, the relationship between Japan and the European Union has not matured to the level of Japan–US relations or EU–US relations. In acknowledging the US, Japan and EU as the three biggest economies in the world, one could reasonably deduce that relationships among economies of similar size and levels of development would well follow similar patterns. But so far, there is no evidence of the symmetrical development of Japan–EU relations. This fact raises an interesting question why Japan–EU relations have not deepened as Japan-US relations have, making this comparison meaningful.

The major difference between Japan–EU relations and Japan-US relations is that Japan-US economic issues can be linked to security issues, as trade-offs, due to the fact that Japan depends on US military umbrella for its national security.[11] In other words, foreign economic policymaking cannot be separated from other policy areas.

The relationship between Japan and the United States has been analysed extensively in light of various IR theories. In the context of the structural change of the international political economy, Japan-US relations and Japan's role in multilateral international relations attracted the attention of numerous academics. These two issues are closely connected, and it is impossible to discuss them separately. Japan's relationship with the United States has been an indispensable factor in arguing what role Japan should or will have in international politics and the political economy. Robert Cox, for example, examined Japan's function in a future world order from the perspective of Japan as a middle power despite its economic strength and capabilities (Cox, 1989; Gilpin, 1990; Vogel, 1992; Johnson, 1992b; Nye, 1993; Van Wolferen, 1991).[12] Many suggested a corollary argument to his, that instead of overtaking the US as a leader, Japan would support and share the burden with the US (Rosecrance and Taw, 1990; Johnson, 1991; Maswood, 1989). While the end of the Cold War made Americans revise their security alliances, the Japanese–US alliance remains one of the main pillars of American security policy (Destler and Nacht, 1991). The current economic crisis in Japan and wider Asia since 1997 has shifted the focus of the debate from Japan's 'international' role *per se* to Japanese domestic reform. Now that Japan seems to have too much trouble at home to take a lead in the global political economy, the once-popular debate on Japan's international role has more or less faded.

Trade conflicts between Japan and the US, however, have been given at least as much attention as security issues by both Japanese and American policymakers and analysts. Consequently, some studies focused on the structure of Japan's political economy, foreign economic policy and decision-making as keys to conflict resolution. On top of numerous articles in newspapers, journals, and magazines, journalists have also written a large number of books on the issue.[13] Government officials have also provided commentary on trade negotiations (Yabunaka, 1991). As for academics, various approaches have been taken to handle Japan–US economic relations. Economic analyses may have predominated,[14] but there have also been a growing number of policy-oriented analyses based on frameworks developed in the IR/International Political Economy (IPE) disciplines in order to deal with the question of Japan's foreign economic policy.

Examples of such analyses include the textile negotiations between 1969 and 1971 (Destler, Fukui and Sato, 1979; Otake, 1979), those involving semiconductors in the mid-1980s and the Structural Strategic

Impediment negotiations (H. Sato, 1991).[15] In order to analyse trade disputes, these studies focused on Japan's foreign economic policymaking, analysing how the determinants of governmental decision-making influenced international negotiations. Throughout these works, the significance of domestic politics in foreign economic policymaking was emphasized. One analysis even declared that the domestic politics of the US and Japan were the most significant determinants in their trade negotiations since 1945 (Sato H., 1991). Such works provide useful guidelines in this book to look into domestic decision-making process in foreign economic policymaking.

Simply concentrating on domestic politics is, however, insufficient to analyse foreign economic policymaking. On one hand, the two-level approach of IR combines domestic and international factors within international negotiations.[16] On the other hand, the transnational approach includes non-state actors such as interest groups and multinational corporations that bridge domestic and international arenas.[17] Nagao, for example, employs the transnational approach in the case of the beef and orange trade negotiations between Japan and the US that terminated in 1988, analysing the influence of farmers' associations on policymakers (Nagao, 1990). Analyses like these clearly convey the importance of transnational actors and interactions between domestic and international politics, giving insight into the process of Japan's foreign economic policy, whether it is directed to the United States or to the European Union.

Transnational approaches used in the analysis of Japan–US relations have further implications that would assist the understanding of Japan–EU relations. In a wider perspective than specific trade negotiations, Katzenstein and Tsujinaka discussed US–Japanese relations in support of a transnational approach to IR (Katzenstein and Tsujinaka, 1995). Reiterating the significance of the transaction of external pressure and domestic politics to analyse Japan-US relations, they concluded that 'the domestic structures of the United States and Japan act like filters which refract differently the transnational relations between the United States and Japan.' (Katzenstein and Tsujinaka, 1995: 109) Such a 'refraction effect' of domestic structures can be also found in interactions between Japanese and European actors. For example, the channels European actors use to gain access to the Japanese decision-making system differ from those Japanese business and interest groups use to lobby the European Commission, as well as national and local governments in Europe.

Furthermore, there is another important reason to include the US in contemplating Japan–EU relations: the US itself is a significant variable in issues between Japan and the EU, influencing decision-makers on both sides. US pressure on Japan regarding automobile trade, for example, directly impacted the European automobile market, since Japanese automobile manufacturers tried to compensate for the slow growth of their sales in the US by intensifying exports in Europe. In this sense, Japan-US trade relations not only provide a model for the study of Japan–EU relations, but also directly impact the latter relationship.

JAPAN'S RELATIONS WITH THE EC/EU FROM IR PERSPECTIVES

So far, while individual trade frictions have caught the public's attention, emphasizing the critical state of Japan–EU relations (Yokoyama, 1993), little work has focused on the causes of this situation, their structures and processes.[18] Trade negotiations, for example, between the Japanese government and the European Commission have taken place on many occasions, but few theoretical analyses were attempted that might enhance our understanding of the bilateral relationship.[19] While negotiations between Tokyo and Washington have often been analysed from the perspective of Japan's foreign economic policy – treating Japan's policy as a factor in the problem behind the negotiations – discussion of Japan–EU negotiations often lacks such a policy-oriented analysis.

This book, therefore, proposes to look at Japan–EU relations from the perspective of Japanese decision-making, involving the Japanese government, policies, interest groups, and politicians that interact with their European counterparts at the same levels as well as across levels. As studies of US-Japanese relations have indicated, it is essential to examine Japanese domestic politics in order to understand its foreign economic policy, which equally applies to the case between Japan and the EU. This statement is specifically tested by the case studies in the following chapters.

Focusing on foreign policy and foreign economic decision-making is an important aspect of international relations, and there are different views on what determines foreign policy: the international setting or system, domestic politics, or perceptions of individual decision-makers.

Differences among these levels of analysis are discussed in the next chapter.

The analysis of Japan's policymaking towards EU is not merely applying the method used in that of Japan-US relations. International bargaining between Japan and Europe comprises different levels and stages of decision-making, involving the European Commission as well as the member state governments. Japanese decision-making in its foreign economic policy towards the EU, thus reflects the multi-layered structure of European decision-making. In practice, for example, Japanese government and businesses have developed close ties with central and local governments and business partners in some of the member states, such as the UK, through manufacturing direct investment, which the Japanese see as leverage for establishing stronger connections with the European Union. In this sense, the unique structure of the EU requires more close attention to the question of levels of analysis: regional level, national level, local level and private actors level.

Although traditional IR theories tend to concentrate their focus on state actors and overlook private business actors, the latter is also important in the decision-making process. For example, business groups, such as *Keidanren* (the Federation of Economic Organizations) have regular contact with their European counterparts and with European officials; and the European Business Community (EBC) in Tokyo lobbies actively among Japanese decision-makers. Such activities by private actors influence, or sometimes even replace, government-level decisions as resolutions for economic conflicts. As the case studies show in detail, for example, some Japanese car makers established friendly relationships with the British government through their direct investment in the UK. This helped the Japanese transplant cars to be excluded from the formal agreement between the Japanese government and the EC. Also, business ties between Japanese and European whisky makers added the Japanese domestic voice to the originally European or at least exclusively foreign lobby, consequentially shifting the point of dispute over the Japanese liquor tax between Japan and the EC.

TIMEFRAME AND THE STRUCTURE OF THIS BOOK

Considering Japan's decision-making between 1985 and 1995, the drastic change of political equilibrium in 1993 is noteworthy because of its potential to cause structural change in decision-making. The Liberal Democratic Party's defeat in the 1993 election shook the more or less unchallenged political balance of LDP dominance, called 'the 1955 system.'[20] Nevertheless, practice of decision-making in Japan so far remains stable, although some elements have come to be questioned and challenged. The comeback of the LDP in the 1996 election did not re-establish the same political situation. In addition, a series of various scandals involving bureaucrats among others have led people to question their trust in bureaucracy *per se*. There seems, however, little change in the policy process, revealed in the daily reports of government-led reforms in newspapers. I believe, therefore, that this analysis of policymaking between 1985 and 1995 still remains valid to a great extent at the time of this writing.[21]

Part One of this book is a review of theoretical frameworks. International economic negotiations, through which Japan's foreign economic policymaking towards the EC can be observed, are problematic because they occur at and across a number of levels (state, private, national, local, regional, etc.). Chapter 1, therefore, discusses such levels of analysis and considers what approach is useful to analyse Japan's foreign economic policy decision-making. Chapter 2, in turn, examines the structure in which such decision-making is carried out.

In Part Two, the first two case studies examine two major trade issues between Japan and the EU. Case I, concerning the automobile industry, obviously impacted many people in Japan and Europe. In this case study, the transnational relations between Japanese automobile companies and the British government constitute an important factor. Cooperation between them significantly impacted decision-making within the EC, which in turn influenced negotiations between the Japanese government and the European Commission.

Case II examines the trade dispute involving the Japanese liquor tax. The intensity of this dispute did not correspond to the size of the industry or its importance in the domestic economy. A similar example might be the textile trade conflict between Japan and the US a quarter of a century ago. This is precisely the sort of case in which domestic politics must be taken into account in order to comprehend the issue's impact on international relations. Also the role of international organizations, namely the GATT and later the World Trade Organization (WTO), was quite important in the process of the dispute.

Case III, the Joint Declaration between Japan and the EC was an attempt to resolve conflicts fundamentally: to structure a solid basis for Japan–EC relations to manage recurrent economic conflicts. Wider context of international political economy particularly counted more in this case than in individual trade cases. Yet actors involved in this case were more limited than other case studies, due to Japanese domestic context.

I chose the three cases to examine, since each represents different aspects of Japan's foreign policy towards the EC/EU. The automobile issue attracted the most attention among the economic disputes between the two because of the importance of the industry to the economy as a whole on each side. The liquor tax issue demonstrates how an exclusively domestic issue became an issue of international dispute, requiring a transnational approach. It was also the first case between Japan and the EC to be brought to the GATT and later became the first case of the WTO, attracting greater attention in Japan and Europe as well as globally, beyond what the size of the industry would imply. The last case, the Joint Declaration, was the first serious attempt to establish political ties between the two sides, though the results have not proved particularly fruitful.

In the conclusion, decision-making in the three case studies will be compared, using the theoretical frameworks described in Part One. All three cases involve different actors as the main decision-makers in Japan, though the first two cases, being in the economic sphere, follow similar patterns of negotiations among bureaucrats and business circles while the third lacks business interests. Nevertheless, analyses of transactions between Japan and the EU – whether for economic interests or for diplomatic purposes – indicate the validity of some models of decision-making for Japanese foreign economic policy. The picture that emerges from this decision-making analysis, in turn, contributes to a deeper understanding of Japan–EU relations.

PART I

Approaches to Japan's Decision-Making towards the European Union

CHAPTER 1

Analytical frameworks – contributions from IR perspectives

In attempting to examine Japan–EC/EU relations from an international relations perspective, the first task is to determine the level and object of analysis for this particular relationship. Focusing on foreign policy decision-making is one approach to observe international relations. In the context of Japan–EU relations, Japan's decision-making towards the EU is a window through which one can perceive the relationship between them. This book focuses on Japanese decision-making, whereas EU decision-making towards Japan is dealt with as a complementary factor to explain the relationship. Simultaneously, transnational as well as foreign actors have penetrated the decision-making process in the domestic arena. Foreign pressure – *gaiatsu* – has been a keyword to explain Japan's foreign policy, especially with the United States.[1] Such external influence is often indispensable even when considering 'domestic' policymaking.

However, state-to-state pressure is only one of the major variables in Japanese decision-making. Foreign firms, multinational corporations, cross-border alliances and other non-state actors also play significant roles in the foreign economic policy process. Including non-state actors in the policy process requires decision-making models to integrate transnational actors and the structural influence of foreign actors. This means that in viewing bilateral relations between Japan and the EU, traditional state-centric analysis may overlook an important part of the relationship: the activities of private actors and cross-level interactions.

At the same time, the division between foreign and domestic policy itself has become increasingly obscure. The following is a walk-through of theories and models that have been discussed for decades but nevertheless have been neglected or simply overlooked in the study of Japan–EU relations. Applying these well-established theories to Japan's decision-making towards Europe may clarify the nature and process of this often neglected bilateral relationship.

LEVEL OF ANALYSIS

Regardless of the variety and difference of opinion among theoretical schools in international relations, it is generally accepted that foreign policy is an essential element of international transactions – such as trade negotiations – and reflects the structure of the relationship among states. For the study of foreign policy, in turn, it is necessary to consider all its different determinants, although researchers differ as to which level of analysis should be emphasized to explain the results of negotiations (Moravcsik, 1993: 3–17). The question of levels of analysis is particularly important within the context of Japan–EU relations, as well as wider international relations, because negotiations occur at and across different levels.

Although there is no consensus as to which is the most appropriate categorization of the different levels of analysis, the model proposed by Kenneth Waltz in his seminal work, *Man, the state, and war*, is often referred to as the starting point for many studies. His model concentrates on three levels: the international, domestic and individual levels (Waltz, 1959).[2] The international level of analysis, represented by systemic theories, focuses on international settings as the most significant factor contributing to international relations. States are the main objects, and this analysis makes two key assumptions: that states are fundamentally unitary by nature in their purposes and similar in their preferences and behaviour. States are in fact dealt with as though they were individuals. Expressions such as 'Tokyo decided . . .' and 'Britain insisted . . .' are abundant in literature based on the international level of analysis, as well as in casual usage. Such personification of states is legitimized by considering that states have their own interests, as opposed to partial interests, within societies (Mastanduno, Lake and Ikenburry, 1989). This can be taken to the extreme, however. '[The] analogy between nations in international politics and a coordinated, intelligent human being is so powerful that we rarely remember we are reasoning by analogy.' (Allison, 1971: 252)

As for the second assumption that all states behave in a similar way in any given international situation with a given position, a state's behaviour is seen as a consequence of international settings and not of its unique domestic characteristics (Singer, 1961). Nineteenth-century European history exemplifies this, where all states and would-be-states (i.e. Germany and Italy) pursued war in order to maximize their territories, which directly backed up their power regardless of their differences in domestic politics (Hinsley, 1963: Chapters 9 and 10). Another significant assumption in this level, directly linked to the first assumption, is that decisions made by states are rational for their purposes. This argument about rationality leads to some models of decision-making that will be discussed later in this chapter.

The domestic level of analysis, by contrast, focuses on intra-state elements for foreign policy decision-making as variables independent of international settings. The behaviour of states is the central subject of study in this level of analysis, which is common to the first level, but the primary explanation for state behaviour lies in domestic rather than international factors. In contrast to the international level of analysis, this emphasis on domestic politics allows states to be dissimilar in behaviour and weakens the assumption that states are unitary. Stressing the point that states are not monolithic organizations, this level of analysis highlights the variety of interests within a state and the procedures to select interests to pursue, opening up what is often referred to as the 'black box' in international relations literature. Some of the works on US foreign policy have taken this approach. For example, Graham Allison's models, discussed in a later section, focus on domestic explanations for the state's decisions (Allison, 1971).[3] Peter Katzenstein's *Between Power and Plenty* is a collection of works on foreign economic policies, including not only the United States but also Japan and other advanced industrial states, analysed from the domestic perspective (Katzenstein, 1978).[4] While this second approach generally sees international relations as a consequence of domestic politics, it also allows for the inverse: 'the second image reversed' says that the international system is also a cause of domestic politics and structures (Gourevitch, 1978).

Third, the individual level of analysis focuses on individual women and men within governments and decision-making bodies. It borrows various perspectives from other academic fields, such as psychology and sociology, including belief systems, cognitive maps and operational codes used to analyse foreign policymaking (Holsti, 1976; Steinbruner, 1974; G. Snyder and Diesing, 1977). Given that both international and domestic environments are not isolated objective variables but rather subject to individual actors, these actors' cognitions, including any psychological biases, are deemed to influence directly a state's actions. Robert Jervis, for example, suggested various misperceptions of individual decision-makers – such as the misperception that people tend to think foreign countries are more centralized than they actually are – implying that the assumption of a unitary state is not always valid (Jervis, 1976: Chapter 8).

Although mixing different levels of analysis is not generally accepted (Moravcsik, 1993: 6; Singer, 1961: 91), there have been several attempts to link levels, partly in response to the increasing complexity across domestic and international politics. In linking levels, it is still necessary to be aware of how selected levels are intertwined; this distinguishes it from random mixing of levels of analysis. Earlier attempts include 'linkage politics' as a study area in the 1960s, which supposed linkages between national political systems and their environments (Rosenau, 1966; Rosenau, 1969; Takayanagi S., 1971). While it was more or less obvious that foreign policy analysis needed to take into account both international and domestic politics, linkage politics attempted to invent a formula to combine international and domestic variables in policymaking (Hanrieder, 1967). In the end, however, attempts at theorizing linkage politics were abandoned because of the excessive complexities of the research object. A state's domestic politics can be complicated enough, but when attempts were made to integrate the domestic politics of multiple states and international politics, the task became hopelessly difficult (Yamakage, 1989: 222).

In the 1980s, a renewed attempt to join different levels of analysis emerged: a two-level approach, in which the close interrelation between domestic elements and international bargaining power indicates a linkage between those levels of analysis (Putnam, 1988; Evans *et al.*, 1993). This approach suggests a way to analyse international negotiations by examining the extent to which each side can compromise its domestic pressures to accommodate the other side's demands. This model has already been used in analysing trade issues between Japan and the United States.[5] Although this two-level approach was not the first to combine international and domestic politics in analysing international relations, it provided the first concrete model of how one should link them.

One of the variations of the two-level approach distinguishes three forms of domestic-international interaction, depending on the participants in the interaction: transgovernmental, non-state-to-non-state and cross-level (Knopf, 1993).[6] By sorting transnational interactions into three kinds, the model clarifies different levels of interactions among governments and non-state actors. The dual framework of the EU's external policymaking – the Union's administrative organ such as the European Commission on the one hand and member governments on

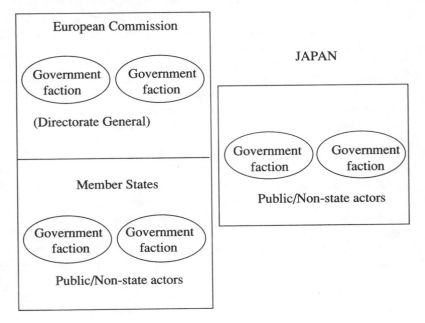

Figure 1.1 Transnational negotiations

the other – has to be fully considered in interactions with Japan. Furthermore, the model also includes public or non-state actors whose interests and behaviour are separate from those of governments, even though a government faction may share a common interest with them.

Including non-state actors is a significant change from traditional IR perspectives. The transnational approach is a major example of new perspectives that explicitly involve non-state actors. It dates back to the 1970s (Keohane and Nye, 1971; Katzenstein, 1978), although it declined in the 1980s before its revival in the 1990s. One of the main arguments of the transnational approach is to discard the state-centric view of the traditional IR approach (Keohane and Nye, 1971: xxiii–xxv, 371–9; Keohane and Nye, 1974).[7] The state-centric assumption distinctively appears in the international level of analysis, but both domestic and individual levels of analysis also usually focus on state actors.

Transnational relations are defined as 'regular interactions across national boundaries when at least one actor is a non-state agent or does not operate on behalf of a national government or an intergovernmental organisation.' (Risse-Kappen, 1995b: 3)[8] This perspective is, therefore, particularly suitable to look into interactions across levels (international–domestic levels, or state–subnational–private levels).

The transnational approach does not suggest that the state is no longer important in international relations. Rather, a current approach bridges the gap between 'those who theorise about international relations and about domestic politics' on the one hand, and the tendency of the transnational approach to neglect structures of governance on the other (Risse-Kappen, 1995b: 16). The two-level approach also emphasizes transnational relations in its analysis of cross-border phenomena (Knopf, 1993).

Generically, domestic structure matters in considering international relations in such a way that domestic structure is a lens through which international relations 'refract'.[9] At the same time, domestic politics alone does not provide sufficient explanation for international relations, particularly because of the penetration of transnational actors into domestic politics. Again using the analogy of a lens, the image on the other side of a lens (international relations) emerges when a light or input from outside (foreign or transnational influence) goes through the lens (domestic structure). In order to consider the influence of transnational relations, it is necessary to examine the decision-making process in domestic politics, in which domestic and transnational actors interact to formulate foreign economic policies.

The rapid development of economic interdependence in the global system has gone so far in the last couple of decades that the traditional perception of power could not alone explain the behaviour of states. Some theorists have restated the claim that states no longer have exclusive jurisdiction over domestic affairs, with the loss of sovereignty to international organizations, multinational corporations and others.[10] Furthermore, considering the increasing significance of transnational actors and foreign pressure on domestic politics, distinguishing international politics from domestic politics has become less important. As a result, interest in transnational relations has recently been revived (Risse-Kappen, 1995a).

In addition to transnational approaches, various other arguments also emphasize the phenomena of interdependence in international relations, paying particular attention to the role of non-state actors (Keohane,

1990). Even in interstate negotiations that clearly weigh governments as the most important entities, the relative correspondence of state to society (for example, the role and responsibilities society expects of the state) has changed, thus departing from the state-centric view. The statesman, for example, who directly participates in international negotiations, can be considered as 'a pure "agent" of society, seeking to maximise domestic political support.' (Moravcsik, 1993: 16)

The departure from the state-centric view of international politics can also be found in the neoliberal argument that 'institutions (in international society) may be a significant factor in promoting international co-operation in ways that neorealism has failed to appreciate.' (Powell, 1994: 326–7) Such institutions have not and may not in the near future overcome the nation-state system, but their significance is so great in people's perceptions that there are strong motivations to sustain the current system (e.g. a liberal trade regime) and international organizations (e.g. the GATT[11] and the WTO).

Criticism of the state-centric view is also reflected in decision-making analysis. In addition to government officials, the role of non-state actors in the private sector and other non-governmental organizations is now regarded as having considerable significance. Non-officials were once considered to have 'access' to the decision-making process but not to be essential actors in it (R. Snyder *et al.*, 1962: 41–2). The distinction between decision-makers and other influential actors was described as analogous to 'the distinction between legal power and influence.'(Frankel, 1963: 5) Unlike security and military issues, economic issues between states almost necessarily involve private sectors whose interests are directly concerned. While governments are principal decision-makers of macroeconomic policy, individual issues such as trade negotiations often allow private actors to take the initiative to settle the issue. As a result, such private groups need be considered in examining the decision-making process.

Traditionally, however, IR decision-making studies focused exclusively on government decisions. While neorealists remain focused mostly on state actions – those of politicians and administrators in the executive branch of government (Mastanduno *et al.*, 1989: 458) – and assume that the state has a distinctive purpose aside from society, this approach may not be particularly appropriate in the case of Japan–EU relations. When a decision-making approach is taken to examine Japan's foreign economic policy towards the

EC/EU, the role of non-state actors is particularly important. For it is private economic interests that have strongly motivated the bilateral relationship. Most state-level contact between Japan and Europe has been initiated by private interests. Hardly any issues between them convey a vital and obvious national interest, such as military security, that illuminates 'the state' as opposed to 'the society'. As a result, each side pursues interests that cannot always be defined as 'national' interests. Sometimes domestic groups such as consumers associations have more of a common stand with foreign entities than with domestic producers. In other words, diversity of interests among government, industrial sectors and other non-state actors makes it difficult to define what national interest is in the context of international economic relations.[12]

Therefore, in order to solve the question of Japan's decision-making towards the EU, relations among state and non-state actors within and across borders need to be fully considered. As the transnational approach points out, various levels of communications – between transnational industries, between bureaucratic units across borders, among national governments within the EU and between industries and the European Commission – are indispensable elements for analysing decision-making, especially for foreign economic policy. The following case studies examine such multifaceted communications. These transnational interactions comprise a great part of the decision-making process.

DECISION-MAKING APPROACHES

As international negotiations greatly reflect and depend upon domestic politics, domestic decision-making is consequently a crucial determinant of international affairs. Graham Allison's *Essence of Decision* provides a clear and widely accepted categorization of three models of state decision-making (Allison, 1971), while a fourth model focuses on the psychological factors of individual participants in the decision-making process. These four models, however, do not reflect the transnational development in international political economy, in that the models focus exclusively on state decisions and private actors' roles are deemed as marginal. In order to introduce transnational relations into decision-making, a fifth model is necessary.

Models of Decision-Making

First, the rational actor theory suggests that decisions are made for certain purposes, and in the sense that decisions-purposes relationship is parallel to the means-ends relationship, such decisions are rational or analytical (Allison, 1971: 10–38).[13] For government decision-makers, there are usually various choices to take, and according to this theory, rational calculations are made to judge which choice is the best for the nation. Realists often stand on this model to interpret states' behaviour, which in their view is the most important element of international affairs.

Many critics, including Allison himself, have attacked the model's assumptions. Even when one assumes that decision-makers are capable of making perfectly rational judgement, options for decision-makers may well emerge only after a considerable time lag. Therefore, at any given moment, a decision-maker cannot necessarily calculate the costs and benefits of all options to make the most effective decision. Even if one could consider all the alternatives, it would still be doubtful whether a person can calculate accurately the probability of success for each option. As for the behaviour of a single isolated individual, Herbert Simon stated that it is impossible to reach any high degree of rationality (Simon, 1976: 79). As a consequence, it is just as likely that a supposedly rational decision may not produce the most desirable result for the original purpose. Moreover, in the case of a state's decision in particular, a nation would not likely have an absolute notion of its goals. There would hardly be unanimous agreement among decision-makers on what is national interest. Therefore, what is deemed rational for one may well be irrational for another. Peace and national security, for example, can be incompatible options with each other. Therefore, the 'rationality' of a decision-maker's choice could well be against the national interest and thus 'irrational' to opponents.

Nevertheless, the rational-choice theory remains influential for many political scientists. By utilizing game theories, originally established in the field of economics, rational-choice is deemed as a most sophisticated theory of decision-making. George Tsebelis, for example, developed a concept of 'nested games', by which he combined multiple conditions (or in his terminology, 'arenas') for a decision. He argued that those decisions deemed sub-optimal to an observer might in fact be optimal if one considers the wider context in which the decision was made (Tsebelis, 1990).

The second model is called the organizational process model. One variation is the bounded rationality theory that assumes a limitation on rationality derived from organizational environment (Simon, 1976). According to Allison,

> [it] emphasizes the processes and procedures of the large organizations that constitute a government. According to this Organizational Process Model, what Model I (the rational actor model) analysts characterize as 'acts' and 'choices' are thought of instead as *outputs* (italics in original) of large organizations functioning according to regular patterns of behavior (Allison, 1971: 6).

According to this model, decisions are made via mechanical or automatic procedures, avoiding a complicated or almost impossible calculation of rationality. Simon explained that an organization, particularly an administrative one, would provide members of the organization who are decision-makers with 'a psychological environment that will adapt their decisions to the organization objectives, and will provide them with the information needed to make these decisions correctly.' (Simon, 1976: 79)

This model alters the definition of rationality by suggesting that decision-makers' rationality was not to search for the optimal choice but a satisfactory one. According to Allison, 'In choosing, human beings do not consider all alternatives and pick the action with the best consequences. Instead, they find a course of action that is "good enough" – that satisfies.' (Allison, 1971: 72) In that sense, rationality in political science is subjective and procedural, but not objective or substantive (Simon, 1976: 297). In consequence, this type of decision-making process avoids (1) the preference of ordering, (2) the explicit calculations of alternatives and outcomes, and (3) the optimizing process that forms the core of the first model (Steinbruner, 1974: 53). The bounded rationality model gives a practical way of dealing with difficulties ignored by the rational actor model, though at the same time it loses sight of the ideal goal of the whole process (G. Snyder and Diesing, 1977: 346).

Decision-making models can roughly be divided into two types, one for single decision-makers, and the other for multiple decision-makers. The rational actor model presumes a unitary decision-making body. The second model presumes a multiple number of individuals participating in decision-making, but an organization could maintain a consistent and unitary nature by providing standard operational codes to the individuals who are members of the organization. In this sense, the organizational process model is also the first type. The following models, on the contrary, focus on the varieties of and differences among individual decision-makers.

The third model, the bureaucratic politics model, focuses on the rigidity of bargaining strategies within an organization, especially when encountering negative information. This model, contrasting with the first two models, interprets the 'irrational' decision-making in a bureaucratic area.[14] In Allison's words, the object of the analysis in this model is governmental actions, which he called political resultants:

> *resultants* in the sense that what happens is not chosen as a solution to a problem but rather results from compromise, conflict, and confusion of officials with diverse interests and unequal influence; *political* in the sense that the activity from which decisions and actions emerge is best characterized as bargaining along regularized channels among individual members of the government (Allison, 1971: 162).

Assuming multiple groups – such as bureaux, departments, and ministries – exist in government and can all be identified as partisan, the model supposes that decision-making is a process of building a majority coalition and that a central decision-maker has to select one option among those offered by the interested parties.[15] Bureaucrats 'pull and haul', (Allison, 1971: 171) working *with* and *against* each other in the process of policymaking in order to achieve majority coalitions (Bacchus, 1974: 15).

Although bureaucratic politics model was originally based on the American political system, it attracted much attention among Japanese researchers. Some accepted the model quite favourably, specifying the prerequisites and issue areas for which the bureaucratic politics model would be appropriate for analysis, and concluded that the bureaucratic politics model would be most applicable in social and economic issues rather than in military strategic issues (Shindo E., 1973). However, some critics claimed that the model could only be valid for pluralist political systems like the United States (S. Smith, 1980: 31-2; Tokito, 1985). And yet the fragmented nature of Japanese government agencies, to be further discussed in the following chapter, may satisfy the prerequisite for the model's applicability.

The fourth model transfers the level of analysis to the psychological aspects of decision-makers. Steinbruner, Jervis and others developed a cognitive process model (Steinbruner, 1974; Jervis, 1976).[16] A decision-maker, according to this model, cannot always recognize changes in the international environment and other types of change. Moreover, recognition does not necessarily imply accurate, objective observation. The decision-maker's perception of the change can be influenced by his or her personal belief systems and images.[17] While other models are based on the systemic level, either international or domestic, this fourth model stands in the individual level of analysis. (See the first section of this chapter.)

None of these models are able to explain the totality of decision-making by themselves. In order to reduce gaps between a model and reality, there have been attempts to link the models. Soon after *Essence of Decision*, for example, Allison revised his models with Halperin, combining the second and third models (Allison and Halperin, 1972). Smith introduced works discussing linkages between the bureaucratic politics and the cognitive approaches (S. Smith, 1989: 126–8). Such a combined approach may be appropriate for the case of American foreign policy, since the President plays a significant role and his cognition influences bureaucratic politics.[18] In contrast, however, it does not seem applicable to the cases of Japan, since the Japanese Prime Minister does not have an equivalent power over decision-making as the US President.

What is common to all four models above is that their focus is on state-level decision-makers, concentrating on governments and government officials. Even among critics of the bureaucratic politics model, there is no argument to expand the model to include actors outside of state organizations. For analysing foreign economic policymaking, however, it is insufficient to examine only the decisions made by state officials, as decisions by private firms – whether multinational, foreign, or domestic – may greatly influence governmental decisions. Analysis of governmental decision-making should not be limited to the chief of government or top bureaucrats (Yamamoto Y., 1990: 23). Thus it is useful to refer to the transnational approach in studying decision-making. In other words, decision-making analysis should be extended across levels (state or private) and national borders. This does not mean that the role of states and members of state organizations could be replaced by private actors. What culminates as a state decision, however, is a consequence of negotiations among domestic bureaucrats (as the bureaucratic politics model suggests) as well as cross-level negotiations among domestic and foreign governments and private actors. For example, Japanese firms establishing cooperative relations with European actors such as British government, helped the Ministry of International Trade and Industry (MITI) in negotiations on automobile trade.

The bureaucratic politics model, particularly its perception of 'political resultants', provides a basis for the fifth model: transnational interactions of various participants of decision-making, whether government officials or private interest groups, pressure the central decision-maker and domestic bureaucrats. In this transnational decision-making model, a fundamental difference remains between governmental actors and private actors in terms of legitimacy. Only the former can represent the state's interests at international negotiations, including multilateral arenas such as GATT negotiations and WTO panels. Interactions between bureaucrats and private interest groups, however, should be given attention, since it is not a simple one-to-one relationship. Interest groups typically contact not only one but various government organizations, and vice versa. Foreign firms and interest groups pressuring governments directly across borders can have such a serious impact on both the internal and external policies of that government, that those foreign pressures should be treated as 'partisan' in the third model.

When considering the Japan–EU relationship, transnational actors are indispensable because private economic activities have so strongly developed that relationship. Analysing Japan's decision-making towards the EU, a non-state-centric perspective must be used in order to include these actors who are deeply involved in the decision-making process of foreign economic policy.

Application to Japan's Foreign Economic Policy

In order to study Japan's foreign economic policy towards Europe, the decision-making models discussed above can give useful insights to help consider how decisions are made that form such policy. There are already numerous works with an emphasis on Japan's industrial policy, trade policy and other economic related policies. It is said, however, that in the tradition of Japanese politics the policymaking process was not considered as important as efficient policy-*execution* by bureaucrats (T. Ishida, 1986: 23).

Arguments of Japanese decision-making disperse in various academic disciplines.[19] Japanese foreign policymaking is often discussed in the context of diplomatic history,[20] while domestic policy is handled by public administration. Decision-making studies in Japan's international relations have so far had limited impact on the study of Japan's foreign policymaking.[21] Within such limitations, however, the MITI, Ministry of Finance (MOF) and other ministries are recognized as the most significant players in Japanese decision-making, and in-depth research on these ministries, including some case studies, has been carried out, although the case studies are almost exclusively on Japan-US trade issues.[22] Therefore, it is yet to be seen whether Japan–EU relations have a comparable decision-making mechanism, as found in the studies of Japan-US relations.

As for the dichotomy between single-person models and group decision-making models, it seems that Japanese decision-making units within the government have such a high unitary character that one could safely use an analogy between a single person and such a unit. These units correspond to divisions within ministries of the central government. Officials in the same division work in one large room. This very characteristic feature of Japanese bureaucracy is called '*ohbeya-shugi*' (collective office mentality) (Shindo M., 1992: 102–3; Omori, 1985: 88–90). Core personnel who deal with actual policymaking in ministries – the division chief and deputy division chief – do not have individual offices but rather share one big room with their juniors. Within such a working environment, the implicit code among officials contains more significance than the organizational process model has expected for American cases.

For certain types of behaviour, such as routine work, the organizational process model is convincing. Sato Hideo, for example, specifically refers to the Ministry of Foreign Affairs (MFA), MITI and MOF as examples of the organizational process model, where policies are seen as products of a quasi-mechanical process based on standard operating procedures within the organization (Sato H., 1989: 46). Admittedly, most of the tasks of these ministries are largely routine, and therefore a semi-automatic decision-making process can explain the features of the Japanese decision-making body. The organizational process model is less compelling in examining the Japanese response to EU trade conflicts. Although tasks concerning trade conflict occur only too frequently, they are not in the strict sense routine. In each case, in order to represent the interests of the Japanese economic sector(s) in question, ministry officials must fully comprehend the domestic situation and build, to a certain extent, a mutual trust between the sector(s) and themselves. Regular contacts and consultations between government officials and representative of economic sector(s) are indispensable for that purpose, extending so far that private sectors practically take part in policymaking.

In addition to domestic interest groups, European pressure groups backed by European governments including the European Commission, have frequent, direct contact with the Japanese government. Japanese government negotiations, whether with domestic interest groups or with European governments, require flexibility to reach a conclusion and usually involve compromise, instead of following the routine code blindly.

Also within the Japanese government, the differences between the interests of bureaucrats and politicians are important. Politicians, especially major cabinet members and high rank officials of the governing party, are significant decision-makers, although opposition party politicians can also play an important role.[23] Politicians who specialize in specific policies are called *zoku-giin* ('tribe politicians'). Their function varies from co-operating with bureaucrats and endorsing their policy proposals to fighting against bureaucrats in order to protect the interest of their supporters, such as private interest groups [e.g. Japan Automobile Manufacturers Association (JAMA)]. The nature and role of 'tribe politicians' will be discussed more in the next chapter.

The bureaucratic politics model, which has been widely discussed and criticized (Krasner, 1973; Steiner, 1977; S. Smith, 1980; S. Smith, 1989; Art, 1977), still seems to be widely applicable to Japan's policymaking. Furthermore, some of the criticisms made of the model – namely that it fails to explain American decision-making adequately – may not be appropriate to Japan. Empirical evidence suggests that Japan may fit the model better. A criticism, for example, that the model assumed incorrectly that leadership is weak in American decision-making, does not influence the applicability of the model in Japan's political system. Unlike the US President, the Japanese Prime Minister cannot pick his own staff.[24] Consequently, he has only a very limited number of staff who would be loyal to him. Therefore, those who give the Prime Minister advice and policy options are part of his given environment. Such advisers are mostly bureaucrats, but also include some LDP colleagues and big business representatives. Other ministers have often only limited influence on the Prime Minister. In addition, ministerial seats are decided by the political struggles among party factions, not by a Prime Minister's own choice.[25]

As for partisans in the bureaucratic politics model, various divisions, bureaux and ministries correspond to such actors in the model. While the homogeneity of officials could be extended as far as a bureau, rivalry and clashes of interests between different bureaux within a ministry as well as between ministries are frequently witnessed. Otake Hideo adapted this theory to interpret Japan's case, acknowledging that the fundamental significance of the model was to recognize that one's opinions and ideas are determined by which position he or she occupies ('where-you-stand-depends-on-where-you-sit').[26] While some of Allison's critics asserted there was little evidence for this maxim in the US, the Japanese political and administrative systems seem to provide it.

Regarding the fourth model, there are not many occasions when individuals' decisions determine crucial state action of Japan. As a consequence of consensus-making as a code of society (Befu, 1990),[27] the role of individuals tends to be less visible, although exceptions exist.[28] Apart from occasional issues with serious diplomatic problems, no individual has been seen to be distinctly influential in decision-making, especially since the 1980s. Alternatively, instead of focusing on the perceptions of a single decision-maker, it is possible to refer to 'groupthink' in order to examine *ohbeya-shugi*. As Janis pointed out, groupthink does not always result in fiascos, but may produce positive outcomes (Janis, 1972: 13). Decision-making in the Japanese bureaucracy can be studied from the perspective of groupthink, although there is a serious difficulty in collecting sources for contemporary foreign policy as well as domestic policy; thus it is difficult to conduct empirical research.

Considering the close relationship between the bureaucracy and the private sector, interest groups should be included in the analysis of decision-making process. Furthermore, the role of foreign pressure and the impact of multinational corporations also need to be fully examined. Thus, it is useful to introduce the transnational decision-making model that provides a framework to integrate the transnational impact into the decision-making model.

It should be noted here, however, that in studies of the Japanese political economy, *gaiatsu* (foreign pressure) has become a common term to describe the likeliness of concession by the Japanese government to foreign government pressure, particularly that of the United States, supported by private interest groups. There have been several works on *gaiatsu*, but not many of them discuss it in the wider context of the transnational trend (Calder, 1988; Schoppa, 1993).[29] Considering that *gaiatsu* is often utilized by the Japanese government, or sub-governments, in order to convince opposing domestic groups, it is not a matter of simple foreign relations, but a good example of transnational relations in which interest-based coalitions can be made across borders. In this sense, there should be more to exploit from studying this Japanese practice for IR theorizing.

POLICY TAXONOMY

The applicability of decision-making models depends on the type of political system as well as the type of policies in question. Politicians are sometimes more important in the decision-making process than bureaucratic actors, while other times bureaucrats totally dominate the process. There are also occasions in which private business actors assume the initiative in dealing with foreign trade relations, thus influencing the governmental policy process to a great extent. In this sense, policy taxonomy is important to discern the correlation between policy type and policymaking process (R. Snyder *et al.*, 1962: 95; Lowi, 1972). Without going into too detailed categorization, the following distinguishes certain policy types in order to apply decision-making models in appropriate cases.

A group of policies has a hierarchical structure in a way that policies that set abstract framework determine concrete policies that would implement the former. In other words, a group of policies are structured in a way that a concrete policy is a means to carry out the purpose set by a policy of a higher level (Yamaguchi J., 1987: Chapter 1). Policies of the most abstract level are to deal with structural issues and providing a general direction to the issue concerned. Among various governmental plans and actions, this type of policy indicates which issues should be given primacy, and in what direction the government is heading. The issues handled by such policies are 'political' in a sense that politicians are more closely involved with, or further take initiatives in, the decision-making process. The room for bureaucrats to manoeuvre in this area is limited. At best they could have some influence on politicians' ideas through regular contacts, but such influence is only indirect to the policy itself (Yamaguchi J., 1987: Chapter 2).

On the other hand, implementing policies accompany government's actions and influence individuals and private groups (clients) by

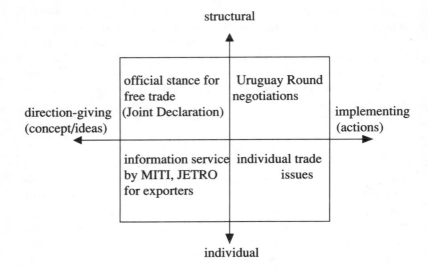

structural

official stance for | Uruguay Round
free trade | negotiations
(Joint Declaration) |

direction-giving | | implementing
(concept/ideas) | | (actions)

information service | individual trade
by MITI, JETRO | issues
for exporters |

individual

Figure 1.2 Types of policies

affecting their interests. Those concrete policies are provided with a
suitable budget, human resources and other resources.

In the case of Japan's foreign policy towards Europe, it is hidden
behind various short term goals designed to soothe economic friction.
The Japanese government is sometimes said to act not on the basis of
a certain policy but on an *ad hoc* basis.[30] As for Japan's relations with
Europe, no issues involve national security or ideology. Instead, most
of Japan's policies relevant to Europe fall into the category of partial
economic interests of the society and stress implementation rather than
conceptualization.

As will be discussed later, the relationship between politicians and
bureaucrats has been one of the major focuses of the political system
of Japan, determining who is important in state-level decision-making.
A popular argument is that 'tribe politicians' of the LDP have risen
in importance as the main decision-makers while bureaucrats have
experienced a relative decline. Such a simple description of 'who-
is-most-powerful' is inadequate and denies the variety of policies
that determine the role and power of politicians and bureaucrats. In
certain areas, politicians can take the initiative to make policy, while
in other areas, administrative officials are responsible for both planning

and implementing policies. Therefore, it is meaningless to generalize which actor is more powerful than another (Muramatsu, 1981: 161). What matters is the correlation between the policy area and the type of actors who are important decision-makers for a particular issue.

More important question in the context of this book is what type of policy Japan's decision-making towards the EC deals with. By specifying the type of policy, one may find which relevant actors should be emphasized in the decision-making process. In practice, individual trade conflicts are handled according to the implementing, individual-functioning policies, whereas the issue of political cooperation, symbolized by the Joint Declaration, is higher in the degree of abstractness. The total trade balance and macroeconomic policy co-ordination are structural issues that require direction or a certain principle set by a larger framework.

This chapter walked through some analytical concepts and tools that are essential in examining Japan's decision-making towards the EU. The question of level of analysis is, on the one hand, in a way prerequisite when analysing international relations such as between Japan and the EU. On the other hand, its importance should be reiterated in the rise of cross-level interactions exemplified by transnational relations. It is through the decision-making process that transnational relations act on domestic structure and thus try to influence international negotiations. While there are several models of decision-making, patterns of decision-making depend on the type of policies. In the context of Japan's decision-making, who is the core decision-maker and who influences him depends on the type of policy that is involved.

Domestic structure refracts the behaviour of decision-makers including transnational actors in international relations. Thus the next chapter reviews the Japanese domestic structure in order to determine what kind of lens it is through which decision-makers endeavour to influence and negotiate with each other.

CHAPTER 2

The Japanese political economy and decision-making structure

Since domestic structure refracts the influence of domestic as well as foreign and transnational actors, Japanese domestic structure is the next question. It is the arena in which various actors negotiate, compromise, manoeuvre, and even try to force their way as the bureaucratic politics model for decision-making illustrates. In the context of Japan's decision-making towards the EU, who in Japan makes important decisions and policies? What is the structure of Japan's decision-making?

Examining Japanese domestic structure, there are different views of institutions that comprise the power structure and decision-making mechanism. The formal structure, which is parliamentary democracy in Japan, does not specify the location of actual power in foreign policy decision-making. Strong bureaucracy combined with indifferent politicians used to be a common picture for Japanese policymaking, despite severe criticisms against the inefficiency and corruption among bureaucrats. Yet arguments vary as to what degree bureaucrats dominate decision-making and how much political and economic leaders matter.

On the other hand, the EC/EU has a unique structure that has two different levels of decision-making: the Community/Union level and the member state level. Japan's attitude towards the EU responds to this unparallel structure. At trade negotiations in the 1980s, for example, when the Commission had difficulty in harmonizing member states' opinions, Japan preferred directly negotiating with individual member states. To the extent that it is necessary to understand the interactions between Japanese and European actors, I also review the EU structure of decision-making. The later section focuses on the EC after the Single European Act of 1987, as its results greatly changed the power and roles of Community institutions.

THE DOMESTIC STRUCTURE OF
JAPANESE POLITICAL ECONOMY

There are two main schools to interpret the power structure of Japanese political economy: the bureaucracy dominance model[1] and the pluralist model. A third perspective, using the concept of corporatism, is not a completely separate school of thought from pluralism, although it originally challenged it (Schmitter, 1979a: 14). Furthermore, revisionism provides a popular view of Japan, particularly in the United States. The essence of revisionism is, however, not an original interpretation of the Japanese political economy, but its value judgement. The major difference among them is in the relationship and power balance among the various actors including bureaucrats, politicians, and business groups.

The Bureaucratic Dominance Model

As its name indicates, this model deems the bureaucracy to be the centre of power. It perceives the current Japanese bureaucracy as a continuation of the pre-1945 bureaucracy, when the authoritarian state strongly controlled the nation in order to modernize its society, economy and military organization. The most authoritative work establishing this model originated from studies of Japanese public administration (Tsuji, 1958; Tsuji, 1969). In this model, central government bureaucrats control the entire country. Politicians in the governing party depend on them for policymaking, as a result of which the Diet, constitutionally the sole legislative organization, becomes merely a place for formal rites. According to this model, the tight control and regulation exercised by economic ministries facilitated the rapid economic development in the 1960s and quick recovery from the oil shock in the 1970s. The model insists, therefore, that one need look no further than the processes and procedures within the bureaucracy. Furthermore, the emphasis on economic development over other policy areas has made economic ministries – namely the Ministry of Finance (MOF) and Ministry of International Trade and Industry (MITI) – the most powerful of the ministries.

From this viewpoint, political leaders would just follow scenarios prepared by bureaucrats. Their main role is merely to support bureaucratic decisions. In practice, the government party, which until 1993 was invariably the Liberal Democratic Party (LDP), defends bureaucratic policy proposals against the opposition parties, when issues are taken at the Diet. For issues not sent to the Diet, including most foreign economic policies, the role of political leaders is even more limited. Political leaders appear as figureheads at international meetings, but they are instructed in the minutest detail by bureaucrats about how far they can compromise or how strongly they must hold their positions; practically, they are told what to say. Therefore, according to the bureaucratic dominance model, there is often no room for politicians to manoeuvre with their own initiatives in foreign economic policymaking.

There are cases, however, in which political leaders have played important roles in decision-making, particularly at the structural level (see Figure 1.2 in Chapter 1). The textile trade conflict with the US in the 1960s, for example, spilled over from an individual-implementing policy concerning the textile industry that was consequently linked to a structural policy of Japanese security relations with the US (Destler *et al.*, 1979; Otake, 1979).[2] In this case, the Prime Minister and the Foreign Minister had significant roles, and to a certain extent, took initiatives while the bureaucracy functioned to implement the political will. More recently, former Prime Minister Nakasone Yasuhiro in the 1980s (Angel, 1989) and Ozawa Ichiro in the 1990s indicated personal interest in foreign policymaking,[3] although it is hard to recognize how far Nakasone's views were reflected in actual policy or how much influence Ozawa accepted from the bureaucracy over his own ideas.

Chalmers Johnson emphasized bureaucratic dominance in Japanese foreign economic policy, and considered the influence of bureaucrats over politicians and business circles to be so strong that both the political and economic fields were controlled by bureaucrats. In *MITI and the Japanese Miracle*, MITI officials are said to have had near-total control over Japanese industry (Johnson, 1982). In a more recent article, Johnson distinguished three different approaches to explain the bases of Japanese power, all of which put the bureaucracy as the centre of power, though in different contexts (Johnson, 1992a). As for the MOF, it is widely admitted that its Budget Bureau represents the strongest power within the bureaucracy, since other ministries, political parties, and businesses of all sizes have a critical interest in the budget policies (Itoh D., 1967; Kuribayashi, 1991).[4]

The power of bureaucracy can be also recognized from a personnel perspective. Johnson surveyed the close link between government officials and big business; the former obtains high-rank positions in the latter when they retire from government organizations (*amakudari*

– descent from heaven).[5] He concluded that the ministries used this connection between government and big business to influence private firms (Johnson, 1995: 141–56). Officials who become politicians after retiring from government service can also increase their former ministries' influence on political parties, although their destination used to be exclusively the LDP.

On the other hand, *amakudari* can be interpreted as a tool for reciprocal influencing. Industries find hiring ex-MITI officials convenient, allowing quick access to ministerial information. When in government, the LDP uses ex-officials to temper demands from their former ministries. A Prime Minister or Finance Minister, for example, would mobilize ex-MOF officials in his party to suppress the MOF's inclination to a policy of retrenchment. Because of the seniority rule running through Japanese society in general, but particularly strongly in the bureaucracy, former senior-rank officials have considerable influence over their old offices. At the same time, a study of Japanese political parties proved that this same seniority rule disadvantages ex-high-ranking bureaucrats in the realm of party politics because of their late start as politicians (Sato S. and Matsuzaki, 1986: 39–51).

Those who adopt this model to explain Japan's political-economic system are critical of the system they define. Tsuji Kiyoaki asserted that the non-democratic Japanese bureaucracy was founded in pre-war traditions and decision-making structures. Characteristics of bureaucratic decision-making according to Tsuji were inefficiency, dispersed responsibility and lack of leadership (Tsuji, 1958; Tsuji, 1969: 158–62). In addition to such old arguments vehement criticism of the bureaucracy emerged along with various scandals in the mid- to late 1990s.[6] Furthermore, decision-making among these elite is viewed as so consensus-oriented that policies often become *ad hoc* remedies or mere compromises (T. Ishida, 1986: 24).

In the Western liberal principle, bureaucracy as a governmental organization is supposed to be a politically neutral institution responsible for the fair distribution of resources to the nation. Political parties, on the other hand, at least originally, represent people who share common political ideas and/or interests and therefore do not necessarily represent the interests of the entire nation. In reality, however, public administration and politics are inseparably intertwined so that strict demarcation of roles between bureaucratic and political elite is difficult. The 'bureaucratization of politics and politicization of bureaucracy' seems to be a worldwide phenomenon (Rix, 1988: 61–2).

Still, it is particularly prominent in Japan because the long dominance of the LDP has made the border between the bureaucracy and the political system very ambiguous.

Western researchers who support this view cite the corruptive tendencies that develop within an atmosphere of close relationships among the political, economic, and bureaucratic elite.[7] While this model strongly emphasizes the bureaucracy rather than other political or economic leaders, it also ascribes to the power elite or elitist model, which holds that Japanese political and business circles are inseparably connected to the bureaucracy, comprising a united power nucleus (Fukui, 1977b).[8] One of the most well-known terms for this model is 'Japan Inc.', suggesting the most extreme, conspiratorial image, though this has been considered obsolete for some time (Curtis, 1975: 35–6).[9] On the other hand, a similar image of Japan possessing a united strategy to dominate the global economy remains attractive to some.[10]

The Pluralist Model

The pluralist model arose as a challenge to the bureaucratic dominance model. While the latter criticizes the status quo, the pluralist model commends the Japanese system as a valid form of liberal democracy. As Japan succeeded in its post-war economic recovery, the state's further aims became obscure, and the bureaucracy's role also became less certain and needed adjustment. The increasing variety of interests and dispersed sources of influence made traditional bureaucracy unable to respond effectively to society's needs. Even in terms of economic development in the 1960s, a questionnaire survey showed that neither bureaucrats nor politicians regarded the bureaucracy as important as the efforts of business or the industriousness of individuals (Muramatsu, 1981: 30–1).

Pluralism itself was much discussed in the context of American society. Whereas American political scientists were enthusiastic about it in the 1950s and 1960s, Japanese researchers were keen to apply pluralist models in the 1970s to the Japanese political economy.[11] Unlike the bureaucratic dominance model that posits continued bureaucratic dominance since pre-WWII, pluralists argue that bureaucracy fundamentally changed in the process of democratization following Japan's defeat in 1945, especially through the new Constitution in 1947. Consequently, the pluralist model stresses the restraints on bureaucratic power and the influence of political parties, especially the LDP, in decision-making. As the legitimate source of government lies in the Diet, the bureaucracy can act only within the framework determined by the party in government. Therefore, the bureaucracy is subject to political parties (Muramatsu, 1981: 293–9, also Chapters 4 and 8). From a similar viewpoint, some describe the relationship between politicians and bureaucrats in Japan as a principal–agent relationship (Ramseyer and Rosenbluth, 1993).

The limit of bureaucratic power over the political sphere can be clearly seen in a number of case studies, including those involving automobile recalls and the textile trade conflict with the United States (Otake, 1979). In analysing the influence and limits of political, economic and bureaucratic actors, Otake Hideo designed theoretical frameworks distinguishing different types and spheres of influences that could yield favourable consequences. That is, to a certain extent, and in certain areas, bureaucrats, big business and other interest groups can force their will upon political leaders. However, they have to succumb to the political will when politicians are determined not to give in to such bureaucratic or business pressures.

The pluralistic perspective also challenges the elitist model in general by emphasizing the competitive relationship among elite (Muramatsu and Krauss, 1984). While the bureaucratic politics model criticizes the corruptive relationship between the bureaucracy and the LDP, pluralists interpret the relationship as one of 'checks-and-balances'. Therefore, pluralist models maintain that the Japanese bureaucracy 'functions as a pivot for policy-making', despite emphasizing the importance of political actors in decision-making (Muramatsu and Krauss, 1987: 536–54).

As the variety of interest representation in the society increased (e.g., issues of welfare, local infrastructure, environment, education, etc.), politicians became more involved in various levels of decision-making. The bureaucratization of the LDP gave birth to *zoku-giin* (tribe politicians) or specialists in certain types of administrative responsibilities, including transportation, construction and agricultural subsidies (Inoguchi and Iwai, 1987; Sato S. and Matsuzaki, 1986). In addition to those distributive aspects of administrative responsibilities, some politicians began to specialize in the redistribution function of the government, such as taxation, welfare and health, and education, all of which impact the entire nation rather than limited and specific economic sectors. Some *zoku-giin* have more knowledge of their specialty than bureaucrats, therefore preventing bureaucrats from exercising a free hand in drafting policy proposals.

Ex-officials who have become politicians usually join the tribe of their former specialty to bestow their expert knowledge. The pluralist model also emphasizes another active role of political leaders in decision-making, as mediators. The fragmentation of the bureaucracy into ministries and bureaux, representing partial interests in various private sectors, fosters occasional stalemates in ministerial conflicts. Some powerful politicians, particularly LDP executives, obtain roles as mediators for such conflicts.

The pluralist model also points out that targets of interest group activities are 'sub-governments', not the government at large. Interest groups lobby individual ministry bureaux and the LDP *zoku-giin*, realizing the competitive relationship among these domestic decision-makers (Muramatsu and Krauss, 1987: 549; Pizzorno, 1981: 273).

Whereas elitist models include the big business circles, or *zaikai*, as one of the inseparable power elite, pluralists emphasize their relative independence of the political and administrative elite. Ogata Sadako pointed to conflicting interests between big business and the government, introducing a concept of three hierarchical levels of economic groups; the top level is *zaikai*, the second *gyokai*, and the third is individual firms (Ogata, 1977: 214–18). Although the definition of *zaikai* varies (Curtis, 1975: 36–8; Yanaga, 1968: 32), popular usage of the term means big business leaders, particularly those represented by four groups.[12] Another definition of *zaikai* requires *zaikai* members to be more than successful employers; it also necessitates participating in politics in an unofficial way, such as having personal contacts with a Prime Minister (Misawa, 1977: 182–3). Nevertheless, such access cannot simply imply *zaikai* influence on the political elite or agreement with government policy, as political decisions do not always reflect *zaikai* interests (Curtis, 1975: 49).

Gyokai is equivalent to an industrial sector, such as textiles, steel, electric power, banking and retailing, usually organized as a trade association. It is at this level that industries have close contact with responsible bureaucrats, as the *gyokai* represents interests of a sector as a whole against the government or foreign pressure. *Zaikai*, on the contrary, does not represent any particular industrial sector, but mediates conflicts among *gyokai* and coordinates national economic goals with the government (Allinson, 1987).

In addition to domestic interest groups, foreign interests are an important element in decision-making in Japan. Whereas *gaiatsu* refers to purely foreign influence, transnational actors whose nationality is mixed also exert pressure on Japanese decision-making. Transnational actors such as Japanese subsidiaries in Europe and international business alliances lobby and influence state decision-makers.

While the academic trend in Japan inclined to pluralism in the 1970s and 1980s, pluralist development seems to have stopped short. Critics of pluralism point out the virtual homogeneity of interests represented. The interests of other social groups were hardly realized effectively at the same level as those of LDP supporters (Yamaguchi J., 1989). However various the actors in decision-making are, interests of weaker minorities remain underrepresented in the decision-making sphere since they have no access to key decision-makers (Stockwin, 1988b: 11). Even among LDP supporters, the interests of 'important' supporters are given priority over those of smaller or financially weaker interest groups. In foreign economic policy, such an unequal treatment of interest groups by governmental decision-makers is also clearly seen. The liquor industry, for example, had political connections with the LDP, but agricultural interests were deemed much more important in the LDP's agenda. As a result, the tariff on imported liquor was nullified to appease trade partners, while agricultural products were exempted from the GATT Uruguay Round. Likewise, the interests of Japanese whisky makers were the first to be compromised in the liquor tax dispute, whereas *shochu* makers, who had stronger political clout than whisky makers, managed to make the government withhold longer for their interests. (See Chapter 4.)

Pluralists' positive evaluation for *zoku-giin* is also controversial. While pluralists accept a positive role for the *zoku-giin* in that they compete against bureaucrats over policymaking, others view *zoku-giin* intervention into bureaucratic decisions as the source of political corruption.[13] At best, the relationship between *zoku-giin* and bureaucrats is that of co-operation, not of 'checks-and-balances'.[14] In taxation policy, for example, tax tribe *zoku-giin* cannot counterbalance the bureaucrats, since they share a common ideological goal for tax policy (Yamaguchi J., 1993: 75–9).

Therefore the pluralist assumption that policy decision-making is carried out in free competition among various actors does not have any evidence in reality. It is for this reason that adjectives such as 'patterned' or 'compartmentalized' were put in front of 'pluralism' to describe Japan's situation (Muramatsu and Krauss, 1987; Sato S. and Matsuzaki,

1986: 153–72). Such an adjustment may be insufficient, however, to distinguish the Japanese model of pluralism from the elitist model. While the pluralist term 'tripod system' reflects the importance of the three pillars – the bureaucracy, the LDP, and big business (Hosoya, 1977b: 5-10) – it is questionable how essentially different it is from the elitist model or the bureaucratic dominance model. In the elitist model, the elite co-operates with each other because they share common interests against non-elite. The exclusion of non-elite from decision-making was deemed to be the most important element of foreign economic policy and its resulting success (Pempel, 1978).

Political instability since 1993 may have left policymaking to the bureaucrats almost exclusively (Suzuki, 1994). Even with the return of the LDP to the government with various coalition partners, it is hard to judge how bureaucracy's role may change in Japanese politics. The administrative reform that began in 1993 with the Hosokawa government and continued through the Hashimoto government in 1996 accelerated curtailing the power of bureaucracy. A series of scandals involving a number of bureaucrats were revealed, which have severely undermined the status of bureaucracy. Simultaneously, some politicians have acquired a reputation of capable policymaking, and the number of bills brought up by members of the Diet is increasing.

The Corporatist Model

The third approach to analysing Japan's political economy is through the concept of corporatism. Corporatism is a system of interest representation in which interest groups are organized in a singular, hierarchical order, headed by peak organizations, and most typically the state intermediates labour and capital in a corporatist society (Schmiter, 1979b: 13).[15] Comparative studies of corporatism rank Japan as less corporatist than most Western European countries (Tsujinaka, 1986a: 232). As for the definition of corporatism, arguments vary in levels from macro- (national) to meso- (within an industrial sector) to micro-level (within a firm).[16] Focusing on the intermediation of organized interests within a society is one of the most popular views (Schmitter, 1979b).

While both pluralism and corporatism focus on interest groups as the major actors in decision-making, the characteristics of interest representation divide the two schools. In corporatist society, according to the theory, interest groups do not compete in a free market; rather 'unions and organized capital are always likely to prevail.'(Berger, 1981: 13)[17]

The theoretical development of corporatism has been supported by empirical studies of Western European countries,[18] but Japan has hardly been taken as a corporatist model (Tsujinaka, 1986a: 232). Nevertheless, a neo-corporatist approach may be useful to understand some features of the Japanese political economy. As is shown in criticisms of the pluralist view, government tends to give LDP interests priority, therefore enabling bureaucratic support, whereas other interests have fewer opportunities to press their cases. A common feature among various types of corporatism is that interests are organized by states, coinciding with the Japanese bureaucratic notion that every matter is under some bureaucratic jurisdiction.[19]

Two decades ago, Pempel and Tsunekawa called Japan 'corporatism without labour' (Pempel and Tsunekawa, 1979). Nakano's 'corporate pluralism' (Nakano, 1986b)[20] recognizes the existence of competition among 'actors' in policymaking (so it is pluralistic) and at the same time draws attention to the oligopolistic change in political parties as well as in business and to the cooperative attitudes of labour and the opposition parties towards the LDP. Differentiating between corporatism and an inclination towards corporatism, Tsujinaka points out a trend of 'corporatization' (Tsujinaka, 1986a)[21] in Japanese politics, which accelerated including the labour sector in the 1970s and the first half of 1980s (Tsujinaka, 1986b: 282–97). Zeigler included Japan in a group of Asian 'Confucian' corporatist systems (Zeigler, 1988: Chapter 5).

The coalitions created by the Social Democrats with the conservative parties in 1993 seemingly indicated the direction suggested in Nakano's article, at least at the political level, although at the economic or social levels there was no evidence of any widening participation of labour in decision-making. In some of the political scandals, it became clear that a system of government-controlled interest representation exists in Japan, organizing the selection and realization of interests. In the Recruit Scandal in 1989, for example, the 'procedure' for a new economic sector or a newcomer to a sector to establish its representation channel involved illegal actions.[22]

Nevertheless, some essential elements of the corporatist state seem to be lacking in Japan. First, even if there has been progress in recognizing labour's participation in the political economic system, it is still limited. Historical arguments about corporatism highlight labour participation in decision-making above almost all other interest groups (Maier, 1981), casting doubt on the meaning of 'corporatism without labour'. There seems little use in conceiving corporatism without labour when such a model looks identical to an elitist model. Aside from the overall theoretical debate between pluralism and corporatism, the debate in Japan's case seems to have less significance for understanding the Japanese political economy.[23] Without referring to either school, for example, Richard Samuels coined a term, 'reciprocal consent', by which the balance between bureaucracy and private firms in decision-making was ably explained (Samuels, 1987).

Second, a neo-corporatist state is expected to have a unified purpose in the maintenance of economic and social order (Williamson, 1985: 8). The rivalry and severe competition among bureaucratic organizations in Japan are at odds with this assumption. In addition, the LDP break-up suggests that the LDP system of organization is no longer a suitable way to represent interests at the national level. The birth of new parties may reflect the existence of interests that have been insufficiently represented or simply ignored.

Third, in terms of foreign economic policy, corporatist decision-making cannot explain transnational connections among firms and their effects on economic policy. Since corporatism originally focused on domestic interests and their representation in domestic politics, transnational linkages do not seem to be considered in corporatist models. In the automobile sector, for example, Japanese automobile industry interests are not exclusively represented through MITI. Instead, the industry sometimes is inclined to negotiate directly with foreign governments and industries. The liquor industry, for its part, is divided into sub-groups in terms of interest representation, one of which, whisky makers, sometimes shares a common interest with foreign whisky makers rather than with other domestic liquor producers. The transnational linkage of economic interests induces more complicated relations between states and private sectors than the original corporatist models expect. In the context of Japanese–European relations, the Japanese government may attempt to unite domestic interests to confront European pressure, but the definition of domestic interest is no longer self-evident in the widespread transnational business relationship.

Revisionism

Revisionism is not a school of thought that can be directly compared with the three above, but rather a movement to see Japan as outside the framework of generally 'Western' political science. Its impact on Japan's foreign economic relations, particularly with the United States but also with the EU, is far from negligible, though it seems to have lost momentum.[24] Until the early 1990s revisionism was quite popular among American academic, journalistic and political circles as emphasizing differences between the Japanese political economy and that of the West. It challenged the traditional idea that capitalism is the same the world over and deemed the Japanese capitalism is challenging and even threatening the Western, original capitalism.

The assertion that Japan is unique is nothing new for the Japanese people; there is considerable support for the idea that they are different from others. Some have questioned the actual applicability of Western theories to the areas of international politics and political economy (Yamamura and Yasuba, 1987: 1, 3–4). Johnson and E. B. Keehn, for example, discount applying a rational choice model to Japan's decision-making on the grounds that it ignores historical background and is totally Anglo-American centric (Johnson and Keehn, 1994). In their view, ahistorical arguments prevent a true understanding of Japan, which raises the question of confrontation between history and political science. Regarding decision-making, the revisionist school often stresses the importance of government officials, which makes it indistinguishable from the elitist model in substance.

Revisionism also encompasses some general ideas of the so-called 'Japan-bashers'.[25] The purpose of revisionist arguments was to accuse Japan's 'uniqueness' that is 'unfair' by Western standards.[26] In a sense, revisionism itself was a way of interpreting Japan–US relations rather than a solid framework to explain Japanese political economy. Yet the popularity of revisionism was a reflection of strained relationship Japan had with the EU as well as with the US.

THE STRUCTURE AND CHARACTERISTICS OF THE JAPANESE BUREAUCRACY

Regardless of which decision-making model is used, bureaucracy clearly positions itself at the core of decision-making in Japan, while other actors are sometimes neglected despite their significant roles in the decision-making process. Even in the pluralist framework, bureaucrats' participation in decision-making has never been questioned. As a consequence, the role and function of non-bureaucratic actors should be understood in conjunction with decision-making within the bureaucracy. Therefore, it is necessary to examine the structure of Japanese bureaucracy, which determines a significant part of the decision-making.

Kent Calder argues that bureaucratic decision-making can be divided into two types: taking initiatives (proactive) and responding to *gaiatsu* (reactive). According to him, the latter is usually the primary function of the bureaucracy in Japanese foreign relations (Calder, 1988).[27] However, assuming that the Japanese government remains passive in foreign economic policy is over-generalizing. Even though European pressure often prompts negotiations over economic policy between Japan and the EC, the Japanese government has now and then taken the initiative in the bilateral relationship. Case III, for example, shows that the Ministry of Foreign Affairs (MFA) of Japan initiated the Joint Declaration between Japan and the EC.

In the process of policymaking, most dossiers go up the bureaucratic hierarchy.[28] Divisions in each bureau of a ministry are usually the basic units handling an issue, and division chiefs are responsible for initiating plans to be sent up to their seniors and colleagues. Despite the importance of their tasks, however, division chiefs tend to remain anonymous in international negotiations (Omori, 1985: 88). Members of a division, including its chief and his deputy share an office (*ohbeya-shugi*),[29] and as a result they cultivate a united approach and attitude within the division. This does not deny the commitment of senior level officials, such as bureau directors, who appear to be responsible for decisions in external negotiations. They are closely consulted during the original planning process by the divisions. When difficulties occur in negotiations between different bureaux or ministries, one way to break through the deadlock is to elevate the level of negotiation to that of higher rank officials, a technique used in international negotiations as well. This technique also formalizes the resulting agreement, at which stage the actual negotiations have almost been finalized by lower level officials, simply leaving higher rank officials to sign the agreement.

What means success for a bureaucrat is to bring his or her policy into enactment. By doing so, that bureaucrat heightens the reputation of his or her ministry and enlarges the ministry's jurisdiction, budget and positions. Such behaviour is based on 'the ministerial bias' or 'the department's philosophy' (Muramatsu, 1981: 154–5). Japanese bureaucrats identify themselves with their original ministry, and apart from relatively short secondments, they usually stay in the same ministry until they retire. This enables ministries to retain institutional memory and loyalty to the organization, thus exacerbating the confrontation between ministries (Kusano, 1989: 74).[30] Strong rivalries among ministries are well known and called '*sekushonarizumu*' (sectionalism).[31] A European diplomat admitted that one of the most striking differences between Japanese bureaucracy and that of his own country was the fragmentation of the former. Different ministries in Japan tend to be indifferent to other ministries' policies, rather than showing a united opinion on the same issues.[32] On the other hand, the competition among groups or agencies within a government has been analysed extensively in North America and Western Europe, providing many insights applicable to Japan (Imamura, 1985).

To apply the bureaucratic politics model to Japanese foreign economic policymaking, it is necessary to make some assumptions about Japanese bureaucratic behaviour. First, instead of a powerful government chief deciding all policy issues, the ministry responsible for individual issues – i.e. the MOF for macroeconomic policy, the MITI for trade, and the Ministry of Foreign Affairs (MFA) for diplomacy – makes the final decision after the 'pulling and hauling' undertaken with other actors including *zoku-giin* politicians and interest groups. When an economic issue contains political implications, political leaders may need to make the final decision. In this sense, no permanent office, like the American presidency, makes a final decision. Most actors are equal, but there is always one that takes the top position, depending on the type of issues involved.

Second, Japanese officials are supposedly trained to suppress individuality and originality. The *ohbeya-shugi* reinforces the homogeneity of divisions within ministries. Therefore, it is more likely that personnel in the same division would have the same purpose and approach towards the issues at hand, such as trade issues between Japan and the EU. While a division could be deemed as a single actor, different divisions, bureaux or ministries may have opposing views. In other words, those decision-making actors within the same government do not always share a common purpose or belief system (Kusano, 1989: 55).

Third, bureaucrats are not supposed to pursue perfection in their policymaking, but to compromise on a moderate solution (Simon, 1976: 297; March and Simon, 1958: 140–1). Muramatsu accepts the validity of the 'administrative man' whose rationality is not absolute, but is rather satisfied with a moderate solution. He describes bureaucrats behaving in 'an adapting and rational' manner (Muramatsu, 1981: 22). In accepting this pattern of behaviour, however, there remains a question. In what sense is the bureaucrat's behaviour adapting and rational: for policy objectives or for his or her promotions and professional career?

DECISION-MAKING IN THE EUROPEAN COMMUNITY

While academic discussion of decision-making in Japan has so far been limited to domestic actors, the importance of cross-level transactions, indicated in Chapter 1, suggests that transnational actors have become influential in economic policy decision-making. In addition to non-state actors, the multiplicity of levels of actors in Europe, including the European Commission and member state governments, significantly influences Japan's decision-making towards Europe. Therefore, the decision-making structure in the EC/EU needs to be reviewed.

Decision-making in the EC differs greatly from Japanese decision-making. While the Japanese system of decision-making is hierarchical and formal, decision-making in the EC is disparate, often dispersed and as often mutually antagonistic as cooperative among the Commission, the Council and member states.[33] The institutional change of the EU by the Treaty of European Union in 1993 will not be discussed, as the Treaty did not significantly affect ongoing communications between Japan and Europe. The following is limited to examining the European structure of decision-making *vis-à-vis* its relations with Japan.

Governmental interactions between Japan and the EC can be divided into two areas: political and diplomatic on the one hand, and economic on the other, depending on which different bodies in the Community are responsible. For trade matters, because of the Common Commercial Policy based on Article 113 of the Treaty of Rome in 1957, the European Commission handles negotiations with Japan, whereas member states give a mandate to the Commission or voice their demands to the Commission via a Council organization, namely the 113 Committee. Within the Commission, DG I (external relations) and DG III (industrial policy) are usually responsible for trade matters with Japan.[34] The Commission acts as a negotiator and signatory on behalf of all member states for trade agreements as long as the issues fall within the Community's competence. Still, the Commission needs a mandate agreed to by the Council in order to act in place of individual member states.

The 113 Committee also has an important role in trade policymaking. The Committee is always consulted before the Commission takes action towards external countries such as Japan. Even when issues do not involve all member states, each member state can bring its trade concerns before the 113 Committee so that the Commission can pursue international negotiations on their behalf with its Japanese counterpart. The case of Scotch whisky is a good example, discussed in detail in Chapter 4. Since the Single European Act came into force in 1987, trade policy has relied on the possibility and practice of majority voting in the Council (H. Wallace, 1990: 222). In general, the common commercial policy seems to function well in the case of trade with Japan. However, there have been cases in which member states exhibited differences in the Council, making it difficult for the Commission to harmonize a common European policy towards Japan.[35]

A large number of interest groups lobby the Commission as well as the member state governments, since private industries have the right to call directly on the Commission to investigate allegations of third country trade barriers (for example, Japanese taxation system) injuring Community industries (Sargent, 1985: 229–53). Interest groups recognize the capability and necessity of the Commission, although the definition of the Commission's competence still provokes disputes. In other words, the Commission does not monopolize jurisdiction over trade and other issues, therefore interest groups have to look to both the Commission and member governments for support (H. Wallace, 1996: 58). The European Business Community, one of the most important interest groups in trade with Japan, lobbies extensively to the Commission, the member state governments and the Japanese government through its Tokyo office. Interest groups of each member state also lobby actively both in Brussels and in Tokyo. Actual examples of their activities are discussed in the following case studies.

For diplomatic and political issues, on the other hand, member state governments exert more independent strategies, although the Commission retains prerogatives for making drafts and initiating policy proposals on behalf of the Community/Union. While the Commission, particularly DG I, is equivalent to a national foreign service, the Council of Foreign Ministers often determines EC/EU foreign policy. In contrast to trade agreements, the Commission is not the sole signatory for the European side. Rather, the government holding the Presidency of the Council represents the member state governments in political treaties and agreements.[36] This does not mean, however, that relations between the Commission and the Council are adversarial (Ludlow, 1991: 87–8).

HYPOTHESES

As a conclusion of Part I, I raise two hypotheses on the applicability of theories to Japan's decision-making towards the EU. The existing state-centric IR approaches have been challenged as cross-border transactions have increased. Responding to such a challenge, the hypotheses to be tested are as follows.

First, if transnational relations, especially in the economic sphere, have developed to the extent that it influences domestic politics, Japanese decision-making involves new elements that go beyond the framework of the bureaucratic politics model. Second, if the policy area differs as the taxonomy suggested in Chapter 1, the centre of decision-making in Japan also shifts accordingly.

In addressing the first hypothesis, while public administration studies have extensively discussed the decision-making processes within the bureaucratic system, international relations can add a new dimension to the analysis of decision-making by focusing on interactions among actors across levels and borders. The bureaucratic politics model has been influential in describing decision-making but criticized in that it does not explain the role of non-state actors, particularly transnational actors. Furthermore, the reality of cross-level transactions across borders goes beyond the framework of traditional IR. The following cases test the necessity of a transnational approach in examining Japanese decision-making in the foreign economic policy arena, by studying domestic actors along with their European counterparts. The first two cases, involving trade issues, allow the first hypothesis to be directly examined. Extensive contacts at different levels as well as across levels between Japan and Europe indicate the wide range of participants in the decision-making process, although the Japanese bureaucracy is still deemed to be the most desirable point of contact by both European businesses and government officials.

Various levels of communication between Japan and Europe have developed. Japanese firms expanding into Europe and European firms penetrating the Japanese market have increased the number of contacts with each other. Communications between the European Commission and the Japanese government, on top of those at the national government level, have also grown, along with direct contacts between governmental agencies (including the Commission) and private (business) actors.

Regarding the second hypothesis, the contrasting case studies indicate a correlation between policy type and decision-making process. The link between foreign policy process and issue area has been discussed in the context of international comparison, arguing that issue areas rather than political structures determine the type of policy process (Zimmerman, 1973; Evangelista, 1989). Although the comparison between Japanese and European political structures is implied in the following case studies, the purpose of seeking a correlation between policy area and decision-making process here is to solve the question of Japanese foreign policy decision-making.

This hypothesis may be further divided into two assumptions. First, an individual-implementing policy (see Figure 1.2),[37] in which a foreign economic issue is categorized, allows bureaucrats to assume the most prominent role in supporting Japanese industrial groups, leaving political leaders merely to distribute the restricted amount of benefit among domestic interest groups. Second, when the issue is related to more structural matters, such as the tax system and overall foreign policy revision, the decision-making process involves political leaders as more significant actors. This difference in decision-making process has been described as the 'politicization' of Japan–EU relations. Between the end of WWII and the early 1980s Japan–EC relations were free from politicizing economic policy issues (Rothacher, 1983: xi). In contrast, since the mid-1980s, politicization of economic issues has characterized their relationship. Economic problems between them began to seek political solutions. Also the movement of building political relations has emerged, though it occurred slowly and only after the dramatic collapse of the Soviet bloc in 1989. By distinguishing different types of policies, however, 'politicization' can be understood not only as a gradual change in the general relationship between Japan and the EU, but as the expansion of policy areas.

Regarding the question of decision-making actors, different ministries are responsible in the following case studies. In each case, a main bureaucratic body is supposed to make the final decision, over which other bureaucratic as well as business groups try to exert influence. The inputs from transnational communications – i.e. between Japanese sub-governments and European industrial groups, between Japanese industrial groups and European Commission and member state governments and between businesses across borders – significantly impact state-to-state level negotiations.

The difference in actors' roles and influences in decision-making between the cases can be explained by focusing on the type of policies. Typical trade issues, such as automobiles (Case I), involve the implementing-individual level (see Figure 1.2). Therefore, the role of bureaucrats is expected to be more significant in decision-making than that of politicians. Taxation policy in Case II, however, involves potentially national structural changes, thus the role of politicians is important. Case III, which is not a trade issue and is thus fundamentally different from the first two cases, shows the MFA's attempt to lead structural policy changes, while it simultaneously tried to avoid other actors' intervention. As a result, the Joint Declaration never became an important agenda item among political leaders, nor did it attract other ministries or business interests. Thus what the MFA achieved did not add up to structural policy in the end.

Consequently the aggregation of those case studies from different areas will exhibit patterns of decision-making for Japanese foreign economic policy. In so doing this book aims to see the relationship between Japan and the European Union with a clearer view.

PART II

Case studies

Gathering case studies is in a way like accumulating circumstantial evidence. They are not as implicating as a murder weapon, for example, but even circumstantial evidence can certainly set a detective on the right track. The following three cases cover different issues and settings and together they crawl near to the conviction. The automobile dispute illustrates the European concern about Japanese imports, the severest bone of contention between Japan and the EC in the 1980s. The liquor tax dispute signifies another type of problem, namely Japanese market access. In parallel with the rising concern over non-tariff barriers (NTBs) in international trade in general, the EC regarded NTBs as important stumbling blocks to balanced trade with Japan. While those trade frictions characterized the bilateral relationship, diplomatic efforts were made to restructure the whole relationship to help resolve trade disputes.

The following three chapters share the same structure for the purpose of comparison. The first section of each chapter provides background information, including problematic areas between Japan and the European Community. This section includes US influence on the specific issue. Japan–US relations invite comparison to Japan–EC relations, and third party US interests in Japan–EC trade relations may influence decision-makers in Japan and Europe. The second section considers each issue from the Japanese perspective, focusing on the role of Japanese actors in the decision-making process, and the relationships among them. The third section details the European perspective in a similar fashion. The discussion here focuses on the structure and actors of European decision-making to the extent that they mattered to the Japanese decision-makers. Through these sections, where and how transnational relations were established, who the transnational actors were and how the context of domestic politics mattered in the international negotiations become clear. The fourth section offers a chronological description of each issue, focusing on international negotiations at the governmental level. Finally, the concluding section summarizes the meaning and consequences of international trade negotiations, assessing the transnational influence on domestic decision-making.

CHAPTER 3

Case I – The automobile agreement and domestic factors

Automobile disputes symbolized the troubled trade relations between Japan and the European Community in the 1980s and culminated in the agreement between the Japanese government and the EC in July 1991.[1] This agreement stipulated that free trade in automobiles be completed by 1999 and set a transitional period to allow European manufacturers to adapt. Since the agreement, officials from the Japanese government and the European Commission have held biannual meetings to control the flow of Japanese cars into Europe.

Japan's automobile trade policy towards the EC is one of the main puzzles in understanding these negotiations. This puzzle can be broken down into two questions: what kind of relationship existed between the Japanese automobile sector and the Ministry of International Trade and Industry (MITI), and to what extent did MITI influence the automobile industry? European pressure on Japanese decision-making and the relationship Japanese car manufacturers cultivated with European governments, in particular the British government, also shaped the automobile agreement of 1991. Although the role of bureaucrats is essential, the independent role of industrialists in these automobile negotiations reflects the tension between the bureaucratic dominance approach and the pluralist approach of Japanese decision-making.

BACKGROUND AND PROBLEMATIC AREAS

The importance of the automobile sector is apparent as the sector proportionately reflects a country's economic size and strength with various related industries such as steel, electronics, rubber and other car parts. Understandably, some European countries have been very sensitive to Japanese car imports, particularly after witnessing the decline of the US motor industry after Japanese expansion into the US market. Japanese automobile exports to the US grew rapidly in the 1960s, reaching one million units in 1970. The figure rose steadily until the United States demanded voluntary restraint in 1981. This practice of voluntary export restraint (VER) seriously concerned Europeans who feared it would redirect Japanese car exports towards the European market.

In addition to this general trade imbalance, the automobile sector carried other specific reasons for concern: an overcrowded European market, pressure for change caused by the Single Market Programme, the question of how to treat Japanese cars made in Europe and the US factor.

The European Market

The most distinctive feature of the European automobile industry was that it had a constant problem of overcapacity. This was particularly true for the passenger car market. As many as six major manufacturers claimed more than 10 per cent of the market share, though none of them boasted a decisive lead over the others. Japan's participation – whether by export or transplant – in such a close game among European makers naturally caused considerable concern and bitterness (Yoshida, 1990). Japanese car imports had been a sore point in Japan–EC relations since the end of the 1970s, which led to MITI monitoring since 1986. Compared with the American car market, the European market was highly protected, allowing a less spectacular trade deficit from Japanese car imports. Before the 1991 car agreement between Japan and the EC, only 20.8 per cent of the EC's trade deficit to Japan was caused by car trade, compared with 59.0 per cent for the United States (MITI, 1991).

Although the term 'European market' may imply a single uniform entity, it was composed of twelve individual markets, at least until 1993 when the Single European Market programme was completed. As a result, specific circumstances of individual countries shaped Europe's response to Japanese automobile imports. On the one hand, highly protectionist countries, such as France and Italy, had and still have quite strong domestic manufacturers and imposed quantitative controls on Japanese car imports. France allocated Japan a quota of 3 per cent of its market share (85,000 units in 1991), whereas the Italian government admitted only 13,000 units in 1991, including those distributed via other member states.[2] Britain also set a ceiling for Japan's market share of 11 per cent (see Table 3.1). On the other hand, those countries

France	3% of market	Government allocates quota to importers.
Italy	3,300 + indirect (p.a.)	Importers apply for licence, registering Japanese cars with the government.
Spain	1,200 (p.a.)	Same as above.
Portugal	10,000 (p.a.)	Same as above.
U.K.	11% of market	SMMT* and JAMA's agreement. JAMA† allocates quota for Japanese makers.
Other EC states	No official restriction	-

Table 3.1 *The restriction of Japanese car imports in EC countries until 1993*

* SMMT: Society of Motor Manufacturers and Traders
† JAMA: Japan Automobile Manufacturers Association

without indigenous car manufacturers, such as Denmark, Greece and Ireland, assumed a more liberal trade stance, allowing the free flow of Japanese-made automobiles. In contrast to these two groups, Germany did not have any formal barriers, but managed to keep the market share for Japanese cars at around 15 per cent, much lower than shares in Denmark, Ireland and other non-restricted markets. Some believed a 'gentlemen's agreement' allowed for a stable appearance of Japanese cars in the German market as well as in Belgium and the Netherlands (Hindley, 1985: 66),[3] although Japanese manufacturers denied this and attributed the relatively smaller Japanese presence in the German market to the strength of German manufacturers.[4]

The Single Market Programme

In 1987, when the Single European Act of the EC was ratified by member states, the programme to complete the Single European Market started at full speed. The so-called 1992 programme led to the closer convergence of national policies within a single Community policy, a policy more liberal and less regulatory than those of most member states. In other words, the programme forced those countries with protectionist policies to face the prospect of freer competition with Japanese manufacturers, along with tougher competition from other European manufacturers. At the same time, the programme of unifying the twelve markets into a single European market motivated

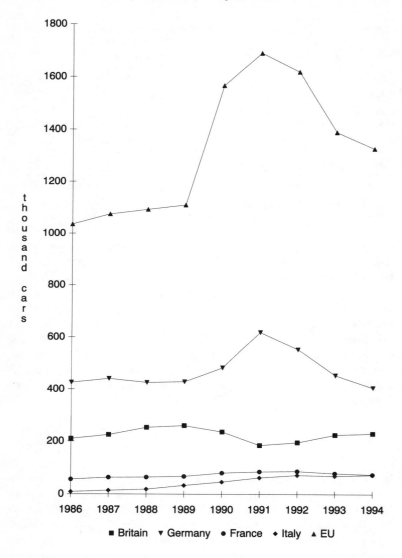

Figure 3.1 The new registration of Japanese cars in European markets ('000)

Source: Economist Intelligence Unit, *European Motor Business, Japanese Motor Business,* and *International Motor Business,* 1987–95.
* Twelve member states (1986–89); fifteen member states plus Norway and Switzerland (1990–4).

Japanese automobile manufacturers to invest in production within the EC. The potential profits from the emerging single biggest market lured them, and they also feared the creation of a 'Fortress Europe' that would discriminate against foreign products and prevent Japan from benefiting from market expansion. Japan and other countries outside the EC were seriously concerned about the potential protectionism of the programme.[5]

As a result of the Single European Market, national quotas for Japanese car imports became anachronistic, as cars could enter freely via member states not having import restrictions. This meant that the Single European Market might extinguish one or even more European manufacturers due to accelerated competition. Not surprisingly, the notion of free competition with Japanese manufacturers found few supporters within the EC. Both governments and manufacturers protected by national import quotas strongly resisted their termination. (See the sections on European governments and manufacturers later in this chapter.)

The Directorate General (DG) IV of the European Commission, responsible for competition policy, was part of the small minority to encourage free trade. Commissioner Bangemann's plan on behalf of DG III (responsible for industrial policy and the internal market) advocated a Community-level automobile policy including the termination of national import restrictions by 1990 or 1992. Based on his belief in liberal trade policy, Commissioner Bangemann requested the Industry Ministers' Council to abolish import restrictions on Japanese cars.[6]

Neo-classical economists also favoured eliminating all trade restrictions, citing the negative effects of VERs (Curzon and Curzon, 1987). In concrete terms, critics believed that VERs increased consumer costs and delayed restructuring of the European automobile industry, though other forms of trade restrictions, including import quotas, also hampered restructuring. It was suggested that even a tariff barrier would be less harmful to the competitiveness of manufacturers than VERs (A. Smith and Venables, 1991: 190).

In one calculation of the costs of the British VER, an analyst concluded: (1) the VER disadvantaged customers by raising the price by 10 to 15 per cent, excluding luxury-type cars, which were hardly affected by the price difference; (2) tariff revenue was lost by discouraging people from buying Japanese cars; and (3) 'those who would have purchased a Japanese car in the absence of the VER have been diverted by its effects to a less-preferred car from another source.' (Hindley,

1985: 86–7.) This last cost may be questionable, but over 130 million sterling pounds was calculated to be lost, to the disadvantage of British residents. Although at the time there was only British Leyland – and now there is no purely national car manufacturer – this analysis concluded that VER benefits for British manufacturers would not outweigh the total costs of the VER (Hindley, 1985: 88–91).

In 1988 Japanese business circles became almost panic-stricken at the prospect of a stronger Europe as a rival economic power and of protectionism excluding the Japanese from the benefit of the Single Market. Fears of European protectionism lingered, even when the collapse of communism in Eastern Europe and the unification of Germany in 1989 diverted Japanese attention from the EC integration movement itself, as they appeared to strain the EC and its integration engine, Germany. While EC officials repeatedly tried to reassure other countries that the Single Market was not intended to build a 'Fortress Europe', the Commission nonetheless made an exception to the principle of free circulation of goods within the Community against Japanese automobiles. Japanese concern became greater when, as late as January 1991, the Commission still authorized some EC member states to monitor 'indirect' imports via other member states, based on Article 115 of the Rome Treaty.[7]

Japanese Cars 'Made in Europe'

Japanese foreign direct investment (FDI) in Europe significantly increased as a result of the 1992 programme (Kume and Totsuka, 1991; Turner, 1991: 110–13). The sharp rise of the yen against the US dollar after 1985 also facilitated Japanese FDI in Europe; this accounted for the general trend of Japanese manufacturers transferring production abroad. Without the great appreciation of the yen, it would have been impossible, or non-profitable, for manufacturers to shift production to Europe.

In addition to the revaluation of the yen, the stagnated and saturated Japanese domestic market forced firms to look for new markets to increase output (Dassbach, 1994). For the same reasons as American car manufacturers had in the 1920s, Japanese car manufacturers began European production in order to compensate for slow growth in the domestic market.

After all, European integration affected the timing of the Japanese investment rather than determining whether companies should invest or not (Thomsen and Nicolaides, 1991: x). In Honda's case, for example, it was not the 1992 programme in particular but Honda's basic policy to 'produce where there is demand' that led to its decision to invest in the Community.[8]

In extensive studies on Japanese FDI in the EC[9] and its impact on trade, some analysts argue that FDI was a substitute for trade and its purpose was to avoid or mitigate trade friction (Micossi and Viesti, 1991; Kume and Totsuka, 1991[10]). Others found a complementary relationship between Japanese FDI and exports to the EC (Buigues and Jacquemin, 1994: 171; Thomsen and Nicolaides, 1991). Prior to the Single European Act, Japanese FDI in the European Community increased considerably around 1984, supposedly in an attempt to circumvent anti-dumping procedures. The scale of FDI, however, was much smaller than the boom in 1988–90. The substantial increase of Japanese FDI towards the EC started in 1988 (JETRO, 1994: 16). This means that when the Single Market became a realistic idea in 1985 by the publication of the Cockfield White Paper that advocated the benefits of market unification of member states, few Japanese companies realized the full implications.

Nevertheless, the belated effect of the 1992 programme on Japanese manufacturers was prominent. Whereas the programme encouraged trade liberalism within the Community, external trade was not explicitly discussed when the programme was announced, adding to Japan's concern. The impending Single Market apparently provoked Japanese FDI in the automobile sector also. Among approximately 60 Japanese car and car parts manufacturers that had established their factories within the EC by 1993, only seven of them had done so before 1984 (JETRO, 1994: 105–67). Although European headquarters were established much earlier, actual production by Japanese car makers in Europe had to wait until the second half of the 1980s.[11] NMUK, Nissan's British subsidiary, was established in 1984 and began production in 1986; Toyota in Burnaston, Derbyshire and Honda's Swindon factory both produced their first cars in 1992.

The rush of Japanese car factories into the EC area provoked criticism among the Europeans. They derided them as 'screwdriver plants' because they mostly used imported Japanese parts. France resisted most strongly. In 1988 the French government, supported by domestic manufacturers, objected vehemently to accepting such cars as European-made and sought to include them in the Japanese import quota. The concept of 'local content' became the focus of the argument, which was much confused with the origin rule of products in the Community. The Community had adopted the Kyoto Convention, defining product origin as the place where the last substantial transformation that adds value to the product is carried out (Zaimis and Chance, 1992: 13, 22–3). Therefore, neither proportion nor amount of local content defined the origin of products. In addition to this rule, products with 60 per cent or more of locally made parts were customarily, as well as legally, approved as EC products.

The French government, however, insisted that unless the Nissan Bluebird made in Sunderland consisted of 80 per cent or more of locally produced components, it had to be treated as a Japanese import and subjected to quotas. The Italian government also sought to treat NMUK's products as Japanese imports. The British government backed the Japanese manufacturers in resisting French pressure and announced officially that local content should be decided between the host country and the manufacturer.[12] In the end, the Commission managed to make France guarantee that British-made Nissans would be excluded from the import restriction.[13] Italy also agreed to mitigate restrictions on these cars but said that it would not agree to European status for Japanese-badged cars.[14]

Japanese manufacturers, however, provided the final solution to this dispute by introducing more local or regional subsidiaries as a trade-off to the higher local content. Nissan, the first to produce in Europe, took the longest time to raise its local content, but nonetheless reached 80 per cent by 1990. Toyota and Honda had the advantage of coming later and took less than two years to clear that hurdle after beginning production. In Fuji's case, however, their plan of a green field investment in France with a 20,000–30,000 per annum level of car production was abandoned because of the 80 per cent local content demanded by the French government.

As Japanese manufacturers managed to raise local content, as required by the European governments, some suspected that 'the hidden purpose of the import restriction was to promote local production in Europe.' (Tsukada, 1992) To some, the end of the dispute over local content signalled that the French government merely intended to promote Japanese FDI in France.[15] Such a positive attitude toward Japanese FDI can be explained by its effect on the manufacturing sector of the host countries. In Britain, productivity in the car-parts sector reportedly improved significantly since the launch of Japanese car manufacturers in the country.[16] In a study of Japanese manufacturing FDI in the UK, job opportunities in the automobile sector increased; the trade balance experienced a substantial surplus; and additional exports caused by Japanese car factories in Britain outweighed the additional imports (R. Strange, 1993: 385–420).

FDI in the European automobile industry was not new. Two US automobile giants, Ford and GM, established European subsidiaries as early as the 1920s and are now members of the top six manufacturers in Europe. Although their investment strategies were different to start with (Ford choosing a green field site in 1924; GM buying Vauxhall in Britain in 1925 and Opel in Germany in 1929), their European branches both remain highly independent of their US parents, with their research and development function separate from American parents and local content set at more than 90 per cent. Although these American companies seem to be totally 'Europeanized', they were allowed full membership in the Association of European Automobile Manufacturers (ACEA) only in 1991, since the former body, the Committee of Common Market Automobile Constructors (CCMC), had never permitted American participation. Through the American experience, therefore, Japanese manufacturers were well aware of the sensitivity of Europeans.

The boom of Japanese FDI itself ceased after 1992, when the euphoria of the Single Market died down and a global economic downturn simultaneously set in, severely impacting the Japanese economy for a long time. According to Japan External Trade Research Organization (JETRO)'s poll in 1993, 82.8 per cent of Japanese manufacturers in Europe admitted some negative impact of the economic downturn on their businesses, of which 38.7 per cent decided to lay off some personnel, 36.6 per cent reduced production and 31.8 per cent abandoned investment in infrastructure (JETRO, 1994: 7). In such circumstances, automobile makers were not an exception.

US Influence

The US factor cannot be neglected when considering the psychology of decision-makers in Japan and Europe, as well as the nature of the world automobile market and automobile production. The US government carefully monitored the negotiation process between Japan and the EC and the concluding accord of 1991, wanting Japanese transplants in the United States not to be counted as Japanese cars in the quota.

There was, therefore, another area of transnational relations between Japanese manufacturers in the US and the American government that could be considered.

The tremendous pressures from the US and Europe that Japan open its market highly impacted Japan's automobile trade policy since the 1980s. Although Europe has been successful – as exemplified by Rover Japan – in establishing its own distribution channels and easily signing up new distributors, the Europeans insist that the special relationship between Japanese manufacturers and distributors (*keiretsu*) made it harder than it would have been in other markets.[17] Thus the EC agrees with the US analysis that Japanese automobile market is protected by NTBs. In this sense, the US and the EC were allies.

Simultaneously the US and the EC were rivals competing in the same international market, including the Japanese market. While American car exports increased in the early 1990s, the Germans in clear contrast saw their exports drop by almost 30 per cent. Among US exports, a significant amount was produced by Japanese manufacturers in the US: 49.3 per cent of car imports from the US were produced by Honda and 14.6 per cent by Toyota. Despite the rapid growth of these Japanese transplants in the US, the most successful manufacturers in the Japanese imported car market were all German manufacturers: Volkswagen, BMW and Mercedes-Benz. German and American attitudes contrasted over the Japanese market. BMW, for example, tended to be rather quiet in trade disputes due to the importance of the Japanese market for its export strategy (out of 510,112 cars produced in 1993, BMW exported 28,532 to Japan).[18] Meanwhile the American Big Three (General Motors, Ford and Chrysler) often exerted glaring pressure on the US President and Congress. The German preference for free trade reflects this attitude, even in the context of Japanese exports and transplants in Europe. However, the so-called revisionist view, advocating that the EC and national governments take a similar stance to the US, did become more evident, as the revisionism gained popularity.[19]

The intense bilateral trade negotiations between Japan and the United States raised European suspicions that Japan would compromise with American demands at the cost of European interests. In February 1992, for example, when the Japan-US agreement on automobiles allowed for a doubling of Japan's purchase of American car parts, there was strong criticism in Europe.[20] Some also worried that the American attitude might cause European protectionism to re-emerge.[21]

A similar case reappeared in May 1995 when Japan was to reach a bilateral deal with the United States to set up a 'voluntary' plan to increase foreign car parts purchases. The European Commission threatened both sides to bring the case to the World Trade Organization (WTO).[22] As Japan and the US finalized the agreement at the end of June, the EU succeeded in participating in monitoring the agreement.[23] According to the EU, the unilateral sanction of imposing a 100 per cent tariff on Japanese luxury cars that the US threatened to do, simply contradicted the WTO and its principles. During this dispute, the EU was careful not to take definite sides between Japan and the US.

JAPANESE DOMESTIC ACTORS

Now that the contexts in which the automobile disputes took place are covered, the next question is the contents, namely: who participated? As Chapter 2 reviewed, Japanese actors are largely classified into three groups: bureaucrats, politicians and economic interest groups.

Bureaucrats

The Ministry of International Trade and Industry is the most important government organization for the Japanese automobile industry. MITI's role is, as its name suggests, making and implementing industrial and trade policy, though these two domains are so closely related to each other that sometimes it is impossible to distinguish between them. In the early stages of the postwar period when economic recovery was a central concern of Japan, both areas of MITI's jurisdiction were key factors. Historically the ministry emphasized industrial policy more, with trade policy providing a supplementary role. In the wake of serious trade friction, however, trade policy became more prominent.

Since Chalmers Johnson's seminal *MITI and the Japanese Miracle* was published in 1982, it has been widely accepted, especially in the English-speaking world, that Japanese industrial success derived from MITI initiatives. MITI's importance and power, however, tended to be overemphasized regardless of the stage of Japan's development. In his book, Johnson discussed the period between 1925 and 1975, attributing the rapid growth of several industries to tight government control, mainly by the Ministry of Commerce and the Ministry of Munitions in the pre-war period and later MITI.

In reality, various MITI projects turned out to be ineffective, if not abject failures. Oil industry policy is one example. In 1974, MITI was widely accused of irresponsible administrative guidance for cartels (Namiki, 1989: 61–113). Instead of overestimating the power and effectiveness of MITI, Daniel Okimoto specified MITI's role as providing 'a framework for communication and consensus building between government and business' and by doing so, preventing 'excessive meddling by the political parties' in industrial policy (Okimoto, 1989: 232).

The automobile manufacturers neither enjoyed nor wished for such strong intervention by MITI (Cusumano, 1985: 20, 403–4). MITI's main responsibilities to the automobile industry were to provide protection through trade policies and to nurture the industry. During the 1950s and 1960s, MITI protected the automobile industry through high tariffs, a commodity tax to give advantage to domestic products compared to imports, import restrictions via foreign currency control, and foreign investment restrictions. The government nurtured the industry by providing financial support. *The Law Concerning Special Measures for Development of the Machinery Industry* (1956) enabled automobile primary-parts producers to take low-interest loans from the Japan Development Bank, and secondary-parts makers from the Small Business Finance Corporation. Nevertheless, such financial support given to the automobile industry in the 1950s and 1960s was considerably less than that given to other heavy industries (Calder, 1993: 110–11, 169–70). Whatever financial advantage the Japanese automobile manufacturers had enjoyed ended in April 1971, when capital liberalization, although only nominal at that time, took place.

In any case, it was manufacturers rather than MITI that forged most technological and managerial innovations. MITI planned to mould the automobile sector as it liked, though failed. Neither the 'people's car plan' of 1955[24] nor the plan to reorganize makers through mergers and acquisitions in 1961 won the manufacturers' support, thus neither plan materialized. As those plans implied, MITI favoured a few big manufacturers rather than the medium-sized makers that have been the actual pioneers in developing technology. For example, Honda and Mitsubishi first developed anti-pollution devices, followed by top makers such as Toyota and Nissan (Mutou, 1984: 289). Auto industry development was not, therefore, totally designed by MITI as it had wished.

Regarding industrial policy in general, providing a suitable environment is the most important function the government can do to benefit industry (Lindbeck, 1981).[25] MITI's 'pick winners' policy for the automobile industry in the 1950s and 1960s did not accomplish this; neither did the European 'national champions' policy in the 1970s and early 1980s. The result of such policies shows the limited efficiency of state intervention in industry. Nevertheless, even after Japanese manufacturers established international positions, MITI tried to control the industry rather than leave it to market forces. MITI's supervision of domestic investment to bring about an economic upturn illustrates the ministry's concern for oversupply, as well as its skepticism of the Japanese producers' ability to adjust.[26]

However, MITI was effective in developing the automobile industry by reserving the domestic market for domestic manufacturers until they became powerful enough to compete with American and European manufacturers. Foreign exchange control and tight regulation on imports were the most common tools for this purpose.

In addition to protecting and nurturing, MITI also negotiated with its foreign counterparts on trade issues. Since the maturity of Japanese manufacturers, MITI has maintained the upper hand over the automobile industry mostly in this area. On the issue of exports to the EC/EU, many decisions were at MITI's discretion: MITI handled negotiations to estimate European market growth; MITI decided the scale of total Japanese exports; and MITI allocated export quotas to individual makers. From 1986 until the 1991 agreement, MITI monitored Japanese exports to the EC. The participation of Japanese manufacturers in MITI policymaking was not usually exposed to the public, in that their more important contacts were often held at an informal level. Establishing export limits and allocating quotas to individual manufacturers inevitably involved hearings. Major firms submitted their own estimates of the European market, their own sales growth and other makers' sales growth, from which MITI officials supposedly calculated their estimates.[27]

MITI's attitude towards FDI was encouraging to the extent that it helped to divert trade frictions, particularly with the EC and North America. In the practice of foreign investment, however, MITI did not actively promote FDI in Europe. Admittedly, excessive industrial FDI could lead to a hollow-out in the domestic economy, in which case MITI was obligated to be cautious in advocating production transfer abroad. Nevertheless, MITI tried to create a favourable environment for FDI (Kuroda, 1990: 29–31). The Asian region absorbed most Japanese capital outflow, to which the government tacitly consented out of necessity, to maintain the competitiveness of Japanese-brand products against the steep rise of the yen. In 1980, when the United States demanded that the Japanese government encourage FDI and VERs towards the US, MITI agreed and requested Nissan and Toyota to launch transplants there. Although they were not legally obligated to do so, both companies started planning for FDI. When Nissan was about to establish production facilities in Britain, MITI was notified of the process, but to the media, MITI remained under the shadow of its UK counterpart, the Department of Trade and Industry (DTI).

In summary, MITI's control over the automobile industry was more effective in trade policymaking than in actively promoting the industry. MITI's trade policy did certainly influence car makers' production and marketing strategies in a direct manner. The industry, however, usually attributed any success to its own efforts with full pride, not to those of MITI. This weakened MITI's grip on the sector. While MITI's favours tended to be directed towards the top manufacturers, the international business expansion of medium-sized manufacturers, such as Honda, Mitsubishi and Suzuki, indicated that success was possible without MITI's attentive support. MITI often tried to influence industrial sectors in general through administrative guidance, which did not require legislative enactment to back up its authority; but this lesser formality made the obligation vague. Nonetheless, industrialists usually followed administrative guidance and other non-legally binding instructions, if only out of fear of retaliation from the ministry.

Japan's trade policy since the 1980s aimed at controlling the speed and degree of liberalization in the domestic market, in contrast to the apparent protectionism of the 1950s and 1960s. Despite implicit protests from the manufacturers, for example, MITI 'requested' Japanese manufacturers to provide a show room at special rates (almost nothing) for foreign (exclusively American) cars.[28] On the other hand, in the case of the car parts dispute with the United States, settled in June 1995, manufacturers were more willing to compromise from an earlier stage, while MITI's attitude was more intransigent.

As for promoting trade, MITI has several external organs, the best known being the Japan External Trade Research Organization. JETRO's initial function, as its name clearly indicates, is to promote trade and particularly since the 1980s imports.[29] In terms of automobile trade with the EC, JETRO's main functions include researching the global economy and promoting public relations with foreign countries in such areas as the Japanese economy, trade, industry and economic policy. While JETRO often provides foreign information to Japanese traders, automobile firms tend to rely on their own individual information gathering. Therefore, information collected by JETRO on automobile issues is mainly used by MITI. A substantial part of JETRO's personnel at the senior level are from MITI. MITI also sends its personnel to the office of the Machine Export Promoting Union in Brussels. Although those officials on secondment do not formally represent MITI, their role is essentially the same as other MITI officials abroad such as at embassies. Thus, MITI maintains wide information network through various routes.

Not all automobile trade issues were dealt with by MITI, as trade issues expanded to include the various problems of NTBs. A major example was the issue of *shaken* (Japanese MOT tests), clearly under the Ministry of Transport's jurisdiction. Thus, when the EU pressed for deregulating these tests, MOT officials carried out these negotiations with the European Commission.

Finally, the Ministry of Foreign Affairs was the formal representative body in international negotiations, especially for GATT-related issues. The First Division of Western Europe in the Asia and Europe Bureau (hereafter WE I) was responsible for political relationships with the EC, and the First Division of International Economic Affairs in the International Economic Affairs Bureau (in Japanese abbreviation, KK I) handled economic relations with the EC. Thus both divisions were consulted in trade negotiations with the EC. The MFA tends to be more conciliatory than other ministries.[30] It was sensitive to Japan's reputation and wished to cooperate in a liberal trade regime. In practice, however, the MFA had little influence on decision-making in trade policies, as other ministries had principal responsibility. In cases of trade issues with the EC, the general power of the WE I was quite limited because European issues in general ranked lower in priority than, for example, American issues. The KK I, for its part, tried more vigorously to participate in the car agreement, insisting that the agreement should be compatible with the GATT principle, i.e. no formal quotas. The actual consequence of the agreement was a monitoring system, which did not explicitly break the GATT rule. Consequently, MITI carried out official negotiations for other aspects of the agreement without much intervention from the MFA.

Political Leaders

The role of politicians in the automobile industry was not as apparent as in other industries, and thus it was almost negligible, particularly in trade issues. While representing general industry and commerce was deemed to be one of the most profitable activities of LDP politicians, as indicated by the fact that *shoko-zoku* (industry and commerce tribe politicians) was the biggest tribe of all, the automobile industry itself did not attract many Diet members.

The two different aspects of *shoko-zoku* account for this. On the one hand, they look after the local constituency consisting of small- and middle-scale enterprises. On the other hand, they represent the interests of a sector, focusing mainly on big business interests, through which they achieve financial support (Inoguchi and Iwai, 1987: 182–5). In exchange for support from industrialists, these politicians typically allocate benefits within a regulated domain and protect the interests of the whole sector against pressure from the domestic bureaucracy or foreign competitors.

In the case of the automobile sector, car manufacturers were all considered big businesses,[31] allowing no occasion for *jidosha-zoku* (automobile tribe) politicians to distribute interest among manufacturers, except for export quota allocations. Even these were determined by MITI without involving political implications. Therefore, *jidosha-zoku* could only protect the general interests of the entire sector, and thus there was a relatively thin relationship between politicians and the industry. The cases in which *jidosha-zoku* politicians could be active were mainly taxation problems, government subsidies and domestic regulation changes, i.e. issues routed through the Diet.[32] The automobile industry itself tried to build a stronger tribe for its sector.

Jidosha-zoku's influence on trade policy, however, seemed small and indirect. In trade issues with the EC/EU, European interest groups and government officials lobbied or met *jidosha-zoku* politicians, but their influence remained subtle.

Industry

Nine big businesses comprised the passenger car industry, and they acted as a single interest group. Japan Automobile Manufacturers Associations (JAMA) was one of the most powerful and vocal bodies among all industrial interest groups. Individual firms tended to rely on JAMA to express their opinions as a whole industrial sector rather than commenting independently on foreign trade issues, as their European and American industrial counterparts did. This made JAMA appear to be a highly united organization. In practice, however, the function of JAMA was formal rather than substantial. For example, in the case of the gentleman's agreement with the Society of Motor Manufacturers and Trades (SMMT) of the UK, both MITI and the DTI were closely consulted. MITI's administrative guidance and other forms of instruction were addressed to JAMA, but actual documents were directly delivered to each manufacturer.

Even though Japan had a domestic market of considerable size, it was considered too crowded to sustain nine automobile manufacturers. For the passenger car industry itself, there were two world-class giants and four medium-sized firms. Domestic competition expanded to export markets, where each maker made huge efforts to gather its own information, rather than rely on MITI or JAMA. In the second half of the 1980s, when Japanese exports to the EC grew gradually under MITI monitoring, most manufacturers had offices in Brussels,[33] although they had not started direct manufacturing investment, except for Nissan.

The success of individual manufacturers – particularly that of Toyota, Nissan and Honda – attracted enormous interest, encouraging a variety of research projects on the Japanese automobile industry. Such research did not indicate much governmental lead of industry growth any more than in other countries (Cusumano, 1985; Womack *et al.*, 1990; Garrahan and Stewart, 1992). As mentioned earlier, in contrast to the Big Two of Japan, namely Toyota and Nissan, medium-sized manufacturers had little support from the government, as seen in MITI plans of the 1950s and 1960s. Although their survival and subsequent success in international markets were supported by government protection of the domestic market and financial encouragement of overseas investment (Garrahan and Stewart, 1992: 16), medium-sized manufacturers, especially Honda, maintained a slight distance from MITI and led technological innovation.

The Relationship among Actors

Despite the widespread image of a tight relationship among Japanese political, bureaucratic and industrial leaders, the automobile sector showed relatively little interdependence among them. The strongest communication channel among the three was between the industry and MITI; this channel was nevertheless weaker than that of other industries, as mentioned earlier. Politicians could provide little benefit to either MITI bureaucrats or industrialists. MITI relied less on tribe politicians than other ministries did. When necessary, coordination or arbitration within the industry was taken care of by MITI with the help of JAMA – in other words, without LDP intervention. Compared to other ministries, MITI did not produce many LDP politicians from its former members, which was often used as a measure to foster a close relationship with the LDP. As a result, political interference, such as over personnel issues in MITI, provoked intense conflict.[34]

Regarding the relationship between MITI and the automobile sector, the famous *amakudari*, a custom by which former high-ranked officials get executive jobs in private firms, was not as common in the automobile industry as in other sectors. The majority of boards of major car companies consist of indigenous personnel, whose whole career is in the same company (Cusumano, 1985: 76).

For industrial development, as described above, car manufacturers were less dependent than other industries on MITI. Trade policy decision-making involved hearing from individual manufacturers, co-ordinating their opinions and winning their assent. In responding to foreign pressure, the automobile section of MITI sounded out manufacturers' interests, which were then reflected in MITI's opinions at international talks with foreign counterparts. In the case of negotiations with the EC, manufacturers were united under the common position of JAMA and left the international negotiations to MITI (McLaughlin, 1994: 151).

MITI offered the industry various interventions, regardless of their efficiency. The industry had no choice but to listen to what MITI said, but did not necessarily follow its advice. For example, Mitsubishi and Chrysler established a capital tie-up in 1969, despite strong opposition from MITI (Ogata, 1977: 223–3). In contrast to the 1950s when the industry needed heavy government protection to catch up with foreign car makers, manufacturers in the 1980s were capable of competing with their international rivals without government intervention, even in international markets. Although it was within MITI's jurisdiction through JETRO to provide auto manufacturers with the necessary information for launching direct investment, the importance of JETRO's role was minimal. Undoubtedly MITI's information was useful for those who tried to start any business in foreign countries. Automobile manufacturers, however, had been selling cars in Europe for a couple of decades before starting local production, setting up their distribution networks and their own business relations. Honda, for example, clearly and proudly credited choosing Swindon as its factory site to its own knowledge accumulated for over 20 years in Europe.[35] Nevertheless, manufacturers tended to feel obliged to maintain close communications with JETRO or MITI.

While big business in general has a close tie with the LDP, comprising a part of the power elite structure of Japan,[36] business-politics relations in the automobile sector was not as tight as in some other economic sectors. In July 1989, for example, the LDP lost the Upper House election, and it believed that the lack of cooperation from the automobile industry on the consumption tax issue attributed to its defeat. Around this time the relationship between the LDP and automobile industry was relatively cold.[37] JAMA officially supported the LDP and reportedly even contributed 5 billion yen to the party.[38] In terms of elections, on the other hand, most automobile workers were mobilized by the Social Democratic Party (SDP) through trade unions.

EUROPEAN ACTORS[39]

European actors operate under a different decision-making structure than Japanese domestic actors. The European Commission began to attract the attention of Japanese industrialists as well as bureaucrats in the 1980s, as it became less restricted in negotiating with full responsibility. Simultaneously, despite the common trade policy in principle, individual member states were allowed to pursue their own trade policy under Article 115 of the Rome Treaty. National governments of the member states, especially in Britain, Germany, France, and Italy, have always significantly impacted automobile trade policy with Japan. For the EC and the Commission, coordination among the member states was a key factor for successful negotiations with Japan. The last, but not least, significant actor was the automobile industry in Europe. Its influence on respective national economies strengthened its political clout and lobbying power.

Governments of the Member States

Before the 1991 agreement, national governments in four member states were responsible for unilateral control over Japanese cars entering into their national markets (see Table 3.1). In France, the government established 3 per cent quotas for registering Japanese cars. In this case, Japanese manufacturers did not limit exports to France themselves, but rather left French importers to allocate quotas to individual Japanese makers (i.e. how many cars each Japanese maker could get registered by the French government). Italy, Spain and Portugal had more or less similar unilateral ceilings for Japanese cars, through licensing the importers.

The French and Italian governments have been the most serious opponents of the Japanese automobile industry. Their hard protectionist policy was a corollary of their 'national champion' industrial policies: French Renault and Italian Fiat have both been strongly supported by their respective governments. These manufacturers, plus French Peugeot, depended heavily on their own domestic markets, and their presence in other European markets was considerably weak. They were the most vulnerable to competition with Japanese cars, and the French and Italian governments intervened directly to impede Japanese imports.

In contrast, the British government left the job of controlling Japanese imports to the industrialists, preferring this practice to an obviously protectionist policy, at least on the surface. The British government also actively encouraged Japanese investment in the UK, with tax credits for inward investors, for example. This inevitably led to rather frequent contacts between British government officials and Japanese manufacturers. Margaret Thatcher, as Prime Minister in the 1980s, was particularly enthusiastic about Nissan's inward manufacturing investment, at least partly because Japan had already marginalized trade unions in industrial and political life, a major agenda item of her government (Garrahan and Stewart, 1992: 5–6). Japanese FDI, encouraged by the UK government, positively impacted the British manufacturing sector. As was shown in the earlier section, the UK government, especially the DTI, regarded products from such plants as British-made. This British attitude usually met with French antagonism, complicating Japan's perception of the European Community. Nonetheless, the cooperation between Japanese automobile manufacturers and the British government provides a meaningful example of transnational relations.

The German government assumed an even more liberal stance than the UK, again at least on the surface. Since German manufacturers, such as VW, BMW and Mercedes-Benz, were highly competitive both in European and international markets, the German government strongly supported a liberal trade policy. Even in the Japanese market, German makers, particularly those of specialty cars, successfully increased their share. Therefore, the German government needed be cautious not to provoke protectionist retaliation in Japan.

Individual member states, therefore, pursued their own automobile policies, including separate contacts with MITI and other Japanese actors. The British Embassy in Tokyo, for example, included DTI personnel, whose tasks included regularly contacting MITI officials, Japanese manufacturers and sometimes political leaders interested in automobile trade issues. At the same time, individual European embassies communicated with EC delegations as well as with each other, although different approaches to the car issue among member states remained.

The Commission of the European Community

It was never easy for the Commission of the EC to co-ordinate such various national automobile policies. Even though the Single European Act promised the Commission sole authority to handle external trade in principle, the Community's automobile policy did not take shape immediately. In the meantime, the Commission merely mediated between member states over such conflicts as France and Britain's differences over local content requirements for cars from Japanese transplants in Britain. (See the earlier section of this chapter.)

When Martin Bangemann assumed office in 1989 as the Commissioner responsible for the DG III, dealing with the internal market and industry, the direction of the Community's policy changed significantly. It is noteworthy that the change in personnel transformed the Community policy to the opposite direction. Together with Commissioner Leon Brittan, then responsible for the competition policy (DG IV), Commissioner Bangemann aimed to liberalize automobile policy at the Community level and replace protectionism in some member states. The issue of Japanese cars presented a major obstacle to co-ordinating national policies into a Community policy, and the

Commission had to threaten reluctant member states to compromise. In practice, Commissioner Bangemann urged member states to reach a prompt decision on the transitional period, failing which, general market rules were to be in force at the start of 1993. At the same time, Commissioner Brittan warned that 'if Community agreement was not reached, the Commission would have to enforce the law by taking legal proceedings against countries which maintained quotas.'[40]

While using strong words in framing a common automobile policy, the Commission was constantly under pressure from the member states. As indicated in the chronology of the negotiations in the following section, Commissioner Bangemann had to retreat from his initial proposition of a liberal, common automobile policy, and compromise with the demands for protection that came mainly from the southern member states, particularly France and Italy.

As for negotiations with the Japanese government, the Commission never acquired nor even sought a formal mandate from the Council of Ministers to negotiate with Japan, as was the normal practice. The Commission opted for informal negotiations with MITI, so that the lack of coordination among member states would not deter them from reaching an agreement with Japan. Even if France had wished to veto the accord, for example, its informality would have made such a measure inappropriate.[41] Such tactics on the part of the Commission caused ambivalent reactions from the member states. The British government, for example, opposed such irregular measures but supported the Commission's stance on the treatment of transplants. On the other hand, the Commission was concerned that France or Italy might resort to national import quotas, which the GATT might find legal. Those countries could then veto a formal draft accord between the Community and Japan and continue their protectionist policies without fear of extra-Community legal sanctions, thus undermining the principle of the Single Market (Mason, 1994: 433).

In its relationship with Japan, the DG I (external affairs) also participated directly, especially at the early stage of negotiations. DG I also worked to settle US concerns that Japanese-badged cars manufactured in North America not be considered as Japanese cars, so that they would not be included in the quotas. The EC delegation in Tokyo, for its part, communicated with Japanese automobile manufacturers as well as with MITI, independently from member states' embassies.

Automobile Manufacturers

It took European manufacturers even longer than their American counterparts to realize that the Japanese success story was worth researching, rather than simply blaming Japan for being unfair (T. Jackson, 1993: 93–107). Because of the industry's size, individual automobile manufacturers often exercised significant political clout over automobile policymaking. Unlike their Japanese counterparts, individual European automobile manufacturers boldly expressed their opinions on car trade issues. Jacques Calvet, the president of the Peugeot–Citroën–Talbot Group, was the strongest opponent of unrestricted imports of Japanese cars,[42] resulting in Peugeot Group's exclusion from the ACEA at its inception.[43] The tone of his argument also provoked strong criticism in Japan (Yoshida, 1990: 122–37). Although European manufacturers realized the inevitability of liberalization of the European automobile market, they demanded a European-wide quota for Japanese imports to replace national frameworks.

While the Commission tried hard to convince member states, the Japanese government made no serious efforts to assuage protectionist countries such as France and Italy. At the same time, however, French and Italian manufacturers' emphasis on the domestic market in their marketing strategies meant that they neglected the Japanese market and consequently exercised little influence on Japanese decision-making. In contrast, the Japanese were highly sensitive to any change in the tone of German manufacturers, who were believed to be sympathizers of free trade. When the president of BMW reportedly admonished increased local production of Japanese transplants, Japanese makers took it seriously as a sign of strengthening European criticism against Japan (Nakamura Tsuneo, 1992: 56).

At the same time as European manufacturers sought to impede Japanese penetration into their home markets, there were several cases of business co-operation between Japanese and European manufacturers, such as: Mitsubishi and Volvo, Honda and Rover[44] and Ford and Mazda. In the case of Mitsubishi and Volvo, the Dutch government participated in their joint venture in the Netherlands, giving an interesting example of transnational relations.[45]

Although each manufacturer brought to bear significant influence on its own national government, indicating considerable political clout, European automobile manufacturers did not easily unite into a single interest group, presenting a functional problem before the ACEA succeeded the CCMC in 1991 (McLaughlin, 1994: 149–56). In part, those who produced luxury cars (for example, BMW) had different interests from mass-producers (for example, Fiat, Renault, VW and Peugeot Group). The lack of internal consensus among manufacturers, particularly on the issue of how to deal with Japanese cars, resulted in poor lobbying ability with the Commission. Individual companies consequently made direct interest representations to the Commission (McLaughlin, 1994: 155). Nonetheless, the transformation of the group into the ACEA, in which they introduced majority decision rules instead of unanimous ones and ostracized the most intransigent Peugeot Group, enabled the industrial group to gain more prowess of its own.[46]

CHRONOLOGY: THE NEGOTIATION PROCESS OF THE 1991 AGREEMENT[47]

In the late 1980s, the expected completion of the Single Market by 1993 necessitated formulating a common automobile policy instead of allowing individual member states to have their own. This meant that the EC needed to co-ordinate twelve individual automobile policies, the main problem being how to open restricted markets to Japanese cars. In the meantime, the principle of free circulation of goods within the Community was suspended in the five countries restricting Japanese automobile imports (see Table 3.1). This allowed these countries to limit indirect imports (i.e. those that come from other member states) on the basis of Article 115 of the Rome Treaty. In order to establish a Community-wide framework that would comply with the Single Market, Japan–EC bilateral negotiations were carried out. In other words, the negotiations derived from the EC policy change, to which Japanese actors needed to respond. Simultaneously, Japanese industrial policy for the automobile sector, including private initiatives for transplants and their transnational relations, was a significant determinant of the negotiation process.

As mentioned earlier, the Commission assumed an informal approach to negotiations with Japan because of EC internal diversities, which Japan accepted. While having officially requested a smooth start of automobile free trade in the Community, MITI was fully aware of the difficulties facing European manufacturers in preparing for free competition with the Japanese. The MFA also participated, not only because of the formality of international negotiations, but also out of concern that the resulting agreement be compatible with the concurrent GATT Uruguay Round talks. The early stage of the talks between Japanese and Commission officials, therefore, included those from the KK I of the MFA. The automobile division of MITI, for its part, met with Japanese manufacturers to decide its position on the form and size of Japanese car sales in the Community.

Consequently, MITI and the Commission contrasted significantly in their management of 'domestic' actors. While the Commission constantly had to negotiate with member state governments and convince European manufacturers during the negotiations with Japan, Japanese automobile makers remained compliant so that MITI did not have to struggle to achieve domestic consensus.

In its approach, the Commission fluctuated between protectionism and a more liberal automobile policy. When Commissioner Bangemann took leadership of DG III in 1989, Japan appreciated the more liberalized policy. His plan, which provided the basis of the Commission's official plan for a common automobile policy, included: (1) abolishing national import restrictions on Japanese automobiles by the end of 1992; (2) setting a transition period after the launch of Single Market in 1993 to allow European makers time to prepare for free competition with Japanese automobiles; and (3) establishing that no requirement of local content be made by member governments. Once talks with the Japanese government started, the second point became the focus of discussion, together with the treatment of Japanese cars produced in the EC. The Commission wanted a voluntary restriction on Japanese imports to be the method of control during the transition period, while France, Italy and even Germany demanded an import quota be set at the Community level. This policy was sought not only because of the principle of free trade, but also because member states could not challenge the Commission on Japanese voluntary restrictions, i.e. what was not the Commission's own action.

Various views appeared in the press about the desirable length of the transition period. In mid-September 1989, European makers, including VW, Fiat and Renault, demanded five years, for which Toyota showed some understanding.[48] However, at a time when the Commission had almost achieved a consensus among European manufacturers in December 1989, French government officials insisted on seven years.[49] Two months later, the Commission released a report indicating that national quotas might be kept for ten years.[50] Throughout 1990, no single view prevailed on the transition period length among the European makers. Jacques Calvet of Peugeot in particular held to his strongly protectionist position, demanding at least ten years. As a result, the European automobile association, CCMC, practically collapsed, and all but Peugeot established a new association, the ACEA, in February 1991.[51] In March 1991, all ACEA members agreed to approximately six to seven years for the transition period.

In January 1990, MITI and the Commission officially started talks over the treatment of Japanese cars in the Single Market. The form of restriction was the main agenda item of the negotiations. The choice was mainly between voluntary export restraints through monitoring by the government (MITI) and the imposition of an import quota by the European Community. The option of sustaining national quotas was dismissed promptly. In the British case, for example, SMMT and JAMA agreed bilaterally in April 1992 to terminate Japan's VER by the end of that year. Consequently, it was decided that MITI monitor the amount of exports to the Community and to the 'restricted' market, and once the form of control was decided as Japanese monitoring, the MFA dropped out of the negotiations.

It was relatively easy for MITI to accept a transition period before total liberalization. The difficulty was deciding on how long this period should be. MITI negotiators had trouble finding the point of agreement, because EC member states seemed too divided to suggest a unified opinion.

Combined with the length of the transition period, whether or not Japanese transplants should be included in the restrictions during the transition made the negotiations even more difficult. From the beginning of the talks, MITI as well as Japanese car makers strongly opposed restricting European-made Japanese cars in any form.[52] The sorest point for the Japanese manufacturers was that after raising the local content as required by European governments, they were still not accepted as being 'made in Europe'. For the European side, too, the treatment of transplant cars was the most significant issue, since other issues (such as the length of the transition period and the quota allocation for Japanese cars) would eventually and ultimately dissolve once the Single Market was completed. Thus, ACEA demanded that the growth of Japanese transplant production be treated as the central issue of any EC–Japan agreement (McLaughlin, 1994: 152). In May 1991, Commissioner Brittan explained the Commission's stance:

Transplant production does not formally contribute to the Japanese share of the Community Market. It does however compete for the same share of the market as Japanese imports. We therefore need an accurate estimate of the number of transplants which are likely to come on stream during the transition.[53]

Both Japan and Europe were conscious of the need for the agreement to be compatible with the GATT. MITI, supported by the MFA, insisted that restricting transplants violated GATT rules.

The conclusion of the matter took an ambiguous form of agreement. The final agreement, 'Elements of Consensus' (hereinafter, the accord), was completed on 31 July 1991. Transplants were not explicitly included in the restriction, but their future treatment was left vague so that the agreement could be accepted by both sides. The last paragraph of the document showed the compromise not to set the treatment of transplants:

> Japanese side will convey to Japanese manufacturers Commission's repeatedly expressed concern that an excessive concentration of sales of their vehicles produced in EC on specific national markets would cause market disruption, and would affect the necessary adjustments of the other EC manufacturers towards adequate levels of international competitiveness.[54]

The quantity of Japanese cars admitted into the European market during the transition period was another difficult issue on which to achieve an agreement. France opposed setting a definite number, insisting that the 'share in market growth' be considered: if the European car market expands, the benefit should be shared between European and Japanese automobile makers; but if there is no growth of the market, the Japanese share should not be increased.[55] Japan, for its part, tried vigorously not to link the figure of exports allowed with local production, but it was flexible with numerical limits as to whether they were set by units or by market share. Consequently, these problems were solved by trade-off. While Japan managed to avoid including local production in the accord, the 'Internal Declaration' attached to the accord stated that 'if demand of any one year is forecast lower than the level resulting from the trend originally assumed, then the forecast level of exports in this period will be reduced by 75 per cent of the deviation.'[56] In practice, it was decided that Japanese imports were to

		EC	EFTA	Western Europe
1986	Units	1,036,000	329,500	1,365,600
	% share	9.8	28.6	11.7
1987	Units	1,075,700	338,200	1,413,900
	% share	9.5	30.0	11.4
1988	Units	1,088,562	370,464	1,459,026
	% share	9.2	31.9	11.2
1989	Units	1,106,547	348,769	1,455,316
	% share	9.0	30.3	10.8
1990	Units	1,219,584	321,298	1,540,882
	% share	10.0	30.8	11.7
1991	Units	1,363,089	299,699	1,662,788
	% share	10.9	31.6	12.4
1992	Units	1,322,557	272,150	1,594,707
	% share	10.5	30.6	11.8
1993	Units	1,169,177	214,501	1,383,678
	% share	11.0	27.4	12.1
1994	Units	-	-	1,330,169
	% share	-	-	10.9
1995	Units	-	-	1,278,254
	% share	-	-	10.6

Table 3.2 *The market share of the Japanese cars in Western Europe*

Source: International Motor Business, 1987-96.
N.B. Because of the European Economic Area and of Austrian, Finnish and Swedish entry to the EC, the separate figures for the EC and the European Free Trade Association (EFTA) are omitted from 1994.

be 1,230,000 by the end of 1999, based on an estimate that the market would be 15,100,000 cars.

In addition, both sides understood that by 1999 when the transition period ended, Japanese local production would reach 1,200,000, although there was no concrete restriction of transplants in the official document.[57] Nevertheless, in the following years when the economic downturn hit the automobile market, Japan and the Community (later Union) argued repeatedly over the market estimate and the practical quota for Japanese imports.

The nature of the accord, that it was not a legal agreement, made it possible for both sides to agree to it. This is clearly seen in a comment by the Secretary General of ACEA: 'The fact that it has no legal base is probably the best reason why it will be respected.'[58] Nevertheless, because the agreement was highly equivocal, it only postponed the problems, notably the treatment of transplant cars.

CONSEQUENCES OF THE NEGOTIATION

The practice of monitoring exports to the EC started a year earlier than had been planned in 1992. Since then, MITI and the Commission have held talks every six months, about coordinating the market estimate, with MITI inclined to be overly optimistic about market growth and the Commission excessively pessimistic. Despite fierce negotiations, however, market forces have worked to moderate Japanese exports. In 1993, although officials from both sides agreed in September to allow 980,000 units, actual exports amounted to only 867,547.[59] In 1994 the gap between the quota and the actual exports even expanded to 993,000 and 815,911, respectively.[60] At the same time, however, Japanese manufacturers in Europe increased production from 360,095 in 1992 to 487,090 in 1993, raising Japan's overall share. At least on the surface, the Japanese government denies any link between the decrease in export restraints and the increase in local production, attempting to maintain the principle that cars made in Europe not have any restriction. Japanese manufacturers explained plainly that the high yen pushed down exports, which encouraged them to increase the sales of transplant cars,[61] and they even expected that the influence of exchange rates might make the export monitoring unnecessary.[62]

The European Commission seems to have a similar view as Japanese manufacturers. An official asserted that, partly because of the rise of the yen, 'it is unlikely that direct imports from Japan will reach this ceiling (for 1995).'[63] European manufacturers, for their part, have been calling for a restriction on Japanese transplants since almost immediately after the signing of the 1991 accord.[64] Manufacturers make this demand both individually and collectively via the ACEA. Although the total Japanese share in the EU market has been stable at between 10.0 and 11.0 per cent since the accord, European manufacturers' caution against the transplants has further heightened, as local production has continued to grow, while exports have declined. In 1996 the chairman of the ACEA was Mr Calvet of Peugeot Group, newly joined, this demand to include transplants in the quotas became even more insistent.[65] Regarding this unsettled situation of the transplants, calling the accord a 'vain attempt' seems justifiable (T. Jackson, 1993: 95).

While European automobile manufacturers tried to impose restrictions on Japanese cars, consumers associations were critical of the accord itself. The UK's National Consumers Council (NCC) claimed that the accord itself was against the GATT rule to apply safeguard procedures on all exporters rather than on a single country, and that total consumer losses would be about £230 for every car sold from 1993 to 1999 (National Consumer Council, 1993: 15). It is also noteworthy that the accord has never been officially available for public viewing, as the NCC explicitly complained, although the contents were widely reported in the press. In contrast, the actual accord was circulated in the form of documents to the manufacturers in both Japan and the EU by their respective bureaucracies. These facts imply the sensitive nature of the accord and the wish not to have it seen as violating the GATT rule.

The governments, however, both in Tokyo and in Europe, remained quiet, showing no sign of revising the accord or setting up another agreement concerning local production. The Commission's 'Communication to the Council and the European Parliament' in February 1994, for example, did not mention the transplant issue at all, instead claiming 'the consultations held so far between the Commission and MITI, in particular those held in 1993, show that reasonable compromises can be reached even in exceptionally unfavourable circumstances such as those presently prevailing in the car market.'[66]

The deepening economic turmoil since 1997, especially the drop of the yen and the wider Asian crisis, dramatically changed the Japanese export scene in general. The recession, with an excessively weak domestic demand, led to continuous growth of the Japanese trade surplus. Automobile trade with the EU was no exception to this trend, though it was largely mitigated by the 1991 agreement.

This case mainly shows that since the development of FDI, what used to be strictly domestic now inevitably involves foreign companies that directly contact the government of the host country. Although this relationship so far applies only to the combination of Japanese manufacturers and European governments, European manufacturers also have direct contacts with the Japanese government, particularly with MITI, as part of their lobbying activities. For example, ACEA has finally established an office in Tokyo for closer contacts with Japanese actors.

In any case, Japanese manufacturers' contacts with European governments, especially with the host country governments of their investment, added an important factor to the state-level negotiations, including intra-EC decision-making. While MITI was fully in control of international negotiations with the EC, Japanese automobile manufacturers actively established transnational relations. It showed a clear contrast to the European situation, where the Commission needed to balance the national differences, which were enhanced by the industrialists' lobbying.

In sum, the accord confirmed the role of MITI in trade control. By avoiding commitment to restricting transplanted cars, the accord also allowed transnational development between Japanese manufacturers and European governments.

CHAPTER 4

Case II – The liquor tax dispute, 1986–95

The liquor tax system in Japan was a long-standing trade issue between Japan and the European Community/Union. While most trade issues involve both domestic and international politics in one way or another, this issue was particularly political in several ways. First, taxation itself is a matter of domestic politics and sovereignty. However, the GATT (General Agreement on Tariff and Trade) regime explicitly prohibited discriminatory taxation on imported products that aimed to protect domestic products (Article III-1). Consequently, this trade dispute was not just a bilateral dispute but also an issue to be handled by the multilateral trade regime. Second, the disproportionate escalation of the issue compared to the economic size of the liquor industry indicates the industry's political influence.

In accordance with the timeframe of this book, this chapter discusses mainly the dispute until 1995, although the role of the WTO in resolving the dispute is crucial. However, since the focus of the analysis lies in the domestic politics realm and its influence on international negotiations, the concluding stage of the dispute itself together with the implications of the WTO will be limited to a short description.

BACKGROUND AND PROBLEMATIC AREAS

The Liquor Market in Japan

The issue of alcoholic beverage exports was constantly on the EC's agenda at regular official meetings between the EC and Japan since the early 1980s. Japan was one of the major importers of Scotch whisky (Hirasawa, 1989: 29), along with other kinds of alcoholic beverages. With the economic downturn in the mid-1980s, Scotch whisky sales decreased considerably while, to the whisky manufacturers' irritation, sales of *shochu* (spirits made of rice, wheat or sweet potatoes) grew rapidly. Although the proportion of European alcoholic beverage

Year	Percentage share of spirituous beverage in EC exports to Japan	Percentage share of whisky in UK exports to Japan	Percentage share of wine in French exports to Japan	Percentage share of brandy in French exports to Japan
1980	3.8	9.7	n.a.	n.a.
1981	2.7	4.5	n.a.	n.a.
1982	3.2	7.1	n.a.	n.a.
1983	2.9	6.3	n.a.	n.a.
1984	2.4	5.0	n.a.	n.a.
1985	2.5	5.1	n.a.	n.a.
1986	2.2	3.6	2.4	5.1
1987	2.5	5.4	2.7	4.8
1988	2.6	5.2	2.7	4.2
1989	3.6	8.1	3.6	6.0
1990	3.9	8.3	3.7	6.4
1991	4.7	7.7	3.7	12.5
1992	4.7	8.9	3.8	12.5
1993	4.4	7.9	3.2	12.2
1994	4.0	6.4	4.0	10.7
1995	2.9	4.6	4.3	8.6

Table 4.1 *Proportion of beverage exports of the EC 1980–95*

Source: MITI, *White Paper on International Trade of Japan*, 1981–96.

exports to Japan was not spectacular, the issue at its height obtained enough importance to be a test case to assess how willing Japan was to co-operate with the European Community.

The Japanese Liquor Tax System

The Japanese liquor tax system was extremely complicated, which the EC began to highlight in the mid-1980s as a trade problem. The tax amount and rate, for example, depended on liquor type, alcohol percentage and beverage grade based on 'quality', this last item an uncommon one among industrialized countries. The complexity of the system was under serious criticism even in domestic circles. In practice, while there was a grading system for traditional beverages such as *sake* (fermented rice liquor) and *shochu*, there was no objective criteria to decide whether a certain product was of 'quality' or not. It was simply up to producers to decide based on their market strategies. The system remained mostly unchanged from 1962 to 1989 despite criticism that

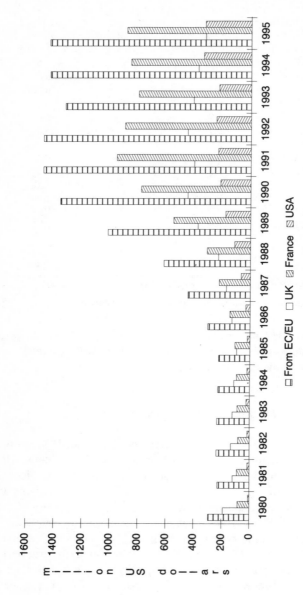

Figure 4.1 Japanese liquor imports

Source: MITI, *White Paper on International Trade of Japan* 1981-96.

the liquor tax system caused structural problems since it did not reflect economic and social changes over time (Ishi, 1993: 236).

Liquor tax law was based on four grounds: (1) it promised substantial income for the government; (2) it would deter people from excessive drinking; (3) the social cost caused by excessive drinking would be paid by drinkers, not by general taxpayers; and (4) those who could afford to drink liquor were assumed to be financially capable of paying the tax because consuming liquor is not a daily necessity for the most part (Kaneko, 1984: 31–2). Legal studies on taxation emphasized this last point as the main reason for imposing a liquor tax, although the Ministry of Finance (MOF) found the first point crucial since the ministry's priority lies in retaining tax revenue.

The Japanese government assumed the stance that the fairest way to levy the tax would be to impose a liquor tax on individual consumers by calculating the total consumption of liquor per year, to which a progressive tax would be applied. As this method of taxation was not practical, other alternatives were investigated, considering two factors: horizontal and vertical fairness, concepts usually used in income tax. Horizontal fairness was achieved by imposing the same tax on liquor selling at the same price per unit. Categorized as a luxury good, the liquor tax would be progressive commensurate with a consumer's tax-bearing ability, to retain vertical fairness.

This, however, resulted in excessive categorization and grading of liquor for the purpose of taxation, based on criteria such as alcohol percentage, raw materials and, in the case of distilled liquors, manufacturing method. The EC considered such tax differentiation as discriminatory against European imports. Especially in the case of whiskies, there were three grades depending on alcohol percentage, providing a basis for different tax rates. Such a grading system levied a higher tax on products with higher alcohol content (see Table 4.2). On the other hand, *shochu* was considered a lower-class drink so it had a much lower tax rate than other spirits, in the interests of ensuring vertical fairness in taxation.

The Europeans asserted that the Japanese tax system formed a non-tariff barrier (NTB).[1] While NTBs, such as complicated distribution systems and exclusive business relationships, are often discussed, directly proving protection for domestic goods and discrimination against foreign goods is usually difficult. The liquor tax system, in contrast, was seen as a clear case of discrimination. The Europeans accused the Japanese of discriminatory differentiation in two areas. First, whisky with 43 per cent or more alcohol was levied at a higher tax rate, while Scotch whisky by definition contains 43 per cent alcohol. Second, tax rates for *shochu* were distinctively lower than those for other spirits. This clearness encouraged European officials to bring the issue to the GATT. When the European Commission appealed to the opening of the GATT panel in 1986, it became clear that the issue was not only a simple bilateral trade dispute between Japan and the EC but also a test for Japan to show its loyalty to the GATT. All the participants in the international trade body considered that the liquor tax dispute resolution would indicate Japan's degree of support for the international liberal trade regime.

Japan was undeniably highly dependent on trade and other external economic transactions and had a large stake in maintaining an international liberal trade regime against the trend of protectionism, which remains true today. Sustaining the GATT was therefore part of Japan's general economic policy, although other countries expressed doubts as to whether Japan took its responsibilities seriously in practice. Later, as the dispute developed, the focus of the conflict moved from factual definition to the interpretation and implementation of the GATT findings.

In addition to this multilateral context, the second half of the 1980s was one of the worst periods in Japanese–European economic relations, as the trade imbalance increasingly worsened for the Europeans, raising tensions between the two parties and consequently politicizing the trade issue.

US Influence

When discussing foreign pressure (*gaiatsu*) in opening Japanese markets, the US most often leads the way. In contrast to many such issues, the liquor tax dispute was not particularly important in the Japanese–American trade relationship. Unlike the case of automobiles, European liquor producers did not feel threatened by aggressive American pressure. While US pressure to open the Japanese automobile market tended to resort to bilateral agreement that would disadvantage European manufacturers, European liquor makers were not worried by such a contingency. Instead, in the liquor tax case, it was the Europeans who assumed the lead in opening the Japanese market. In the course of the GATT panel in 1987, the United States together with some other countries gave their views to the panel, and the liquor tax was included in a list of problematic trade issues with Japan.[2] Nonetheless, American participation in the issue was limited, and consequently Japanese officials and manufacturers did not pay as much attention to it as they did to the European complaint. In other words, the liquor tax issue was mostly bilateral with less US involvement. In this sense, the liquor tax dispute had exceptionally little influence from the US.

The situation changed, however. While the US gave clear but not substantial support to the EC/EU in the 1980s and early 1990s, the US and Canada joined the case in July 1995 at the WTO.[3] In contrast to Scotch whisky sales that declined in the first half of the 1990s, American and Canadian whiskey sales had grown rapidly. The Scotch Whisky Association (SWA) was in close contact with its American and Canadian counterparts to pressure Japan together. For example, the international spirits delegation visits to Tokyo included both European and North American interest groups.[4] Also, global liquor operations stretched across the Atlantic. As a result, territorial trade associations increasingly relied on international members.[5] This is another sign of transnational development among business actors influencing international trade negotiations.

JAPANESE DOMESTIC ACTORS

The Tax Bureau of the MOF, leading Liberal Democratic Party (LDP) members, the LDP's Tax Research Council and liquor producers, particularly *shochu* and whisky makers, comprise the main actors in the liquor tax dispute.[6] Before reviewing the roles of those actors, the domestic context of the liquor tax dispute is discussed.

The Environment

European pressure increased in 1986 partly because the Europeans realized that Japan was about to launch a radical reform of the tax system in the following year.[7] The expected tax reform plan included introducing a new mass indirect tax, which would affect the tax and consumption of alcoholic beverages. British officials dealing with the issue in the mid- to late 1980s denied a direct link between their increasing pressure and the expectation of tax reform. They claimed they had been pursuing the Japanese liquor market for some years and that their pressure was constant. Nevertheless, the Europeans likely calculated that the GATT ruling would push the tax reform in the direction they wanted, and their effort to bring the case to the GATT was seen as a milestone of the process.

In fiscal year 1987, liquor tax revenue was 1,974 billion yen, 4.8 per cent of total government income. Historically, the liquor tax has formed a large share of the total tax revenue, although this has shown a long-term declining trend (Ishi, 1993: 234). Nevertheless, given the MOF's sensitivity about its budget falling into deficit, the liquor tax income was never negligible. Only after the 1989 tax reform did the trend of radical taxation reform reduce the importance of liquor tax revenue in the national budget.[8]

The Europeans' prediction about the timing of the reform was correct, but the LDP government failed to win a large enough consensus even within the party itself for the sales tax,[9] the major component of the tax reform project. The entire tax reform, including the liquor tax reform, was thus postponed. In retrospect, it took two years to recover from the damaged image of taxation reform among voters.[10] With regard to the effect of the renamed indirect tax on liquor as well as other goods, bureaucrats and politicians insisted that it was unthinkable to launch a liquor tax reform earlier than the rest of the tax reform.

A drastic reform of the alcohol taxation system received not only foreign pressure but also some domestic support. *Nippon Keizai Shimbun* (Nikkei), a major economic newspaper, for example, explicitly advocated reform, stating that the system was unfair and far too complicated for consumers to understand and that it presented quite a few theoretical problems.[11] The same paper criticized the MOF and National Tax Board bureaucrats of neglecting reform despite several suggestions made by the Diet and LDP councils on the liquor tax issue. Even within the MOF, a liquor tax study group released a report in 1982 that recommended simplifying liquor categorization and reducing the tax differentials among different types of liquor. At the same time, however, much attention was constantly paid to the medium-range tax reform plan based on the introduction of a mass indirect tax, one of the main government tasks since the Ohira cabinet in the late 1970s. In that sense, the liquor tax issue was always obfuscated in arguments concerning the entire taxation system, particularly over the issue of direct-indirect tax proportion.

The tax issue also highlighted the large gap between the price of imported goods, such as alcoholic beverages, and their original price.

Mere tax and tariff doubled the imported price, however the price was mostly increased by the various 'margins' taken by different actors in the distribution process.[12] Furthermore, the oligopoly in the alcohol market caused leading domestic firms – for example, Suntory in whisky and Kirin in beer – to set artificially high price standards (Cavanagh and Clairmonte, 1985: 160–1). Accordingly, the price for imported whisky and other types of liquors was kept high enough to sustain the price level set by such domestic firms.

Limited distribution channels for imported liquors also raised prices. European liquor makers, who were at the same time exporters, usually chose a sole agent to distribute their products exclusively. These Japanese agents opted to sell imported alcoholic beverages as luxury gifts, which promised a large profit per unit. In the 1980s, however, a parallel import prevailed, which circumvented Japanese agents by importing from a third country. Parallel importers were able to sell alcoholic beverages as cheaply as half the price of that sold by the official agents, because they did not have to pay the premium. The sole agent system was based on the legal licensing system of liquor sales, as was fairly common in other countries. Nevertheless, the licensing system formed an NTB by giving advantage to domestic producers to build a close business relationship with small retailers (Glasser, 1988: 51–4).

The liquor distribution problem was often discussed in the context of distribution *keiretsu* and the issue of the Law Concerning Big Retailers, the law limiting the numbers and activities of large scale retailers, such as chain stores, in order to protect small, family-run local shops. Those two issues composed serious trade disputes between Japan and the United States (Itoh M. and Ishiguro, 1993: 190–3; Mizuguchi, 1992).[13] In the context of Japanese-European relations, however, this distribution aspect did not become a serious subject of negotiations between Japan and Europe. It was possibly because liquor distribution was more difficult to prove to the GATT as an NTB than liquor tax differentiation.

Bureaucrats

The Tax Bureau of the MOF ultimately controlled tax decisions while the National Tax Board was mainly responsible for tax collection. Major tax policymaking, such as drafting tax law, was in the hands of Tax Bureau officials. Below the level of central government were

12 regional Tax Bureaux with jurisdiction over 522 local tax offices. In each Tax Bureau – whether central or regional – a specialized section in the Second Tax Division handled the liquor tax issue with the section chief of the liquor tax and the *shurui kanri-kan* (liquor supervisor). Not all local tax offices were equipped with liquor tax specialists, but 158 local offices had such a post. Through taxation, the manufacturing and sale of liquor was also under MOF jurisdiction by virtue of the Law Concerning Liquor Business Association and Measures for Securing Revenue of Liquor Tax.

Although most problems concerning liquor were handled by the MOF, the Economic Planning Agency (EPA) dealt with the problem of differences between original price and imported price. Nevertheless, the Agency lacked power to initiate reform on the price margin issue, particularly without responsibility for specific sectors and without intensive support from the MOF, MITI and other related ministries. The Office of the Trade and Investment Ombudsman (OTO) within the Agency handled complaints made by domestic importers, foreign exporters and the government or other representatives of exporting countries. Although the OTO directly received most complaints on trade and investment, including those related to liquor imports (384 out of 519 cases in total between February 1982 and July 1994),[14] such complaints were sent to the various responsible ministries, depending on each individual case. Therefore, ministries, rather than the EPA, responded to complaints, thus preventing the EPA from taking substantial steps to open the Japanese market.

The Ministry of Foreign Affairs and the Ministry of International Trade and Industry also held their own opinions but only provided limited influence on government decisions over the liquor tax issue. The MFA's role in the liquor tax dispute was providing a formal representative in international negotiations with the EC. Once the case was brought to the GATT, the Division of International Organization (GATT Division for short) in the Economic Affairs Bureau, was in charge of communicating with the MOF. Simultaneously, the First International Economic Affairs Division handled the interministerial communications, as the division responsible for economic issues with the EC. Since the MFA generally tended to be more compromising to foreign interests than other domestic ministries, the British Embassy and the EC/EU delegation in Tokyo encouraged further MFA involvement in this issue, while the Tax Bureau of the MOF maintained its position and reputation of intransigence. In any case, the MFA could only mildly influence taxation policy. The MOF's grip on the tax issue was so strong that the MFA had little room to manoeuvre, even though it was responsible for formal contact with the EC and the GATT.

Political Leaders

Unlike other trade issues, the liquor tax dispute allowed politicians a significant role, because of the nature of taxation as a redistribution policy. Before the LDP lost its position as the government party in 1993, the process of tax reform in general had to go through two different Tax Research Councils (TRCs): a government council, consisting mainly of MOF officials; and an LDP council. The original draft-making was in the hands of the government TRC.

In the mid-1980s, the government TRC turned out to be a main battlefield between then Prime Minister Nakasone and the MOF over the measure of introducing indirect taxation (Muramatsu and Mabuchi, 1994: 184–6; Kato, 1994: 156–90; Tsujinaka, 1988: 176–9). MOF officials had usually dominated the government TRC, but Nakasone sent his own private brains trust in order to usurp control of tax reform from the MOF. Nakasone did not believe that the MOF could manoeuvre domestic politics, which would be necessary for radical tax reform. In the end, the conflict within the government TRC between the MOF and Nakasone's brains trust concluded with the defeat of Nakasone's plan to impose a sales tax on manufacturers. Consequently, the bureaucrats assumed the lead at this stage of tax policymaking, but it is important to note that the Prime Minister independently influenced taxation policy, though he lacked the power to implement it.

Once consensus was achieved within the government TRC, the discussion moved to the LDP Tax Research Council. Nakasone appointed Yamanaka Sadanori as the head of the LDPTRC.[15] Nakasone recognized that Yamanaka was an expert on tax issues among LDP members and also that Yamanaka's strong personality, as well as his close connection with the *shochu* groups, would be the only means of realizing tax reform.[16] Introducing an indirect tax was particularly important for Nakasone, as he listed it as one of the three pillars of completing the post-war era. Liquor tax reform was part of such an overall tax reform.

The LDPTRC sought to obtain consensus among LDP politicians on the tax reform draft, a difficult task since the tax issue significantly influenced individual LDP members' re-election. As a result, the LDPTRC involved 268 members (Tsujinaka, 1988: 177), half of the LDP members of the Diet. On the other hand, there were only a limited number of tax experts within the LDP who comprised the Committee of the LDPTRC, that is, the *zeisei-zoku* (tax tribe) politicians. While it was comparatively easy to reach consensus about the indirect tax within the Committee, it was difficult to win consent at the general meeting of the TRC.

The *okura-zoku* (MOF tribe), of which the *zeisei-zoku* was a part, was a distinctive tribe among many policy tribes in the LDP, both in terms of its policy interests and its *zoku* membership (Inoguchi and Iwai, 1987: 205-9). The emergence of the *zeisei-zoku* was recognized in the 1980s, later than other tribes (Yamaguchi J., 1993: 75). All the members of the *okura-zoku* were either ex-MOF officials or had experience as a minister or vice minister of the MOF. This was partly because becoming a taxation specialist required a high standard of knowledge and partly because there was little merit for politicians to become *okura-zoku*, thus the tribe attracted few members of the Diet apart from fiscal and tax policy experts. *Okura-zoku* politicians, particularly *zeisei-zoku*, supported the fiscal policy planned by the MOF, defending it against various interventions attempted by other tribes.

In practice, during the indirect tax debate at the end of 1986, LDPTRC leaders avoided a thorough debate among all the members, so that other tribes could not impose their individual interests on tax policy. Consequently, the decision was made without party consensus. Council Chairman Yamanaka behaved too forcefully to be accepted by those outside his close circle. His high-handed style of dealing with the tax issue, especially raising the tax rate for *shochu*, cost him one election. At the Lower House election on 18 February 1990 he failed to hold onto his seat.

Other tribes involved in the liquor tax issue tried to protect the interests of liquor makers. The number of Diet members related to the liquor industry as a whole was estimated to be around 200. These liquor tribe politicians divided into smaller groups, based on liquor type, such as *sake* and *shochu* (see below). In the same way as interest groups would seek government budget allocations in their favour, they tried to avoid tax increases that would negatively impact their businesses. Therefore, the most important function of the LDP politicians in budget policymaking was equally found in the context of taxation policy, that is, to represent the interest of clienteles (Campbell, 1977: 138-42).

Industry

The liquor industry consisted of four major trade associations: (1) *Nippon shuzo kumiai chuo-kai* (Japan Central Association for *Sake* Producers; hereafter *shuzo kumiai*), for *sake* and *otsu-rui* (group B) *shochu*; (2) *Nippon joryushu shuzo kumiai* (Japan Distillers Association; hereafter *joryushu kumiai*), for *kou-rui* (group A) *shochu*; (3) *Nippon yoshu shuzo kumiai* (Association of Wine and Spirits Producers of Japan; hereafter *yoshu kumiai*), for whisky, wine and other Western style spirits; and (4) *Biru shuzo kumiai* (Beer Brewers Association). In addition to these, there were other related interest groups, such as *Nippon yoshu yunyu kyokai* (Japan Alcoholic Beverage Importers Association).[17] Three distributor associations[18] together with the four producer associations constituted the main seven liquor interest groups. In addition to producers, the wholesalers and retailers formed very powerful networks and voting blocs. The number and variety of actors involved in the liquor tax issue tended to complicate the process when any policy change was expected.

For tax purposes, alcoholic beverages were divided into ten different categories, some of which involved different *zoku-giin* politicians. *Shochu*, for example, was originally a type of local spirit of Satsuma, currently Kagoshima, part of which is Yamanaka's constituency. Large numbers of producers of traditional liquors such as *sake* and *shochu-otsu* (group B), were often small, family-run businesses, closely linked to the local community and thus involved in local politics. At the same time, however, small-scale traditional liquor makers were disappearing, which the government recognized as a fact. When the government introduced the 1994 tax reform (as discussed later), it responded with financial support for those who were to be out of business (Okura-sho, 1994: 334-5).[19]

On the other hand, large *sake* and *shochu* firms controlled a major part of the market share, especially in *shochu-kou* (group A) category. In 1989, six big *sake* companies occupied 25.6 per cent share of output, and four major companies produced 50.6 per cent of *shochu-otsu*, whereas 72.4 per cent of the *shochu-kou* market was held by four major manufacturers. As a result, these liquor interest groups exercised political clout in two ways: by financially supporting the associations' lobbying activities, and mobilizing voting power among numerous small and widely scattered manufacturers.

The Relationship among Actors

The liquor tax reform process involved authentically domestic politics because its influence affected the interests of a very wide range of people. Compared to the sales tax or consumption tax (another form of indirect tax introduced in 1989), the impact of the liquor tax was not as wide, but the liquor industry exercised significant clout in Japanese politics. In spite of varying interests among liquor producers, the four major associations issued a united request paper each year, encouraged by the LDP. From the politicians' point of view, this conveniently showed that their clients had strong, united interests in order to manipulate their influence on LDP policymaking. The single common issue among various liquor interest groups was a request for tax reductions on liquor in general.

The liquor tax division in each local tax office supervised the local organizations of liquor producers, facilitating close and well-communicating industry-bureaucracy relations. Their relationship was as tight if not tighter than those involving other industrial or commerce sectors. In contrast to the liquor makers' demands, however, the MOF inclined to review tax rates in an upward direction (Okura-sho, 1994: 336). In this sense, frequent communications did not necessarily mean that the interest groups and the government shared common interests, but the rift between the bureaucracy and the industry was deeper than the Europeans thought during the dispute. Therefore, reconsidering the models discussed in Chapter 2, the Japan Inc. model does not seem to apply. The liquor industry's dissatisfaction with government policy – particularly on the part of the manufacturers of *sake*, *shochu* and whisky – extended to agricultural policy. The liquor makers claimed they were handicapped by being forced to buy domestic grains, which were of poorer quality and more expensive than imports. It was ironic for Japanese whisky makers that liquor market liberalization was the Japanese government's gesture to contribute to international trade. While the government attempted to compensate for the heavy protection of the Japanese agricultural sector in the GATT Uruguay Round, this only added to the burden of domestic whisky makers to purchase domestic grains. In short, agricultural protection made liquor producers a scapegoat by applying a zero-tariff on imported liquors and simultaneously handicapped them with domestic grains.

In terms of political clout, wine and spirits producers were not as well connected to LDP politicians as 'traditional' liquor makers, although even the latter were not considered strong enough to influence MOF decision-making substantially. In order to enhance their political influence, interest groups recruited former MOF officials. The most prominent example was Murayama Tatsuo, the president of *yoshu kumiai* from December 1991. A former MOF Tax Bureau director, LDP Diet member and former Minister of Finance, he was one of the most powerful *zeisei-zoku* politicians. Also, one of the directors of *yoshu kumiai* was Takayanagi Akio, an ex-MOF official and taxation specialist (Takayanagi A., 1993: 81).[20] *Joryushu kumiai*, for its part, appointed Shimazaki Hitoshi as president, another former MOF official who became a Diet member.

Zeisei-zoku politicians and MOF bureaucrats were very close because of their shared backgrounds described earlier. While *zeisei-zoku* significantly shaped tax policy, their fiscal goals were mostly identical to those of the MOF. As a result, *zeisei-zoku* and the MOF did not compete but rather coexisted (Yamaguchi J., 1993: 79).

In contrast, the relationship between the MOF and liquor tribe politicians was not as close. Each one's interests thwarted the other. In the interests of protecting their respective liquor industries, liquor tribe politicians fought MOF attempts to cut subsidies or to increase taxes. Retrospectively, in the case of tax reforms, the influence of the liquor tribe was quite limited. As suggested before, Yamanaka was the head of both *zeisei-zoku* and *shochu-zoku*. Since he was determined to complete the tax reform through introducing an indirect tax, priority was given to tax reform rather than to protecting the Japanese liquor industry. Yamanaka's strong leadership led other liquor tribe politicians to persuade the industry to compromise with political and bureaucratic leaders.

EUROPEAN ACTORS

The Environment

From Table 4.1, it is clear that however important the Japanese market was for European spirits exporters, neither the size of the industry nor the economic impact of spirit exports would make the liquor tax issue one of the longest and severest trade disputes between Japan and the EC. Such disparity between the economic effect and political significance of a trade issue is not uncommon, but one needs to look at domestic politics within Europe in order to explain the gap.

Because of the common trade policy of the European Community, the European Commission formally handled the liquor issue, although clearly one member state, namely Britain, was distinctively active compared with other member states and exercised the biggest pressure on Japan. Domestic politics in the UK largely explains this active involvement. Other member states constantly supported the British stance, but their participation remained limited in contrast to Britain's robust attitude. Considering the amount of French brandy exports, it was peculiar that neither the French government nor the French brandy industry expressed any intention of taking a lead in pressing Japan. Possibly, the French government chose a quieter role in order to avoid possible repercussions on wine trading, even though the share of brandy in total French exports to Japan was bigger than that of wine.[21]

In any case, Britain gained full support from the other member states, particularly those who had a stake in the spirits industry such as France, Ireland, Spain, and later Sweden and Finland, and the issue was treated as a European issue, not merely a British concern. Thus the Commission handled this case without disharmony among the member states, unlike the case of automobiles.

Governmental Actors: At the Community Level and National Level

European involvement in the liquor tax case reflected the dual structure of officialdom: Community level and national level. Thus, major official actors included the DG I of the Commission, the 113 Committee of the Council and the Department of Trade and Industry (DTI) of the British government.

In the British government, the DTI assumed the lead in dealing with the trade dispute with Japan, although the Ministry of Agriculture was responsible for the whisky industry. The DTI brought the issue to the European level meeting, the 113 Committee, which then decided to take up the liquor issue as a European-wide trade problem. Following the standard procedure of trade issues, the 113

Committee gave the Commission mandate to act on behalf of EC member states.

Inside the European Commission, the Far East Division of the DG I directly contacted the Japanese government, while the GATT Division was closely involved in the question of liquor tariffs. The Commission also used politically higher level meetings, such as annual ministerial meetings between Japan and the EC, to pressure Japan. Simultaneously, the 113 Committee played a decisive role in submitting the case to the GATT in 1986.

Individual British politicians also committed themselves to the case. During her tenure, Margaret Thatcher frequently stressed the issue whenever Japanese politicians visited Britain and met with her. John Major, in his turn, also pressed Japan. At the Japan-UK Summit in September 1993, he criticized the Japanese for taking insufficient action to implement the GATT ruling of 1987, which he reiterated by sending a letter to the Japanese Prime Minister in November. Foreign Secretaries also actively supported the DTI by bringing up the issue at meetings with Japanese politicians and at press conferences.[22] DTI Ministers made official visits to Tokyo, demanding that the Japanese government diminish the tax rate differentiation between *shochu* and whisky. In addition, appointing Leon Brittan as DG I Commissioner in 1993 may have further smoothed communication between the British interest group and the Commission.[23] Such direct involvement by political leaders distinguishes the liquor tax issue to a disproportionate extent in terms of the size of the industry in the British economy, suggesting the strength of the whisky lobby.

Industry

The Scotch Whisky Association (SWA) was the most emphatic interest group to put the Japanese liquor tax issue on the EC agenda and to pressure the Japanese government directly. The strength of the SWA as an interest group derived partly from the fact that Scotch whisky is an area-specific product in comparison to other spirits that tend to be produced over a wider area. SWA members were quite tightly united.[24] This highly local feature could have disadvantaged their lobbying power in the EC framework, but it did not. Its voice was strongly reflected in the European-wide spirits industry group, Confédération Européenne des Producteurs de Spiritueux (CEPS), since an SWA representative occupied a leading position in the CEPS.[25] Consequently, the SWA often chose to go through the CEPS in contacting the European Commission, while still directly contacting the Commission itself. The SWA also kept an amicable and open relationship with the DTI. For its part, the DTI heavily relied on the SWA for information on Japanese market access and other issues, which the DTI used in turn to bring the issue to the European Commission.[26] The SWA established a Tokyo office to lobby the Japanese government intensively and maintain frequent contact with Japanese journalists, the *Nippon yoshu yunyu kyokai* (importers association) and Japanese whisky makers such as Suntory, Nikka and Kirin Seagram.[27]

The European Business Community, particularly its Liquor Committee, was another important interest group. A loose organization of individual European business people in Tokyo, EBC personnel overlapped with other interest groups. Its chair was a British national, reflecting the attention given to the Scotch industry compared to other European spirits makers and facilitating cooperation between the EBC Liquor Committee and the British Embassy in Tokyo. The SWA worked closely with the EBC Liquor Committee. While both had a wide range of contacts in Japan, the EBC often handled political contact.

In contrast, producers of white spirits such as vodka and gin – 'like' products of *shochu* as defined by the 1987 GATT findings – were not as active as the SWA. Possibly the Japanese market was not as significant for these producers as it was for whisky and brandy makers. Although there were national organizations for white spirits, such as the British Gin and Vodka Association, there was no European-wide organization for this category of products. As a result, white spirits producers left the issue in the hands of the more active groups, in effect the SWA and CEPS.[28]

Individual producers were also active in their attempts to open the Japanese market, even penetrating into Japanese domestic politics. For example, a member of the Administrative Reform Committee of the Japanese government headed the Japanese subsidiary of a European liquor maker, who raised the liquor tax issue at the subcommittee on deregulation.[29]

CHRONOLOGY OF THE LIQUOR TAX DISPUTE

At no stage of the liquor tax dispute was there any conventional trade negotiation at which officials from both sides assembled for a specific purpose, as commonly found in trade disputes such as the automobile case. In this case, communications were often carried out in more informal and flexible forms at the bilateral level, and in the framework of the GATT and WTO dispute panel. Therefore, the negotiations for the liquor tax dispute did not involve any formal announcement of the result of bilateral discussions. Instead, the word 'negotiations' here meant a wider range of communications between Japan and Europe. The negotiation process can be divided into four phases: (1) 1982–7, until the GATT panel findings; (2) 1987–9, when the tax reform law was implemented; (3) 1992–4, when the issue was revitalized; and (4) 1995–7, the debate under the framework of the newly established World Trade Organization dispute settlement.

Between phase two and phase three there were a few dormant years, during which the European side allegedly waited for Japan's full implementation of the GATT panel findings, while the Japanese believed that the 1989 reform had completed it. Although admitting some improvement from the 1989 tax reform, Europe renewed pressure in the autumn of 1992 for further reform. The EU took the case to the newly established WTO in 1995, and finally the 1997 liquor tax reform plan by the Japanese government satisfied the EU, closing one of the longest struggles between them.

Phase One

The liquor tax issue can be traced back as early as 1982 when the EC demanded Japan open its liquor market, along with others, though at that time Japan did not take the issue too seriously. Considering the highly domestic and sovereign nature of taxation in general, Japan refused to change its taxation system to appease Europe. The Europeans considered the liquor tax system discriminating against imported whiskies in favour of domestic products. At this stage, the EC also cited other trade obstacles in the liquor sector, such as the custom tariff and the Japanese practice of wine labelling.[30]

In 1983, when Japan planned the tax increase on alcoholic beverages, the EC showed its concern. Japanese domestic producers also were apprehensive, fearing that the tax increase could reduce sales. The Japanese liquor producers at least on the superficial level cooperated with their European counterparts to protest the tax increase, but division among Japanese producers limited this cooperation. Among the EC's first list of requests to Japan, released in 1984, was the demand to reduce the tax on medium-class wines, not to resolve the whisky matter that later became the centre of the dispute. This year's tax reform, however, did not affect the taxation system itself, leaving European concerns, such as the grading system among the same types of products and the significant differentiation of tax rates, unaddressed. As its demands were practically ignored, the EC began to intensify its explicit pressure on the Japanese government.

Europe's frustration was exacerbated by a succession of meetings without any remarkable outcome.[31] In 1986 the liquor tax issue started to take on a more political meaning, adding a more severe tone to European pressure. A Commission report to the Council in March, for example, recommended more pressure on opening up Japanese markets, specifically mentioning that the alcoholic beverages sector could serve as an indicator of the Japanese political will to open its market effectively.[32] The European Parliament, on the other hand, noted:

> the early choice of alcoholic beverages as a 'test case' of Japanese willingness to cooperate with the Community, recalling with concern that a combination of product-definition and excise duty are used to create an effective barrier to whisky, brandy and wines entering Japan, with goods complying with European definitions of these products incurring up to ten times as much duty as certain Japanese products sold under the same generic descriptions.[33]

Not only European officials, but also the SWA and the EBC Liquor Committee intensively lobbied the MOF. The SWA, for example, together with other liquor interest groups from Europe and North America, visited Tokyo to exercise direct pressure in October 1986.

Behind such intensifying European pressure was the market situation. British alcohol exports, mainly Scotch whisky, decreased steadily from 1982 for three years after a peak in 1980 (see Figure 4.1). In 1985, France surpassed the UK in terms of value, due to increased demand for wine and brandy, but the Scotch export was struggling. Whisky exports fell 17.7 per cent, whereas both wine and brandy saw steady increases, 5.4 and 9.8 per cent, respectively.[34] In the following years, the difference between the size of the whisky market and that of wine and brandy became even smaller. In correlating Scotch sales with *shochu*, the contrast was even more remarkable. A so-called '*shochu* boom' began in the early 1980s and reached its peak in 1985. Statistics indicated that this boom directly reduced whisky consumption (Jokai Times, 1993: annex 136). This all added to the Scotch whisky makers' fears. The SWA keenly invoked the GATT dispute settlement and worked closely with the Commission so that the SWA could now and then act with the delegated authority of the Commission.[35]

Since April 1986, the MOF and Commission officials had several negotiations that were in a similar style as the MOSS (market-oriented sector-selective) negotiations between Japan and the United States.[36] In July, after a series of unsuccessful discussions between the Commission and MOF officials, the Council warned that the alcohol issue would be sent to the GATT unless Japan accelerated its process of tax reform.[37] The next day, the Commission formally requested consultations with Japan under GATT Article XXII:1 on Japanese customs duties, taxes and labelling practices on imported wines and alcoholic beverages.[38] Two GATT consultations in August and September failed to produce satisfactory results.

Until the last minute, Japan tried to settle the dispute on a bilateral basis, but finally in late October the EC brought the issue to the GATT under Article XXIII:2. The EC claimed that Japan must reform its alcohol taxation system that discriminated against imported products; lower the existing high tax rate on wine and whisky; and re-regulate the indication of origin rules more strictly, especially for wine.[39] The actual request to establish a panel of the GATT was made a week later, allowing some room for withdrawal in case Japan indicated drastic reform and made a guarantee to put it into practice.

During that period, the Japanese Government TRC released a report on tax reform including a reform in liquor tax, which was accepted by the LDP. At the same time, the LDPTRC tried to mould an agreeable tax reform plan for 1987, but the plan did not satisfy European demands.

In December, the annual ministerial meeting between Japan and the Community was held in Brussels, for which the EC asked Minister of Finance Miyazawa to attend to discuss the liquor tax issue. Such ministerial meetings were usually within the jurisdiction of foreign ministers, thus participation of the finance minister had no precedence. In the end, the Japanese Finance Minister could not schedule a visit to Brussels because of the sales tax dispute at home, but this unusual request from the European side intensified Japan's caution. In response to such serious European demands, the MOF presented a proposal to the LDPTRC and later to the European Commission. Its main points were: (1) to abolish the *ad valorem* tax, imposed on special grade alcohol; (2) to reduce the current liquor tax rate; and (3) to abolish part of the grading system among the same types of liquors, such as *sake*, wine, liqueurs and whisky. For whisky, in particular, a five-year transition period was to be given. The Commission, however, rejected the proposals as inadequate.[40] The British government, which then held the presidency of the Council of the EC, also disapproved it, and the CEPS expressed disappointment to the proposal.[41] All these reactions combined to convince the Japanese government that it could not avoid the multilateral panel discussion at the GATT.

At the GATT Council meeting on 4 February 1987, a panel was established.[42] In April, the panel met at Geneva, heard presentations from Argentina, Canada, Finland, the United States and Yugoslavia. In May the Japanese government and the LDP failed to enact the tax reform law because of fierce nationwide opposition to the sales tax, which consequently made the liquor tax reform impossible in 1987. This, some believe, directly influenced the September GATT report approving EC demands.[43]

The panel

> found the grading system for whisky and brandy, the *ad valorem* taxation system applied in Japan, and the differences in taxation between shochu on the one hand and vodka, whisky and brandy on the other to be contrary to Article XIV:2 of GATT, thus endorsing the Community's line of argument about a disguised discrimination system.[44]

This GATT notification forced the MOF to implement a drastic change in the liquor tax as part of the general taxation reform planned in 1988. Finally in November the GATT Council adopted the panel report that confirmed Japanese defeat. The report cited the following points as being against GATT Article III: (1) the grading system, which imposed a higher tax on whiskies and brandies from the EC than those made in Japan; (2) the disproportionate *ad valorem* tax imposed on EC wines, spirits and liqueurs, which was higher than the specific taxes based on the quantity of all liquor; (3) the higher tax on EC liqueurs than Japanese products because differences in contents; and (4) *shochu*, which competed with or substituted for whisky was protected through lower taxes.

Phase Two

In December, the GATT General Assembly demanded that Japan implement the reformed taxation law during the fiscal year 1988. The Japanese representative replied only with an uncertain prospect of reform. At around the same time the Commission reiterated the same request to Japan as before, which the Council of Ministers confirmed with the threat of sanctions in case of delay. LDP leaders, however, had to face the immense difficulty of persuading Japanese interest groups within the time allowed, while trying to win a compromise from the EC to postpone the reform until as late as autumn. Domestic whisky makers fiercely opposed abolishing the grading system, fearing that would seriously damage second-grade whisky sales.

Shochu makers were also deeply troubled by the tax rate increase. In opposing the decision, the *joryushu kumiai* claimed in 1988 that the demand for *shochu* was declining while the demand for imported whisky was growing. Thus, they reasoned, concerning the balance of the spirits sectors, the respective rise and fall of taxes on *shochu* and whisky did not seem to be fair.[45] The so-called '*shochu* boom' reached its ceiling in 1985 (Dodwell Marketing Consultants, 1989: 1–2), replaced by increased spirits imports from Europe in the following years. On the other hand, it can be said that the decline of *shochu* consumption was a natural phenomenon after an extraordinary boom, and thus the relative decline of *shochu* and rise of whisky were not necessarily affected by taxation. Also, the market trend since the second half of the 1980s showed that the total consumption of spirits was in decline, losing ground to beer, despite the growth of imported spirits.

At this stage there was still a perception gap between the Japanese government and the European Commission. Japan assumed that when Commissioner De Clercq visited Japan in December, he must have understood Japan's stance. He had been given a detailed explanation about the difficulties of starting a new taxation system in April 1988. However, on his return to Europe, the Commissioner surprised the Japanese government by expressing disappointment at the delay suggested by the Japanese government. The EC kept insisting on the earlier implementation of the new alcohol taxation before the indirect tax. Various channels were used to press the Japanese government. At the quadrilateral meeting of trade ministers in April, Commissioner De Clercq demanded that Japan clarify its compliance with the GATT ruling on wines and spirits.[46] Also in May, at the summit meeting between Prime Ministers Takeshita and Thatcher, the liquor tax reform was a main concern.

While European pressure remained persistent, discussions moved mainly to the domestic level in 1988, as MOF officials and LDP politicians were determined to launch tax reforms, despite resistance from domestic industries. In addition to the timing of the new taxation, the change of the tax rate on *shochu*, strongly demanded by the British government, also became a focal point.[47] Compared with these points, the *ad valorem* tax and the grading system were abolished at an earlier stage with support from the *sake* producers. The LDP consulted with industry leaders and higher officials of the Tax Bureau and decided on 25 May to raise the tax rate for *shochu* by 75 per cent. Despite the consultation, the decision provoked fierce opposition among major interest groups, including two different grade *shochu* makers.

On 2 June, the LDP held an open meeting with several interest groups to sound out their opinions. Each group expressed its own position rather than co-ordinating with one another.[48] *Shuzo kumiai* for *sake* producers, which also included the *otsu-rui* (group B) *shochu* makers, did not have strong interests conflicting with the GATT decision or European demand. *Shuzo kumiai* demanded that *sake* not be taxed more than wine and that the authority give consideration to second-class *sake* makers. They did not make any claim for *shochu-otsu*. Considering that the tax reform came along with the amendment of the Special Law for the Stability of the *Sake* Manufacturing Industry, providing compensation funds for the *shochu-otsu* (Okura-sho, 1989: 490–1), *shochu-otsu* producers had already agreed to the government plan by this stage.

In contrast, the *kou-rui* (group A) *shochu* makers group, *joryushu kumiai*, expressed their dismay over the plan to raise taxes by 75 per cent on *shochu*. *Shochu-kou* makers criticized the LDP reform plan on the grounds that: (1) the EC's claim that *shochu* was substitutable for and directly competitive with whisky was based on a faulty argument (thus, *joryushu kumiai* also defied the GATT ruling); and (2) that the theoretical reasoning for the tax was not made clear by the authority.

Yoshu kumiai, for its part, demanded a general decrease in alcohol tax to the level of pre-May 1984. This meant that by this stage they had stopped complaining about abolishing the grading system. Like *shochu-otsu* makers, second-class whisky makers had realized that tax reform was inevitable and therefore, they demanded compensation in the form of financial support.[49] Five days after the meeting, the LDP confirmed the 75 per cent rise for *shochu*, and finalized the entire reform plan a week later.

This domestic process indicated that it was political initiative that persuaded interest groups and that the government did not acquire consensus before its final decision. Because of the concurrent problem of the consumption tax, the LDP was highly united and closely co-operated with the MOF as a whole. The MOF itself closely co-operated with MITI, concerning the impact of the tax on various industries and commerce. However, the interests of the liquor industry, particularly that of domestic whisky and *shochu* makers, were not compatible with the government decision. Nevertheless, the political influence of these industrial groups could not change this decision, and consequently, the liquor industrialists reluctantly accepted the government's decision.[50] The new liquor tax law was submitted to the Diet and enacted on 24 December, in time to implement from the beginning of next fiscal year.

In April 1989, the new taxation system was launched, including the new liquor taxation. The final form of this liquor tax reform: (1) simplified the system, abolishing the *ad valorem* tax, through which liquor taxation was unified into a quantity tax only; completely abolishing the grading system for whisky and brandy; and gradually ceasing grading for *sake*; (2) changed the tax rate so that tax rates were reduced for beer, *sake* and whisky and increased for *shochu* and liqueur; (3) redefined whisky and other spirits; and (4) enacted procedural reform for paying manufacturers.

This resulted in a substantial increase in UK whisky imports (see Figure 4.1), including a 65.3 per cent rise in value and a 29.7 per cent, rise in quantity, although Scotch whisky imports had already recorded a decline in 1991 mainly because of the beer boom.[51] *Shochu* makers, for their part, called the tax increase 'Thatcher *zozei* (tax increase)', criticizing the MOF for giving in to the strong pressure from the British Prime Minister.[52]

Phase Three

While welcoming the 1989 reforms, the Community insisted that it did not believe that the GATT panel was fully implemented. In comparing tax rates as a percentage of retail price, whisky was still considerably higher than both types of *shochu*; 36.3 per cent of the retail price of whisky was tax, compared to 21.3 per cent for *shochu-kou* and 13.5 per

| Type of liquor | | Before the 1989 reform | | 1/4/1989–30/4/1994 | | 1/5/1994– |
Category	Subcategory /Grade	Alcohol (%)	Tax rate (Y/kl)	Alcohol (%)	Tax rate (Y/kl)	Tax rate (Y/kl)
Sake	Special	15.0	570,000*			
	1st class	15.0	279,500	15.0	133,700	140,500
	2nd class	15.0	107,900			
Shochu	A (*Kou-rui*)	25.0	78,600	25.0	119,800	155,700
	B (*Otsu-rui*)	25.0	50,900	25.0	70,800	102,100
Mirin	*Hon-mirin*	13.5	74,100	13.5	21,600	21,600
	Hon-naoshi	22.0	63,500			
Beer			239,100		208,400	222,000
Wine	Extract 7% and plus		159,800*			
	Y450/l and plus		60,400*		46,300	56,500
	Others		49,700*			
	Sweet wine	12,0	117,300*	12.0	85,500	98,600
Whisky	Special	43.0	2,098,100*			
	1st class	40.0	1,011,400*	40.0	982,300	982,300
	2nd class	37.0	296,200*			
Spirits	Quasi-whisky	37.0	296,200	37.0	331,400	367,300
	Others	37.0	361,800*			
Liqueurs	Extract	15.0	367,000*	12.0	85,000	98,600
	21% plus	plus				
	Others	12.0	117,300*			

Table 4.2 *The 1989 and 1994 reform in tax rate*

* In addition to the quantity tax as exhibited, the *ad valorem* tax was also imposed on these specific products, differing from one category to another.
Note: After the 1989 reform, all the alcoholic beverages were additionally charged a general consumption tax of 3% of the price.
Source: Okura-sho, *Kaisei zeiho no subete*, 1989, 1994.

cent for *shochu otsu* (Ishi, 1993: 237). Nevertheless, the Commission as well as European interest groups waited for a few years to reactivate their lobbying of the Japanese government to narrow further the difference between the taxes on *shochu* and other imported spirits, especially whiskies. During the short period between the tax reform and the beginning of economic recession in Japan, imported whisky sales grew rapidly, but when the recession started, they stagnated again. Looking at the market situation, whisky sales started to decline during the negotiations, while *shochu* sales grew steadily. Once the grading system for whisky had been abolished, the tax gap between *shochu* and whisky became the focus of the new phase of negotiations.

The economic downturn that started in 1990 changed the market

Categories	1986	1987	1988	1989	1990	1991
Sake	18.5	17.8	17.1	15.8	15.2	14.8
Shochu	7.7	7.0	6.9	5.8	5.8	5.5
Whisky*	4.0	3.9	3.8	3.2	2.8	2.6
Beer	65.8	67.4	68.3	71.0	71.5	72.6

Table 4.3 *Proportion of alcoholic consumption (% in total consumption)*
* This category includes whisky and brandy, both domestic and imported.
Source: Jokai Times, 1993: annex 136.

distribution. On top of the accelerated decline of the spirits market against lower alcohol beverages, whisky lost its gain in 1989 to *shochu* again, although domestic whisky suffered more than imported whisky (Jokai Times, 1993: 3–5, 9). Within the spirits market, *shochu* made remarkable progress from 63.1 per cent of the total of Japanese spirits market in 1990 to 74.5 per cent in January to May 1994, while imported whisky lost its share from 6.5 to 3.8 per cent in the same period.

The EC regarded the situation remained the same as both before and after the 1987 GATT panel. Although the significance of the issue was widely felt among European officials both in Brussels and Britain, the media coverage was not as great as in the 1980s.

Another, and more important difference from the previous stage was that the European actors acquired a Japanese ally, namely Japanese whisky producers, and particularly those who established business alliances with foreign industries. These included Suntory with Allied Domecq, and Kirin with Seagram (although Kirin was a beer maker). These alliances gave useful support to European pressure groups, although Japanese firms were reluctant to be seen as representing European interests. Consequently, Japanese whisky makers explicitly recognized the direct competition and substitutability between *shochu* and the ex-second grade whiskies and requested the government revise

Categories	1987	1988	1989	1990	1991	1992	1993	1994 (until May)
Imported whisky	3.3	3.7	5.8	6.5	6.0	5.5	5.0	3.8
Domestic whisky	26.7	27.0	23.4	19.6	18.1	17.1	15.8	13.4
Domestic *shochu*	63.8	63.1	61.2	63.1	65.0	66.9	69.3	74.5

Table 4.4 *Japanese spirits market (by % share) 1987–94 (until May)*
Source: National Tax Board tax-paid volumes.

the tax difference between *shochu* and whisky (*Nippon yoshu shuzo kumiai*, 1992: 4–6; *Nippon yoshu shuzo kumiai*, 1993: 1–6). Such clear support for the European side by the Japanese producers could not be found in the 1980s. This is seen as an explicit example of transnational development within the industry, apart from governmental interactions. As a result, domestic interest representation obscured national boundaries.

Concurrently, however, the Japanese whisky producers had opposing interests compared to their European partners on the tariff question. They strongly demanded that there be no tariff reduction to allow domestic products to compete against imports (*Nippon yoshu shuzo kumiai*, 1993: 9–10). Although Europeans demanded tariff reduction, this issue was left to the Uruguay Round and concluded with 'zero-for-zero' agreement. Again, Japanese domestic whisky makers showed their lack of political clout.

In May 1992, the Commission produced 'A Communication on Policy towards Japan', in which the tax rate difference among spirits was included in market access problems in Japan. The Council of Foreign Ministers and the European Parliament followed up the Commission's communication in June 1992 and January 1993 respectively. At the annual ministerial meeting between the EU and Japan in January and meetings of senior officials in April, the Commission suggested resubmitting the case to the GATT unless Japan fulfilled its 1987 GATT ruling obligations by 1994, namely to reduce liquor tax differentials among spirits to '*de minimis*' levels.[53]

In June and September, the Commission raised the issue at GATT Council meetings, demanding full implementation of the 1987 GATT findings. The external trade commissioner directly and openly requested that the MOF revise the tax differentials in writing, and later visited Tokyo to repeat the demand. The EU Ambassador in Tokyo presented a report of the same request to the government TRC in December.

The British government was also insistent. The British Ambassador in Tokyo visited the MOF in September 1993 to demand further revision of the tax difference between *shochu* and whisky.[54] This series of pressures at an official level, in addition to private lobbying by individual industrialists[55] and the Liquor Committee of the EBC in Tokyo, led to the 1994 tax reform, which came into effect on 1 May 1994. The MOF explicitly admitted that European pressure influenced the decision of tax reform (Okura-sho, 1994: 337).

This time, domestic opposition to tax reform was much quieter.

Category	Alcohol %	Tax before reform	Tax after reform
Shochu kou-rui	21-30	7,340	9,540
	31-35	28,430	26,230
Shochu otsu-rui	21-30	4,560	6,580
	31-45	16,930	14,910
Whiskies	40	24,560	24,560
Spirits (incl. vodka)	37	8,960	9,930

Table 4.5 *Tax rate on spirits per one degree of alcohol in Japanese yen*
Source: *Okura-sho*, 1994.

Although *shochu* producers explicitly criticized the government's decision to raise the tax rate on *shochu*, further narrowing the tax difference with whisky, the liquor industry as a whole did not resist the tax increase as vehemently as at the time of the 1989 reform. It seemed that the MOF could decide on reform more freely than last time.

The 1994 reform narrowed the gap between *shochu* and whisky to at most 3.9 times per alcohol content, but this did not yet satisfy any actors in Europe (see Table 4.5). In May 1994 the liquor tax was reviewed again, resulting in a further rise of the tax on *shochu*. This time the MOF aimed specifically at raising government revenue through liquor tax, which was not intended in the 1989 reform (Okura-sho, 1994: 336).

Phase Four

The year 1995 was an important threshold for the multilateral trade regime, with the birth of the World Trade Organization. Accordingly, the EC moved the battlefield to this successor of the GATT after the 1994 tax reform. Though the GATT ruling declared direct competition and substitutability among all spirits, including *shochu* and whiskies, the surviving issue of how a comparable tax should be levied on 'similar' but not 'like' products remained.[56] In addition, countries such as Sweden and Finland that produced vodka (defined as a 'like' product of *shochu*), became EU members, giving the Commission stronger grounds to pressure Japan.

Soon after the 1994 tax reform, the director general of the SWA visited Tokyo to lobby further, using strong words and accusing the Japanese practice as a blatant breach of a GATT ruling by one of the world's main trading nations. He also declared that it was the worst case of discrimination in any of the Scotch export markets.[57] Another delegation of European spirits producers went to Tokyo six months later, urging the Japanese government to harmonize its liquor tax in its 1995/96 budget plan.[58] However, individual industrialists and interest groups differed in terms of concrete demand. On the one hand, CEPS as well as an official of *shuzo kumiai* suggested levying the tax on all imported and domestically produced spirits on the basis of alcohol content.[59] On the other hand, an SWA official argued that all spirits, regardless of alcohol content, should be applied the same tax rate.[60] Such criticisms were also made at the political level. The British Trade and Industry Minister during his visit to Tokyo, leading a large trade mission, criticized the tax difference that still remained after the 1994 reform.[61]

While European pressure increased with the threat to call for the WTO dispute settlement procedure, the MOF maintained, at least on the surface, their belief that the 1989 and 1994 reforms were sufficient. Japan's position was rather twisted. At the disclosure of the panel finding in 1987, the Japanese Ambassador to the EC publicly said that although the finding was not entirely convincing, the Japanese government would accept it in full in order to contribute to the stability of the world trade scheme (Tsukui, 1993: 233). This comment meant that despite the GATT ruling that Japan admitted it was obliged to follow, Japan still believed that shochu was not directly competitive and substitutable with other spirits. The *shochu* industry, for its part, also maintained that *shochu* was a totally different product from other spirits.

In June 1995, the European Union officially brought the case to the WTO.[62] The MOF agreed to the bilateral negotiations, although it was unwilling to make any immediate change in tax rates on the grounds that the 1989 and 1994 reforms were sufficient. At the same time, the MOF indicated it would be ready to increase the tax rate on liquor whose consumption was expanding, a condition that applied to *shochu*.[63] Meanwhile, the *shochu* industry kept resisting any tax increase, insisting that the decrease in *shochu* sales would result in an increase in beer and other lower alcohol beverages sales but not whisky.[64] In contrast, domestic whisky makers remained quiet, avoiding open confrontation with the MOF but at the same time implicitly supporting the European position.

As expected by both Japanese and European officials as well as industrial groups, bilateral talks within the framework of the WTO dispute settlement body did not resolve the issue, which led to setting up an independent dispute panel. At the end of January 1996, the first open hearings for the panel were held. Six months later, the panel concluded that the difference in tax rates between *shochu* and whisky was against WTO rules. They stated that:

(1) Shochu and vodka are like products and Japan, by taxing the latter in excess of the former, is in violation of its obligation under Article III: 2, first sentence, of the General Agreement on Tariffs and Trade 1994.

(2) Shochu, whisky, brandy, rum, genever, and liqueurs are 'directly competitive or substitutable products' and Japan, by not taxing them similarly, is in violation of its obligation under Article III: 2, second sentence, of the General Agreement on Tariffs and Trade 1994.

Responding to the WTO decision, the Japanese government decided to raise the tax on *shochu* by 1.6 to 2.4 times while that on whisky was reduced by 58 per cent.[65] By this decision, the difference between the tax rates on *shochu* and whisky, when calculated per degree of alcohol, would be 3 per cent from 1 October 2001.

CONSEQUENCES OF THE NEGOTIATIONS

The results of the tax reform show the difference in influence among interest groups on the MOF and the LDPTRC. Since the government goal in the series of tax reforms was first to secure tax revenue for the national budget and only second to protect the Japanese liquor industry, the government relatively easily forsook the interests of Japanese whisky producers, the weakest among domestic interest groups.

The grading system for the same type of liquors was abolished in 1989, including whiskies, which was the major concern of the EC at that stage. Japanese whisky makers were the biggest opponents of this reform and displayed their bitter resentment. Immediately after the 1989 tax reform, Scotch whisky makers chose not to reduce prices, despite the tax reduction, in order to maximize the profit per unit.[66] Nevertheless, Scotch whisky sales jumped, while former second grade whiskies precipitously declined. Considering that the demand for lower grade whiskies was artificially created for domestic producers (Glasser, 1988: 50), the grading system was hard to justify. The decline of domestic whisky sales was phenomenal. It was a direct result of the decline of the former second grade whisky, as its tax was more than tripled. In volume terms, the consumption of this grade of whisky fell from 137,000 kilolitres in 1988 that was 45 per cent of the total whisky consumption to 16,000 kilolitres in 1993 (Saji, 1994).

Sake makers, on the other hand, accepted the reform in a relatively positive manner. Considering that the original purpose of the grading system in 1943 was to increase tax revenue, the industry had already realized the system's limit of rationality, although it was understood that price stability was kept by the grading system.[67] Given the strength of *sake* producers' political influence, it would have been more difficult for the MOF to abolish the grading system if the *sake* producers had firmly opposed it.

As for the *shochu* industry, the MOF was more prepared to protect it than the whisky makers and determined to keep the tax rate differences between *shochu* and other spirits, even though the *shochu* industry deemed it insufficient. All the tax reforms since 1989 raised the tax rate on *shochu*, while lowering those on whisky and other spirits. As mentioned above, the government decided to subsidize the closure of traditional liquor makers (including *shochu-otsu*) along with the series of tax reforms. In this sense, structural change in the Japanese liquor industry partly derived from European *gaiatsu* and pressure from the multilateral trade regime.

Most important, the transnational cooperation between domestic and foreign whisky producers was an interesting change in Japanese liquor tax decision-making. In addition to business ties established with European manufacturers, domestic whisky producers began to express similar positions as the Europeans against the *shochu* industry. The report made by the *yoshu kumiai* complained about the tax difference between whisky and spirits on the one hand and *shochu* on the other, based on 'slight' differences in the method of production. These complaints were identical to the European Community's claims submitted to the GATT panel.[68] The collaboration of domestic and foreign whisky makers was described in a comment by the chief director of *yoshu kumiai*. He stated in July 1994 that the abolition of whisky and brandy tariffs by the Uruguay Round 'is expected to exert a favourable impact on Japan's liquor industry and liquor market.' (Saji, 1994.)

This statement came despite the thitherto vehement opposition by individual Japanese whisky and other non-*shochu* spirits makers against abolishing the imported whisky tariff. For example, an official of *yoshu kumiai* revealed a bitter resentment against that decision made by MOF bureaucrats, asserting that domestic whisky makers were scapegoats for the Japanese government to show its commitment to the Uruguay Round while protecting the agricultural sector (Takayanagi A., 1993).[69] However, the practical impact of abolishing the tariff on whisky market competition was questionable, as the retail price difference was equivalent to one pound per bottle.[70] Considering that the tariff made only a small difference in price – thus a minor factor for competition – the rift between Japanese and European whisky producers on this matter seemed to be insignificant.

Until the 1989 reform, the traditional framework may have had a valid interpretation. The MOF together with the LDP mitigated *gaiatsu* by incremental changes, which was essentially a consequence of having the conflict between governments presented to the GATT. Thenceforth, however, transnational actors emerged, and their influence on liquor tax policy in Japan changed the domestic structure. The industrial structure had changed, and thus national borders could no longer divide interests strictly. Hence, transnational business relations have developed to enforce state commitment to international organizations, despite resistance from other domestic actors. The relative influence of pure *gaiatsu* has decreased because part of *gaiatsu* is no longer 'foreign'. The emergence of transnational actors, in other words, made the distinction between *gaiatsu* and domestic politics obscure.

CHAPTER 5

Case III – The Joint Declaration between Japan and the European Community

Andreas van Agt, a former Head of the Commission Delegation to Tokyo, once stated that

> Whereas the US is firmly connected, in various ways, both with Europe and Japan, relations between the latter two are poor and brittle, confined to purely economic matters, devoid of a political or cultural dimension – no more than a dotted line indeed. (Van Agt, 1993: 3)

The Joint Declaration between Japan and the EC, signed in July 1991, was to remedy such a situation, although as van Agt pointed out the effect of the Declaration was quite small even some years later.

As the Joint Declaration was not a trade issue, but an issue of traditional diplomacy, this case is inevitably different in nature from the other two cases. Nevertheless, in this case, too, domestic politics was an essential factor in the international negotiations. The actual effect of the Joint Declaration is in some ways open to debate, since it only minimally changed the relationship between Japan and the EC. It had seemingly little direct influence on business activities or domestic politics on either side. Considering the growing importance of transnational relations in international political economy, such traditional diplomacy often looks less important than before in relation to the substantial transactions across borders.

However, in the diplomatic history between Japan and the EC, the Joint Declaration was a milestone. The Joint Declaration was the first serious step to deal with the lack of a political relationship. In Japan–EC relations, political relations have been only slowly catching up with the economic reality. This course of development of the relationship can be interpreted as a challenge to the traditional (neorealist) framework of international relations, since the power-centric behaviour of nation-states does not explain transnational relations.

While transnational relations in the economic sphere have been the main accelerator of developing Japanese–European relations, as the other cases showed, the Joint Declaration was an attempt by Japanese bureaucrats, in particular those in the Ministry of Foreign Affairs (MFA), to provide a framework for further development. Mere accumulation of political contacts at the time of trade disputes could not totally fill the gap on the political side of Japan–EC relations. The MFA was determined not to allow the issue to become one of foreign *economic* policy, and it was ultimately successful. By limiting the issue as a symbolic, diplomatic one, the policy area was defined as an individual-implementing policy of the MFA, thus eliminating the participation of other actors.

The first section of this chapter attempts to answer the question as to why the Joint Declaration was needed. In doing so, the Transatlantic Declaration between the EC and the United States emerges as an important factor, influencing the MFA's policymaking. The following three sections explain the limits of the Joint Declaration through the decision-making process.

BACKGROUND AND PROBLEMATIC AREAS

The idea of building solid political relations with the EC occurred among MFA officials in the midst of structural change in world politics and political economy. The lack of a political relationship between Japan and Europe became increasingly unsuitable in such an environment.

Lack of Political Relations: An Explanation from a Neo-realist Viewpoint

Among works on Japanese–European political relations in the 1980s, most begin by discussing the lack of a relationship between them in the early postwar period and follow with a description of how economic friction began, was exacerbated, and then became politicized (Daniels and Gow, 1983; Drifte, 1983a; Daniels and Drifte, 1986; Daniels, 1989; Steinert, 1985). There is not much point in repeating such descriptions here, but the similarities in the literature itself may be evidence of the non-existence of, or general lack of interest in, the political aspect of Japanese–European relations, as was openly admitted (Van Agt, 1993).

The nature of the relationship was summarized in a comment made in 1988 by the Japanese Ambassador to the UK: 'We don't have a political alliance with the EC, but we share lots of things. We share values, free trading and open market economies among them, and we also share a great security interest.' (The Anglo-Japanese Economic Institute, 1991: 33.) The development of the EC was inward-looking, while Japan concentrated its economic development on domestic as well as US and Asian markets. Except for interests in individual economic sectors, no significant issue between Japan and the EC necessitated a substantial political bond. In general, until the mid-1980s, distance characterized Japan–EC relations (Lehmann, 1982; Wilkinson, 1980).

The reason behind such a distance between Japan and the EC was obvious to neorealists. Assuming that the nation-state is the most essential unit in international relations, whose behaviour is determined by power politics, Japan and the EC logically did not develop political ties, as they did not have any incentives for it under the security umbrella of the US. During the Cold War period, Japan and EC members shared a geopolitical position between the Super Powers with consequent effects on political options for their respective security policies. This common fate, however, did not develop into any bilateral relationship between them (Mendl, 1984). Instead of seeking bilateral cooperation between them as an alternative to their dependence on the United States, both Japan and Europe remained reliant on the United States. Therefore, bilateral dialogue between Japan and the EC was always contingent on US foreign policy (Maull, 1990: 68). Exceptional arguments predicted closer political cooperation between Japan and the EC, given the relative decline of the United States (Drifte, 1983b; The Anglo-Japanese Economic Institute, 1991). Such arguments in the 1980s, however, looked premature and unrealistic.

In addition to the above systemic level of analysis, the domestic level of analysis provides other perspectives on the lack of political relations. The undeveloped nature of political relations between Japan and the EC could be attributed at least partly to the nature of the EC. Although European Political Cooperation (EPC) was set up in 1970 to co-ordinate foreign policy of EC members, it was not within the framework of the EC treaty, and thus foreign policy was excluded from the Community's competence. The structure of foreign policymaking for EC countries is discussed in the later section, but it should be pointed out here that the Community's inability to handle diplomatic policy with one voice – even if the member states were committed to speak in harmony – discouraged Japan from seeking political ties with the EC (Maull, 1990: 63).

As for individual EC member states, political relations with Japan were insubstantial to varying degrees. In contrast, the US had structural ties with EC countries through the North Atlantic Treaty Organization (NATO), though not all the members of the EC were NATO members or vice versa.

In reality, there were a few small gestures of political recognition of each other, practised in the form of regular meetings among officials and ministers. Since 1983, the Japanese Foreign Minister and the EC Troika (three foreign ministers of former, current and succeeding presidents of the Council) have had biannual meetings, although these meetings were arranged at the same time as the Organization for Economic Cooperation and Development (OECD) meetings so that the ministers were to assemble in any case. Annual ministerial conferences, mainly on economic issues, started in 1984 and involved not only the MFA but MITI, MOF and the Ministry of Agriculture, Forestry and Fishery (MAFF). However, they were cancelled more than once, which would be unthinkable in Japan-US or EC-US relations.[1] As a result, it took three and a half years after the third meeting to hold the fourth one. Such examples were put down to Japan's indifference towards the EC (Ishikawa, 1990b: 140–1), even though the real effect of these meetings was questionable.

Japanese and European political leaders met each other on other occasions, such as G-7 ministerial meetings and summits, in the latter of which the president of the European Commission also participates. On these occasions in the 1980s, they agreed to co-operative actions over, for example, the Iran hostage crisis of 1979–80, participation in the Siberian gas pipeline project, promoting East–West dialogue, opposition to American policy in Central America and dissention to some US economic policies, including the running up of a huge budget deficit and the imposition of high interest rates (Mendl, 1986).

Studies of the summit, however, show little sign that Japan and the European countries had any concrete idea to build either bilateral or Japan–EC level political relations, aside from their commitment to multilateral institutions which invariably included the United States (Putnam and Bayne, 1987; Saito, 1990).

Structural Changes in World Politics

Since the end of the 1980s, a dynamic, structural transformation of world politics has forced people to change their perception of the world structure. Most notably, the end of the Cold War, followed by the collapse of the Soviet Union,. meant that both Japan's and Western Europe's dependence on US military power – which had had significant influence on their overall relationship – had changed, though not vanished in any way. Moreover, despite, or regardless of the disappearance of the apparent enemy, the United States did not seem to be a victor. Military expenditures and also the failure of macroeconomic policy had weakened the American economy and compelled Japan and Europe to question US leadership.[2] Even though the US has regained its confidence and economic lead since the early 1990s, the US dominance found at the end of World War Two is largely gone. The threat of US retreat into isolationism looms over in the absence of battling ideologies and in international economic competition with its allies. Consequently, Japan had to revise its American-centric foreign policy,[3] and Europe also needed to reconsider its foreign policy (Keohane *et al.*, 1993).

When considering Japan–EC relations in, this wider context of international political re-structuring, decision-makers on both sides became interested in greater cooperation and desired to build a substantial relationship between Japan and the EC. This new movement synchronized with the theoretical debate of neoliberalism, including the discussion of transnational relations. While the transnational approach has greatly contributed to explaining the actual development of international transactions, however, it does not seem to have the same effect on diplomatic relations.

The transnational approach helped to explain the background of structural change of international politics, which in turn greatly influenced the decision-makers' perceptions. In terms of direct impact, however, transnational elements were scarcely seen, since the demarcation of traditional diplomacy and foreign economic policy remained strong within both the Japanese and European bureaucracies, which will be discussed in the following sections.

If one takes the view of the retreating power and role of nation-states (S. Strange, 1996), the comparative significance of traditional diplomacy consequentially declines in the face of growing transactions involving non-state actors, though not necessarily excluding state actors. Especially in the context of Japan–EC relations where formal diplomatic relations have long been established, actual economic transactions, particularly business relations, develop more or less independently of the state's diplomatic activities. In other words, Japanese and European businesses did not need to pressure their respective governments to enhance their political relationship for the sake of economic interdependence and transnational development. Therefore, the relative insignificance of the Joint Declaration is parallel to the rise of non-state actors in forming the substance of Japan–EC relations. At the same time, however, states obviously retained their function in trade and investment, as seen in earlier chapters. In this sense, diplomacy itself had to shift weight from the traditional sphere to the economic sphere.

Considered from a neorealist perspective, the strain in Japan–US relations was a significant factor in Japan's search for political ties with Europe. The accumulation of trade disputes seemed to have caused mutual distrust between Japan and the United States.[4] If one sees the direction of Japanese foreign policy in the context of seeking balance of power, though largely economic power, it can be interpreted that Japan began to look for an ally other than the US. A Japanese diplomat involved in the Joint Declaration project explained Japan's motives by saying that 'the more general and worldwide change around 1989 and 1990 caused the necessity for revision of the entire Japanese diplomacy, part of which was reflected in the attempt to reinforce political relations with the EC.'[5] In this sense, the increase of economic interdependence was not sufficient to let Japan revise its policy towards the EC, but had to wait until the 1989 revolutions.

On the other hand, foreign policymakers, particularly MFA officials, were seriously concerned that the EC was about to discriminate against Japan as an exclusive target. A former Japanese diplomat, for example, warned that EC integration was a sign of economic-bloc building (Kuriyama, 1991: 113). Partly due to this concern, the MFA sought political ties with the EC to dilute economic hostility. While the European approach to trade problems with Japan was as aggressive as the American approach in the 1980s, the end of that decade found a change in the style of EC pressuring.[6] The Japanese accepted favourably this new, more cooperative European attitude, especially when faced with the threat of American unilateral sanctions.

As for the European side, some advocates of closer and deeper relations between Japan and the EC emerged, although they were a small minority, whereas the majority remained focused on the issues of trade and investment in specific sectors such as the automobile and electronics industries. The EC sought to deepen its relationship with Japan mainly in response to US–Japan relations: if they became strained, the international economy would suffer severe damage, and if US–Japan relations developed further on a bilateral basis, the EC would be left behind (Lehmann, 1989). Nevertheless, while there was a keen sense of alert to the situation that Europe was more or less excluded from US–Japan relations, Europe generally showed little interest in its relationship with Japan (Lehmann, 1993: 120). Even among the advocates of developing Japan–EC relations, many wished for only an economic-centred framework for the relationship (De la Croix, 1989).

This asymmetry between Japanese and EC attitudes partly derived from the different effects of the structural political change caused by the collapse of the Soviet bloc. In concrete, the democratization of Eastern Europe impacted the EC more directly than Japan, which was most clearly shown in those ex-Communist states wishing to join the Community (Michalski and H. Wallace, 1992: 113–20). Understandably, the EC was more urgently concerned with the revision of political relationships with these immediate neighbours than with Japan relations.

US Influence: The Transatlantic Declaration[7]

A Japanese diplomat who participated in preparing the Joint Declaration denied that the Declarations between the EC and the US and the EC and Canada, signed in November 1990, directly caused the MFA to make a similar declaration with the EC. The same official emphasized that the motivation for proposing a Joint Declaration was to revise Japan's foreign policy in order to adapt it to the structural changes in the world political scene. Still, the United States was unquestionably one of the most important factors in Japan–EC relations and the MFA was concerned about any change in transatlantic relations because of their impact on Japan. Therefore, it is imperative to study the Transatlantic Declaration in order to understand why the Joint Declaration was made.

Among MFA officials, the Transatlantic Declaration raised the possibility of securing a political relationship with the EC, despite the very different backgrounds of US–European relations and Japan–EC relations. The Transatlantic Declaration acknowledged officially the equal partnership of the EC and the US rather than viewing the EC as a junior partner (Featherstone and Ginsberg, 1993: 26). It also compelled the US to recognize the EC as more than an economic entity.

On the other hand, for Japan, the Joint Declaration was the first attempt to put in place a foundation for its political relationship with the EC. Japan–EC economic relations also showed different pictures from EC–US economic relations. While the vast majority of US complaints at the GATT were directed against the EC, it was not seen as a sign of serious crisis in overall US–EC relations (Featherstone and Ginsberg, 1993: 127).[8] Economic friction did not hamper political or security aspects of the relationship. In contrast, the trade friction between Japan and the EC was deemed as the gravest obstacle to a smooth relationship. The troubled economic relations and the lack of political ties mutually exacerbated each other in a vicious circle (Lehmann, 1984: 270).

The Transatlantic Declaration reviewed the bilateral relationship between the US and the EC. The importance of the EC as an actor in international political economy was heightened significantly with the launch of the 1992 programme, and the collapse of communism in Central and Eastern Europe, including the Soviet Union, challenged the very foundations of the transatlantic relationship (Featherstone and Ginsberg, 1993: 81–2). In addition, the prospect of a unified Germany at the time was still uncertain, stimulating American concern about potentially having an even stronger economic rival in the EC. These rationales to revise European policy were shared by Japan.

Last but not least, the Transatlantic Declaration exacerbated the MFA's fear that Japan might be singled out in geopolitical restructuring at the height of international economic competition. The rise of trade protectionism heightened such concern in Japan.

In terms of the process of making the two Declarations, Japan seemed to have loyally followed the steps trodden by the United States. It was American initiative, namely, the speech by President George Bush in Boston in May 1989, declaring a new American relationship with Western Europe, and the speech by Secretary of State James Baker in Berlin in December, initiating bilateral talks to create a new political framework for US-EC relations (M. Smith, 1992: 42).

As for the Joint Declaration, the MFA initiated contact between Japan and the EC. The document of the Transatlantic Declaration was more 'cosmetic than substantive' (Featherstone and Ginsberg, 1993: 32) which was appropriate for the MFA to follow in making their draft, since the MFA intended to avoid concrete economic questions. Thus, the Transatlantic Declaration provided a model for the MFA to propose a plan to institutionalize bilateral political communications, rather than to provide an institution for bilateral relations with the EC.

US influence also gave the EC an incentive to promote political relations with Japan. A communication from the Commission to the Council in March 1995 (i.e. even after the Joint Declaration) indicated that precisely because of economic interest, the EU needed to build political ties with Japan. US pressure to open the Japanese market to its exports, particularly in the areas where the EU also had a large stake such as automobiles, automobile parts and the electronics industry, caused serious concern for the EU. While an open Japanese market would benefit European exporters, numerical targets and other bilateral trade concessions the US demanded from Japan would disadvantage European products. Thus, this same communication advocated an increase in 'the weight of the EU–Japan political relationship both for its intrinsic merits and as a counterweight to US influence.'9 The same argument had been claimed by some academics in the mid-1980s, though they were in minority (see Introduction). Within a decade, it became a practical policy alternative in the form of the Joint Declaration.

JAPANESE DOMESTIC ACTORS

The MFA exclusively handled the Joint Declaration. This was mainly because of the highly diplomatic nature of the issue, but it was also because the MFA deliberately managed to avoid involving other bureaucratic organizations, particularly economic ministries. In order to understand why the MFA wished to have exclusive responsibility for the issue, it is necessary to consider the ministry's position among other elite groups.

The Environment: The MFA's Relationship with Other Actors

A fierce rivalry between MFA officials and those in other economic ministries, MITI in particular, could be traced back to the pre-World War Two period (Johnson, 1982: Chapter 3; Fukui, 1981: 296–7). The two ministries competed with each other over trade policy jurisdiction, often on the basis of rather different interests in individual trade negotiations. According to MITI officials, the MFA was generally too willing to acquiesce to foreign pressure, particularly American pressure, while the MFA criticized the parochial inclination of domestic ministries, which were concerned with protecting partial domestic interests.[10] Their rivalry sometimes went as far as mutual contempt. The examination to enter the MFA as a career official was, for example, different from the unified examination for other ministries, including the MOF and MITI.[11] Even such a relatively minor difference gave grounds for added self-esteem to MFA officials against their rivals in other ministries.

The MOF's responsibility and power over macroeconomic policy – increasingly involved with cross-border coordination and cooperation – did not allow the MFA to monopolize foreign economic policymaking. The MOF, however, co-operated with the MFA on certain foreign policy issues. Import liberalization programmes, for example, promoted by the MFA against the opposition of the MAFF and MITI dovetailed with the MOF's interest in reducing the national budget (Fukui, 1981: 296). On the other hand, the MOF vehemently opposed the liberalization of financial services, although even that has changed in the steep decline of Japanese financial firms in the 1990s.

In terms of trade relations with the EC, MITI and the MOF were responsible for individual issues, as the former case studies clearly indicated. As a result, the MFA was often left marginal in the practical decision-making circles for actual negotiations, despite efforts made by MFA officials. The multilateral negotiations of the GATT Uruguay Round fell within the MFA's jurisdiction, and in this sense the MFA was responsible for keeping the bilateral trade policy within the GATT rules. In practice, however, the MFA's cautious attitude to bilateral agreements exhibited little influence on the decision-making of MITI or the MOF.

The MFA's relationship with political leaders was rather weak, especially compared with that of other ministries. Fewer ex-officials of the MFA became politicians, and Diet members were generally indifferent to foreign policy as a whole. Although a foreign policy tribe existed in the LDP, it did not attract many politicians since foreign policy did not benefit them either financially or at election time (Inoguchi and Iwai, 1987: 132–47). Some politicians with strong ideological views participated in foreign policymaking, particularly on security issues, but even they had little interest in Japan's relations with the EC or with individual European countries.

While weak relations with political leaders limited the political clout of the MFA, this same weak link provided the MFA a relatively free hand on many foreign policy issues. Whereas in theory the cabinet is responsible for final decisions on foreign policy, only a few important issues, such as the US–Japan Security Treaty and opening official diplomatic relations with the People's Republic of China, actually depended on decisions made by the Prime Minister (Nakamura Tk., 1993: II, 488–97; Fukui, 1977c). The Diet, for its part, hardly ever became the venue for making foreign policy (Baerwald, 1977).[12]

Although arguably the Prime Minister had taken initiatives in foreign policy since the 1980s (Kusano, 1989: 82–6; Angel, 1989), at least in the sphere of Japan–EC relations, the Prime Minister and Foreign Minister rarely had distinctive roles from the MFA in policymaking. Apart from a few exceptions (Nakamura Tk., 1993: II, 188–97; Fukui, 1977c), political leaders tended to follow the MFA's advice rather than take the initiative in foreign policymaking. In other words, most issues of foreign policy, including EC relations, rarely concerned political leaders. Therefore, MFA decisions usually became the government's final decisions in terms of foreign policy.

For foreign *economic* policy, however, the Prime Minister received advice from other ministries, such as the MOF and MITI and consulted with other LDP politicians, business circles and journalists, thus diminishing MFA influence on prime ministerial decisions (Fukui, 1981: 291). In this respect, the bureaucratic politics model for decision making seems valid, in that different ministries of various power resources recommend different policy options to the Prime Minister (Allison, 1971: 162–9).

As for private economic interests, the MFA had few connections with business circles. Since the development of transnational economic relations, private businesses were sensitive about foreign economic policy, but weak diplomatic relations, for example, did not deter their economic activities. In this sense, private interests were quite independent from MFA foreign policy. Furthermore, in terms of information gathering, the MFA sometimes relied on the information network of private business, rather than vice versa.[13]

In general terms, domestic pressures provided the MFA with leverage in international negotiations. The two-level approach introduced by Robert Putnam argued that a country's 'win-set', the range within which a country can reach an agreement with a foreign partner, is determined by domestic politics (Putnam, 1988).[14] Such a manoeuvre by the MFA applied to the pre-war period as well as to the post-war time. Michael Blaker, for example, discussed Japan's bargaining style in foreign negotiations, adding that MFA officials often asked their foreign counterparts to 'understand the difficult situation in Japan's domestic politics' in order to draw a favourable compromise (Blaker, 1977: 69–71). In sum, the MFA was deemed to be less powerful than other decision-makers. An extreme argument even claimed that the MFA did not have to exist as an independent bureaucratic agency (Muramatsu and Takubo, 1990).[15] It is necessary to consider this relative weakness of the MFA in order to understand the context of proposal of the Joint Declaration. Including economic aspects would have involved the economic ministries, particularly if the Declaration called for any commitment to deal with the trade balance.

From the experience of negotiations with the US, Japanese bureaucrats were conscious of the danger of promising any practical commitments, such as numerical targets, to deal with trade and other economic issues. The initial purpose of making the Joint Declaration was to build political ties so that the Japan–EC relationship was more in balance with the transatlantic relationship. With the reality of economic interdependence between Japan and the EC, the MFA opposed putting any emphasis on economic terms in the plan. The initiative of the Joint Declaration, therefore, came from the MFA, rather than from the entire government.

The Actors: The Organization and Decision-Making Procedure of the MFA

In general, there was a clear demarcation of the tasks within the MFA. For bilateral political matters concerned with a certain country or a region, the respective geographical bureau was the principal body to handle the issue, whereas economic issues involving more than one country were in the hands of the Economic Affairs Bureau. The Treaties Division of the Treaties Bureau was consulted whenever legal documents were exchanged between Japan and foreign governments, and even when negotiations with the foreign counterpart did not involve binding legal instruments, informal consultations were often made. Because the demarcation of works within the MFA was mostly clear, there was not fierce competition over territory for each division. Among the ten bureaux of the MFA, two were directly responsible for EC matters. The First Division of West Europe (hereafter, WE I) of the Asia and Europe Bureau, was responsible for political affairs with the EC, whereas the First International Economic Affairs Division (hereafter, KK I) of the Economic Affairs Bureau had principal jurisdiction over economic matters with the EC.

The procedure for decision-making was usually highly compartmentalized within each division. Despite the routine of interdivision and interbureau meetings, each division maintained its independent attitude. As a result, the MFA was criticized for not having a decision-making mechanism operating on a ministry-wide basis (Fukui, 1977a: 15). Also, each issue tended to be dealt with on its own rather than in concert with other policy issues, a tendency called *'anken-shugi'* ('single-issue-ism', or 'policy-making by improvisation') (Fukui, 1977a: 29). Policies were thus made by 'continual improvisation in response to the specific circumstances and needs of the case at hand,' (Fukui, 1981: 285) deriving from the MFA tradition of distrusting comprehensive long-term planning (Fukui, 1977a: 15–6).

This 'tradition', however, did not seem to thwart the MFA's decision to propose a Joint Declaration to the EC. The focal point of the proposal aimed at long-term foreign policy goals towards Europe, which was qualitatively different from policies to deal with individual issues, such as single instances of trade concerns.

At the same time, however, another 'tradition' of MFA decision-making – limiting participants to a few selected divisions – applied to this case. Outside actors were not invited to the initial planning process, since the demand for or interest in building a political relationship with the EC was not widely seen in domestic politics. Prime Minister Kaifu and Foreign Minister Nakayama were committed at only a superficial level, and neither had very much power in the domestic political scene. Although there was no opposition to pursuing a political relationship with the EC, the MFA acted more or less alone. It did not seek the active involvement of other actors, whether political or administrative. As a result, the impact of the Joint Declaration in domestic politics was debatable. In terms of policy level, the lack of political participants was a consequence of that the Joint Declaration occurred not at the structural level but at the individual level.

EUROPEAN ACTORS

As in Japan, no private EC actors were directly involved in the policymaking of this case. The structure of the EC, however, produced a unique combination of European actors, namely the Commission and member state governments.

The Environment

The EC, and particularly the Commission, had not been enthusiastic about extending relations with Japan into a more political dimension. The Commission's external policy competence was limited to economic aspects at the time of Japan's proposal, while the political sphere remained, practically, in the hands of individual member states. Nonetheless, the Commission's attitude towards Japan was criticized for being indifferent in the wake of structural changes in the international political economy (Lehmann, 1989: 49).

When the MFA contacted the EC on the matter of a Joint Declaration, trade friction was intense, and voices in Europe demanded practical solutions to the trade imbalance. The EC's trade deficit with Japan kept growing and the concurrent automobile agreement was one of the most important issues on the EC agenda in terms of relations with Japan. As a result, some member states, particularly France, demanded to include economic relations in the Joint Declaration, disappointing and annoying MFA officials.

While a few member states, including Britain and the Netherlands, supported Japan's idea of emphasizing the political aspect in the Joint Declaration, the Commission had to insist on including economic phrases due to pressure from other member states. Britain has had the closest relations with Japan among EC members, accelerated by large-scale Japanese investment in the UK. In the diplomatic arena, the British government often openly supported various aspects of Japan's foreign policy. The problem of the Kurile Islands between Japan and then Soviet Union was only one example in which the British government clearly supported the Japanese government (Lehmann, 1989: 48).

In contrast, some countries, including France, had a more distant relationship with Japan, which heavily influenced the Community's stance. In the early stage of negotiations with Japan, a senior Commission official stated clearly that the future declaration 'was likely to add specific clauses on individual economic sectors,' and reiterated the difference between the Transatlantic Declaration which 'was much more to do with security' and the Declaration with Japan that 'will get more into economic questions and mutual access to markets.'[16] This attitude clearly differed from that of Japan, prophesying that later negotiations would be difficult.

The Actors

For EC external relations, the competence of the Commission had been restricted to economic aspects, but the Single European Act (SEA) and later the Treaty of European Union (Maastricht Treaty) extended it to the political sphere. Title III of the SEA incorporated the EPC into the sphere of foreign policy, extending foreign policy beyond external economic relations in EC treaties.[17] Despite the limits of the EPC at the time, its function and competence were sufficient to negotiate with Japan over establishing political relations.[18] As a result, the Commission became officially involved in the activities of the EPC, and the EPC secretariat became part of the EC organization in Brussels.

At the time of the Joint Declaration, the President of the Council, Luxembourg, was responsible for diplomatic issues on behalf of EC member states, within the framework of the EPC, in cooperation with the DG I of the European Commission. Therefore, the foreign service of Luxembourg, the smallest among the member states, was responsible for negotiations with Japan.

There was a rough demarcation of work between the Commission and the Council. While the President of the Council dealt with the political aspect, the economic part of the Joint Declaration was in the hands of the Commission. Within the Commission, the Joint Declaration fell almost exclusively within the jurisdiction of the DG I, since concrete trade disputes were excluded from the negotiations. Therefore, this case contrasted with specific trade issues, such as the automobile and the liquor tax cases, which involved other Directorate Generals. During the process of the case, DG I mediated the different opinions of member states rather than show its own initiative, because of the limited responsibility and jurisdiction over the Joint Declaration as a whole.

In addition to the EPC framework, European states co-ordinated foreign policy with each other in other ways (Wallace, 1978: 35). Foreign ministers of major European countries have often had close communications and co-operated in the formulation, management and implementation of foreign policy. Within the EC framework, the 113

Committee and other Working Groups of the Council of Ministers (such as that on Asia) provided opportunities for member states to sound their positions. Member states also frequently contacted each other bilaterally on various occasions. While there were thus plenty of venues for foreign policymaking in the EC, member states still had difficulty in achieving unanimous policymaking decisions. The accumulation of these intergovernmental contacts may imply that the opinions of individual member states were reflected directly in the Commission's proposal, leaving little room for the Commission to manoeuvre.

CHRONOLOGY

Before the Joint Declaration, there had been similar attempts to build political ties between Japan and the EC. Japan on several occasions expressed its wish to build a political relationship with Europe. As early as 1973, for example, Prime Minister Tanaka Kakuei proposed establishing a closer relationship through a joint energy programme, but it failed to attract support from any European leaders. In 1983, the Nakasone government proposed a permanent forum to discuss strategic and political issues of mutual concern between Europe (through NATO) and Japan, but it was rebuffed by France (Buckley, 1990: 77).

The EC showed little interest in Japan in political terms. Official statements by the Council of Ministers in the 1980s clearly indicated that the EC concentrated on economic matters with Japan, especially the trade balance.[19] The protectionist trade measures by the EC were more or less explicitly directed to Japan. It was said in private conversations that 'EC representatives assure Americans that the (protectionist) measures are directed at Japan, not the United States.' (Greenwald, 1990: 353.)

The inception of the Joint Declaration derived from informal talks among MFA officials of WE 1 and KK 1, headed by Owada Hisashi, then deputy vice minister responsible for political affairs. The talks aimed to make a similar declaration to the Transatlantic Declaration.[20] This early period of policymaking followed the same pattern recognized in the study of Japanese foreign policymaking. As Fukui Haruhiro explained,

> policies and decisions are apparently not always, nor even often 'made' but rather emerge and evolve, with few specific decisions

made by any particular individuals. A policy emerges as part of an 'atmosphere' which is in turn generated not by particular individuals but by the group as a whole. (Fukui, 1981: 284)

Although it is believed that Owada's personal initiative established the whole process – as the Japanese reference was often called the 'Owada proposals'[21] – the process of drafting the proposal was mainly in the hands of lower level officials, such as division chiefs, with which the bureau directors and the deputy vice minister, Owada, agreed.[22]

When the MFA made its first official contact with the EC at the end of 1990, the presidency of the Council was held by the Italian government, but practical negotiations were carried out under the subsequent President, Luxembourg. Suggestions in the 'Owada proposals' included: a regular meeting at the level of head of state, a renewed effort for greater cooperation, a joint declaration including fundamental values shared by both parties, a list of common objectives, the principle of consultation at the highest level, and an indication of procedures to this effect.[23] The first positive sign from the European side came on 19 February 1991 at the Council of Foreign Ministers, when they announced that they were willing to sign a joint declaration with Japan similar to those signed with the US and Canada.

The negotiations at the division chief level took place in Luxembourg, focusing on the political part of the issue. Senior level officials – that is, Deputy Vice Minister Owada, Secretary General Dondelinger of the Luxembourg Foreign Ministry and Deputy Director General Giola of DG I – met in Tokyo and Brussels. At the Tokyo meetings, discussion was limited to the political dimension, as the MFA insisted that political rather than economic issues be stressed in the Joint Declaration.

In contrast to the unity among MFA officials, there was significant discord within the EC. The General Affairs Council on 15 April could not adopt the draft text prepared by the Commission (for economic issues) and the Directors of Political Co-operation (for political issues), because the member states disagreed whether requirements for 'trade openness' should be formulated in the declaration.[24] On the one hand, the UK together with the Netherlands preferred an exclusively political text, corresponding to the original MFA proposal. On the other hand, most other countries, particularly France, wanted to stress economic and trade issues in order to commit Japan to trade concessions. German, French and Italian delegations reflected this opinion in statements asserting that the participation of Japanese 'technical ministers' (MITI,

MOF, etc.) would be important in the consultation process.[25] Despite their demands, however, it was obvious to those member governments that Japan would not accept a text with such an emphasis on economic and trade matters, as Japan's intention was clearly directed to a political declaration equivalent to the Transatlantic Declaration. Consequently, after rejecting the draft texts by the foreign ministers from both sides, the Commission proposed a final text in the beginning of May, maintaining an emphasis on economic issues and the question of market access, in particular.

Involving other economic ministries was totally unacceptable to the MFA, both in principle (because the whole purpose of the Joint Declaration was political, not economic) and in practice (because the negotiations would become too complicated by involving more intransigent, economic ministries and thus because the negotiations would move beyond the control of the MFA). At least the Joint Declaration was never openly dealt with in conjunction with the concurrent automobile negotiations. On the surface, neither MITI nor other economic ministries were involved at any stage in the international negotiations between Japan and the EC on the issue. Thus the MFA refused the European demand for participation of economic ministries.

From 22 to 25 May, Commission President Jacques Delors, together with Commissioner for External Relations Frans Andriessen, visited Japan. Indicating the EC direction for the Joint Declaration, Delors had stressed the need for a better balance of commercial exchanges by respecting the three fundamental principles of loyalty, equilibrium and reciprocity.[26] Japan became particularly concerned about this term 'reciprocity' that Delors used. The term was not defined by either side. In theory, 'reciprocity' was a political not an economic principle, which helped to cultivate a pro-trade consensus (Curzon and Curzon, 1987: 174). Although the EC did not show any numerical target, Japan feared that some concrete obligation to reduce the trade imbalance might be imposed.

On his return to Europe, President Delors criticized the Japanese attitude by stating that 'Japan has only envisaged the declaration as simple rhetoric.'[27] This statement conveys the Commission's persistence in ensuring Japan's commitment to economic relations. At this middle stage of the negotiations, political contacts beyond the administrative level were made. For example, a delegation of Members of European Parliament headed by Bernhard Sälzer, visited Japan as part of the regular interparliamentary meetings.[28] Their function was not to pursue actual progress in the negotiations for the Joint Declaration but to create a favourable atmosphere for it.

Another division-head level meeting took place in early June in Luxembourg, which meant that the draft was still far from being finalized. The Community requested reciprocal commitments on 'balanced access' to each other's markets and other detailed provisions on 'formal and informal barriers to trade and economic activities.'[29] Soon after that, the regular ministerial conference between Foreign Minister Nakayama and the Troika plus Commissioner Andriessen took place, which had originally been scheduled to finalize the negotiations. The prospective Joint Declaration was among the subjects, but any breakthrough could not be expected. After this meeting, a new schedule for the signing of the declaration was set to take place at the Hague (as the presidency was to shift from Luxembourg to the Netherlands for the second half of 1991) after the G-7 Summit meeting in London on 15–17 July.

In the meantime, the MFA tried to enhance EC members' support for the declaration. Tokyo sent a *kunrei* (a communication ranked between an order and an instruction) to several embassies to publicize Japan's intention and hopes.[30] Although they were still short of complete agreement on the text, a draft text was agreed to by the administrators on both sides and proceeded to the Committee of Permanent Representatives (CORPER) of the Council of Ministers, on 26 June; thence to the Heads of Government and State at the EC Summit on 28–9 June. The foreign ministers' meeting in EPC on 10 July then adopted the 'memorandum' brought up from the CORPER.[31] By this time, the remaining problem revolved mainly around one phrase: the 'balance of benefits'. This was changed to 'equitable access on the basis of comparable opportunities' in the memorandum. The Japanese side accepted this new phrase after some reluctance, and France agreed to it much later, only on the day of signing, 18 July. The finalized paragraph for this point stated that Japan and the EC would pursue 'equitable access to their respective markets and removing obstacles, whether structural or other, impeding the expansion of trade and investment, on the basis of comparable opportunities.'[32] The signatories were the Japanese Prime Minister, the Commission President and the President of the European Council, which was now held by the Netherlands. The Foreign Ministers of Japan and the Netherlands were also present, though the Japanese Minister of International Trade and Industry was not, despite the original schedule.[33]

The most visible result of the Joint Declaration was the establishment of political dialogue as stated in the last paragraph, which involved both the Commission and the Council. This consisted of annual consultations between the President of the Council, the President of the Commission and the Japanese Prime Minister; annual ministerial conferences; and biannual consultations between the foreign ministers of the Community (Troika), a Commission representative responsible for external relations and the Japanese foreign minister.[34]

CONSEQUENCES FOR DOMESTIC POLITICAL ECONOMY – OR LACK OF CONSEQUENCES

As the MFA planned, the Joint Declaration emphasized political relations, while economic concerns between Japan and the EC remained unresolved. The Commission's guidelines for its relations with Japan, released ten months after the Joint Declaration, continued to stress economic problems, which angered the MFA. The MFA condemned it as a breach of the spirit of the Joint Declaration.[35] Considering that the Commission had only very limited competence in political affairs at that time, however, the document was inevitably economic-oriented (Bridges, 1992: 14).

On the other hand, the summit between Japan and the EC in the following July showed some improvements compared to the previous sour exchange. The summit concluded with a joint statement emphasizing positive elements in the bilateral relationship.[36] Increasingly, Japan and the now EU co-operated politically. They issued a joint proposal to establish an Arms Register to secure the non-proliferation of weapons of mass destruction and to improve the monitoring of arms sales. The United Nations successfully institutionalized the Arms Register in January 1992. Japan and the EU also dispatched peace-keeping personnel to Cambodia and committed mutual support to the other's surrounding areas. That is, Japan offered assistance to the European Bank for Reconstruction and Development (EBRD), and the EU supported Japan's activity in the Asia Pacific region.[37] Finally, Japan and the EC have co-operated on environmental issues through the high level meetings (Tanaka T., 1995: 438). Political dialogue has improved, although it would be an exaggeration to describe Japan–EC relations as having made a 'qualitative leap' (Bridges, 1992: 11).

The newly established annual meetings between the Japanese Prime Minister and the presidents of the Commission and the Council were carried out more or less successfully, though they tended to be more ritual than substantial. When the fourth meeting scheduled in July 1994 was cancelled because of the collapse of the short-lived Hata cabinet and the following change of governing parties in Japan, there was little to no impact.[38]

On Japan's side, the MFA continued to promote Japan's relations with the EU. Reflecting European pressure to deal with economic issues, the Economic Affairs Bureau set up a study group and released a report in April 1992 (Anglo-Japanese Journal, 1993a). Even though the study group consisted of non-officials – such as businessmen, academics and journalists, as is mostly the case with governmental study groups – the report strongly reflected the opinion of the MFA (Tanaka T., 1995: 434–5). It was pointed out, however, that there was a slight drawback to Japan's pursuit of political relations with the EU, when the Common Foreign and Security Policy (CFSP) in 1993 replaced the EPC. While this change formally included foreign and security policy within the EU structure unlike its predecessor, the MFA was sceptical about the effect of the CFSP to build coordinated foreign and security policy among the EU members (T. Tanaka, 1995: 432). Nevertheless, despite such a report, there was no evidence that the MFA had changed its policy to seek political relations with the EU.

The European response to the report of April 1992 showed disappointment in that Japan had not taken practical actions, for example, in supporting Russia and other countries in the former Soviet Union (Anglo-Japanese Journal, 1993b). Nonetheless, a growing number of Europeans demanded that the EU establish political relations with Japan since the Joint Declaration. The Commission's communication to the Council in March 1995 acknowledged the necessary effort on the European side, even though the main part of the document concerned the economic sphere, including the arrangement between the US and Japan.[39] The Commission's suggestion that the EU support the Japanese bid for a permanent seat on the UN Security Council was a positive sign. Even though the Commission still proclaimed that 'the political dimension of the relationship has to date been under-developed', it referred to the Joint Declaration as a basis for the developing relations between the two areas.

In conclusion, the case is important for two reasons: one is the impact of domestic politics on international negotiations, and the other is the political–economic balance of Japan–EC relations. First, although the Joint Declaration was initiated because of the structural change in world politics, it could not lead to structural policy changes on either side. Excluding economic aspects from the Declaration was vital for the MFA to retain control over the issue, instead of co-ordinating with other ministries. At the same time, however, the MFA confined the policy to the individual level rather than developing it into the structural level.

Second, as a result of limitations imposed by the MFA on the Joint Declaration throughout domestic and international negotiations, the significance of the Joint Declaration to the actors outside the MFA was greatly restricted. It was an attempt to nurture political relations so that they could catch up with the reality of Japan–EC economic relations. In this sense, the Joint Declaration was at most an indirect endorsement of the transnational development in the bilateral economic tie. In the process of making the Joint Declaration, there were no transnational communications attempting to enhance or deter the state-level communications. Even though the automobile negotiations were held concurrently, neither Japanese nor European automobile makers attempted to connect the two issues. In short, there was no non-state actor involved in the making of the Joint Declaration, which by definition was out of reach of transnational approach.[40]

Considering the significance of transnational relations indicated in the other case studies, authentic diplomacy seems to have had less impact on the actual development of overall relations between Japan and the EC. Traditional diplomacy is a transaction practised within the same level, state-to-state. The Joint Declaration process did not include in its scope transnational relations to strengthen the substance of the bilateral Japan–EC ties. While the political relations were to catch up with the economic relations between Japan and the EC, transnational relations seems to have already made a great dash to extend such a lead. The weak impact of the Joint Declaration on the domestic political economy can be attributed to this large lead.

Conclusion

Having been through three quite different case studies, I now return to the theories reviewed in Part I in order to reconstruct a picture for Japan–EU relations from Japanese decision-making perspectives. Part I illustrated that the level of analysis is important not only in traditional IR perspectives, but also, and more significantly, in the rise of transnational relations occurring across levels and borders. At the same time, the way in which transnational and other actors impact decision-making depends on the domestic structure. The case studies test these perspectives.

First, I will compare the three cases. The second section explores when transnational relations matter and to what extent they now influence domestic decision-making. It also examines the correlation between policy type and decision-making process, especially regarding the actors involved. Lastly, the extent to which studies of Japan–EC/EU relations can contribute to wider theoretical studies is discussed.

A COMPARISON OF THE CASE STUDIES

I chose the three most symbolic case studies from a wide range of issues between Japan and the EC since the mid-1980s. Different ministries, though they were all powerful bureaucratic organizations, were in charge of different cases: the Ministry of International Trade and Industry in Case I, the Ministry of Finance in Case II, and the Ministry of Foreign Affairs in Case III. The cases vary in terms of actors, the decision-making process and other factors, yet they suggest a certain image of Japanese decision-making.

The variety of contexts in which each case took place reinforces the ad hoc nature of Japanese decision-making towards the EC/EU. Individual trade issues are not necessarily part of a wider, comprehensive foreign economic policy. Even the third case, not a trade but a diplomatic issue by definition, was handled as a ministry-specific issue and thus involved a very small group of actors. Despite the rhetoric the MFA bureaucrats used, their foreign policy in this case had little to do with structural or direction-giving policies.

Concerning the question of level of analysis, a great contrast between trade (generically economic) issues and traditional diplomatic issues emerges. The trade cases directly involved transnational relations, as the private actors substantially influenced cross-border activities, independent of governments, as well as domestic decision-making. Therefore, cross-level activities were the essential part of the cases. On the other hand, state actors, namely diplomats, exclusively dealt with the Joint Declaration. In this case, relying on an international level of analysis that responds to traditional, state-to-state international relations seems appropriate. A domestic level of analysis, however, is required to reveal the process of making the Joint Declaration from the motivation for its birth to the form of the end result.

The automobile issue was the biggest concern of the bilateral relationship in the 1980s, symbolizing the contentious trade relationship between Japan and the EC at the time. Whereas the EC began to emphasize the Japanese market structure as the main trade obstacle during the decade this book discusses, thus shifting the focus of trade disputes, Japanese exports remained a strong bone of contention.

Transnational relations are particularly important in this case. Since the treatment of Japanese transplant cars was one of the major concerns of the EC, Japanese automobile manufacturers tried hard to stir the governmental negotiations to their advantage. They established a cooperative relationship with the British government, which significantly influenced negotiations between MITI and the European Commission.

Japanese export towards the EC was not merely a bilateral concern but implicitly and sometimes explicitly involved the US. In practice, MITI officials realized that any agreement between Japan and the EC was going to be an American concern, particularly regarding the treatment of Japanese-badged car imports into the EC from the United States.

American trade policy also greatly influenced both Japanese and European industries. A US gain in Japan via intense government-level pressuring could lead to a European loss straightaway. In other words, although Japanese exports caused similar problems in the US and in Europe, the European interest in mitigating Japanese exports was not compatible with the equivalent US effort. The European Commission often showed that its approach to negotiations with the Japanese was markedly different from that of the Americans. The Commission attempted to keep its distance both from Japan and the US and to stay neutral in Japan–US disputes.

On the other hand, the EC and the US shared the same concerns about trade with Japan: how to moderate Japanese exports, while simultaneously opening the Japanese market. The EC often joined the US in criticizing Japan's trade practices, but it now and then left the 'bullying' to the US, as seen in the strong US demand to open the Japanese distribution system to foreign automobile and automobile parts manufacturers. By standing quietly behind the United States, the EC seemed to manage to maintain a 'positive and friendly climate in an atmosphere of co-operation.'[1]

While the automobile trade dispute was tentatively resolved in 1991 and centred on how to control Japanese penetration into the European market, the Japanese domestic system was the major concern in the liquor tax case. The liquor tax issue heavily involved Japanese domestic politics as well as domestic and internal politics within the EC, and consequently enlarged the scale of the issue beyond its economic impact. Therefore, the domestic structure was key to exploring the whole story. For example, the timing of the comprehensive tax reform plan in the mid-1980s provoked Europe to increase its pressure. Also, the difference in political clout between Japanese domestic whisky industry and the *shochu* industry was manifested in the process. While the Japanese government relatively promptly abandoned the grading system that Japanese whisky makers tried to protect, the tax rate on *shochu* remained as a problem much longer.

In contrast to those trade dispute cases that involved various actors, the third case study involved few beyond the diplomatic circle. The inception of the Joint Declaration is allegedly found in the wider, greater change in world politics, to which the MFA responded by reviewing Japan's foreign policy. The MFA intended to make the Declaration its first step in establishing political relations between Japan and the EC. The European side, however, sought to make the Joint Declaration a concrete framework for a smoother economic relationship between them, rather than a purely political agreement as the MFA anticipated. Despite EC efforts, the MFA managed to avoid any specific commitment in economic terms. How differently Japan and the EC viewed their strained trade relations between them at the time accounts for this gap. For Japan, economic friction with the EC was more or less overshadowed by that with the United States, whereas the

Europeans deemed it as one of the most important issues in its external policy. Furthermore, the Transatlantic Declaration raised tension among Japanese diplomats. The MFA was alert to the possibility that Japan might be left out of the new political alliance among the democratic advanced economies after the Cold War.

The trade case studies also highlight the interplay between government and industry in decision-making. While MITI's responsibility to the automobile industry was to protect domestic manufacturers, the MOF's priority was to impose taxes on appropriate sectors so that the national budget would remain soundly balanced. Therefore, protecting the liquor industry was only a secondary task for the MOF. As a result, the automobile sector could potentially exercise more influence on decisions taken by MITI than the liquor sector could on the MOF.

In turn, respective industries also responded differently to foreign pressure. Whereas automobile manufacturers have been internationalized for at least the last couple of decades and can respond to European pressure, the *shochu* industry was purely domestic and more intransigent and followed the MOF's conciliatory decision only reluctantly. On the one hand, the strength of the Japanese automobile industry together with its experience in international competition made it possible for the industry to take a relatively independent, equilibrating stance against MITI. On the other hand, the relationship between the liquor industry and the MOF was more one-sided, due to the industry's inertia and the MOF's almost paternalistic monitoring of it, which included cushioning the declining industry, and more importantly, securing tax revenue from the sector. As for the Joint Declaration, there was no direct involvement of private industry, thus the decision-making was less complicated with fewer different actors.

Despite the differences between the cases, one basic pattern emerges. Bureaucratic actors form the centre of decision-making and are subject to both domestic and foreign pressure. None of the issues needed to rely on decisions at the cabinet level, which may well be the same for other issues, since these three cases were the most politicized among issues between Japan and the EC. As a result, each issue was managed by a different ministry, suggesting little coordination or connection among the issues (Imamura, 1985: 119–27).[2]

The pluralist model assumes that decision-makers are not a unitary group but rather different types of actors, largely divided into politicians, bureaucrats and non-state actors. Focusing on state-level

Automobile Trade Case

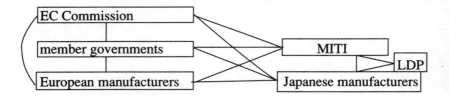

Liquor Tax Case

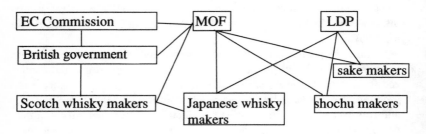

Joint Declaration Case

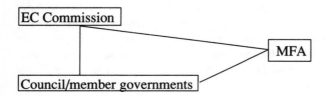

Figure 6.1 The relationships among actors

decision-making, pluralists argue that an actor's influence on individual decisions depends on the area and type of decisions (Otake, 1979). In general terms, Japanese political leaders are supposed to function as mediators for bureaucratic disputes among ministries, according to the pluralist model. Such mediation, however, is carried out by ad hoc political negotiations rather than by systematic policy coordination. The *zoku-giin* politicians were by definition specialists of a certain policy area. Therefore their influence was restricted to a specific area, and their role appeared limited in the case studies, apart from the liquor tax issue. Even in that case, however the joint force of MOF officials and tax tribe politicians subdued the influence of *shochu* tribe politicians. In addition, the lack of active participation by political leaders, such as cabinet members, in all cases indicates that Japan–EC relations have not matured enough to involve structural policy, which in turn would draw political leaders into the decision-making process.

While the pluralist argument has valid points in analysing domestic decision-making, it has so far stopped short in considering the influence of transnational actors in trade cases who pursue their interests in the decision-making arena. Japanese and European firms, often organized into interest groups, strongly influence not only their respective governments but foreign governments, to the extent that decision-making inevitably involves those non-state, cross-border interactions.

In business circles, international partnerships have challenged the traditional meaning of 'national interest', as was seen in the first two case studies and also in a number of industries. Joint ventures among companies across borders, for example, would profit the host country's domestic economy, and thus could mobilize political power in policymaking in the host country. Although automobile makers retain their original nationalities rather than become truly transnational – despite the development of FDI, as is clearly seen in the case of European Ford and GM groups[3] – the relationship between transplanted manufacturers and the governments of host countries affects the latter's trade and industrial policy, and vice versa. In the automobile industry, European makers warned their Japanese counterparts not to cause over-supply in the European market and demanded the opening of the Japanese market. At the same time, technological cooperation, joint ventures and other forms of business links were steadily increasing, strengthening the interdependence among manufacturers. The case of Nedcar, a joint venture between Mitsubishi Motors, Volvo and the Dutch government, provides a good example of cross-border, cross-level interest integration.[4] In the liquor industry, business alliances, such as between Suntory and Allied Domecq, and Kirin and Seagram, also obscure the nationality of their interests, for which they lobby governments 'at home' and 'abroad'.

In general, such industrial initiatives for transnational relations implicitly influence state-to-state interactions, giving a certain direction to settling government-level disputes, or at least delimiting freedom of manoeuvre for governments.

THE HYPOTHESES EXAMINED

The first hypothesis put forth in Chapter 2 was that if transnational development has advanced to the extent that it significantly influences domestic politics, decision-making also involves new transnational actors. First, the conditional phrase of this is seemingly fulfilled only in the case of economic policies. Case III suggests that there is no room to apply the transnational approach to diplomatic issues. Thus, where economic issues are concerned, transnational relations are apt to be an important part of cross-border transactions.

In examining decision-making, the bureaucratic politics model is convenient to perceive the diversity of decision-makers and the relations among them. Considering that the essence of the bureaucratic politics model lies in the concept of 'political resultants' (Allison, 1971: 162), Japan's decision-making towards the EC/EU shows such a feature. However, the range of actors involved is more international, and transnational relations matter more than the original model supposed. Combining the transnational perspective into the bureaucratic politics model has been suggested (Risse-Kappen, 1995b: 9),[5] but it has not been practised in the context of Japanese–European relations.

From the first two case studies, the interactions across borders and levels – i.e. between Japanese government agents and the European private sector, between Japanese and European industries and between Japanese industry and European bureaucracy – have clearly significantly influenced decision-making. Behind the state-level negotiations on automobile and liquor tax issues, lobbying activities from each direction were numerous and intense. In short, the first two case studies plainly show the involvement of transnational actors in the decision-making process.

The Japanese automobile industry was prepared to leave the decision of trade policy to MITI, and the industry itself was also united in its approach to trade and investment with the EC. At the same time, however, it is inexplicable why MITI's control over Japanese cars in the EC market took a monitoring form, unless one looks at not only the pressure from the European Commission and individual member state governments but also the European automobile industry and the GATT that inhibited an outright quota system. Even more directly influential on decision-making was the relationship Japanese automobile manufacturers fostered with the British government through FDI that affected negotiations between the Commission and MITI. As business relations extend across borders, business interests do not necessarily follow the fault line of nationality, most apparently in joint ventures.

In the liquor tax case, domestic interests diverged between the MOF and tax tribe politicians on the one hand, and the liquor industry on the other, as well as among liquor producers of different products. After the 1989 liquor tax reform abolished the grading system of whisky, domestic whisky producers co-ordinated interests more closely with foreign makers. As a result, domestic whisky manufacturers supported the lobbying activities of European whisky manufacturers (the Scotch Whisky Association, in effect), although domestic makers did so quietly so that the MOF would not become hostile to them. The process of deciding the actual taxation reform involved competing industrial groups, both domestic and foreign, and political leaders, which is one of the major features of the bureaucratic politics model. Therefore, when the discussion is focused on a certain issue area, such as individual economic policy, the transnational approach can provide insightful analysis of decision-making.

On the other hand, such transnational influence was not prominent in the process of making the Joint Declaration. While the other cases showed when transnational relations matter, this case indicated when they do not. Without direct economic interests involved, it seems that the transnational approach lost its footing. It is questionable, however, whether one should exclude diplomatic issues categorically from transnational interactions. Japan and the EC had already had stable diplomatic relations, thus developing diplomatic ties was not a serious concern for private companies seeking business opportunities. In contrast, when the political relationship hinders economic connections, private economic actors may well attempt to influence the governmental decision-making system (Fukui, 1977c).

Consequently, the first hypothesis is applicable in specific economic issues, while in diplomatic issue areas the transnational development between Japan and the EU seems to have little effect. Since the object of analysis in this book was Japan's decision-making towards the EU, other issues that involve transnational relations such as the environment, drug trafficking and international terrorism, were out of reach. At least, the case studies show that, in the economic issue area, multinational corporations actively cultivate transnational relations to influence the decision-making process.

The second hypothesis was that depending on the type of policy, the decision-making structure shifts, particularly regarding the position of core decision-making actors. The variety of case studies underscores how decision-making structure and process vary according to policy type. Although bureaucratic actors were always in the centre of Japanese decision-making in the three case studies, other actors held different degrees of importance depending on the policy levels.

The three cases involved clearly different actors and took different courses. The major actors in the automobile case were the bureaucrats and the industrialists who were producers and exporters at the same time. The decision-making for automobile trade policy centred around MITI and the industrial sector, without involving political leaders. Although the relationship between the industrial sector and the bureaucracy was not necessarily always harmonious, the manufacturers vigorously pursued their own interests in cooperation with the responsible ministry bureau. The automobile trade issue hardly involved the LDP or politicians from other parties, though top-level international negotiations were handled by the head of the ministry, invariably an LDP member of the Diet until 1993.

More importantly, from a transnational approach, Japanese manufacturers established strong communication ties with foreign governments through FDI. The British government supported Japanese FDI and consequently influenced negotiations between Japan and the EC over whether transplants should be included in the export quota. While such activities of Japanese private firms were closely observed by MITI, their relations with European actors need to be distinguished from traditional inter-state relations. The substantial part of the Japan–EC relations derives from the activities of non-state actors like multinational corporations.

On the other hand, the liquor tax case involved politicians as significant actors in the decision-making process, although the draft-making of the policy was mainly handled by the MOF. Liquor tribe politicians in the LDP functioned as mediators of conflicting interests, providing compensation to those with compromised interests. Tax policymaking was one of the areas in which tax specialists in the Diet manoeuvre as much as MOF officials. Nonetheless, the participation of political leaders in tax policy did not undermine the role of the MOF, since tax tribe politicians and MOF bureaucrats maintained co-operative relations in policymaking. The relationship between the MOF and tax tribe politicians was distinctive compared with the other tribes (Inoguchi and Iwai, 1987: 205–9). As Chapters 3 and 4 showed, the automobile tribe politicians were little involved in the trade issue, whereas tax tribe politicians participated directly in the liquor tax issue in composing taxation policy in Japan. Even politicians whose careers were based within the LDP and not through the MOF were well respected by bureaucrats because of their expert knowledge. The liquor industry itself had close relations with the LDP and its predecessors historically, therefore the liquor industry communicated its opinions through politicians to the bureaucracy, as well as by direct pressuring. This was reflected in the difference between the MOF and MITI in their relationships with respective tribe politicians.

The Joint Declaration was yet another type of a policy, i.e. a political diplomatic policy, although it could not avoid the economic dimension because of the nature of Japan's relationship with the EC. Initially, the Joint Declaration was part of a grand revision of Japanese foreign policy to respond to structural changes in world politics, though the effect of the Declaration was expected to be small. Despite European demands, particularly from France, that the negotiations include concrete economic commitment, the MFA resisted strongly, wanting to retain exclusive control and not include economic ministries such as the MOF and MITI.

There was no practical participation of political leaders in the decision-making either. Apart from the security area, there was no foreign policy tribe, thus the basic relationship between the bureaucracy (MFA) and politicians was even weaker than that of MITI and *shoko-zoku* (commerce tribe). If political leaders play an important role in making diplomatic policy, it is usually not tribe politicians, but the Prime Minister and Foreign Minister. In the making of the Joint Declaration between Japan and the EC, however, political decisions at the ministerial level were not needed, despite difficulties during the negotiating process. This lack of participation by political actors was precisely because the policy proposed by the MFA to seek political ties with the EC was not a structural change in Japan's foreign policy.

The automobile issue was handled independently from other issues including the Joint Declaration, and the main problem was to decide how to control the number of Japanese cars in the EC market. Therefore, it was an individual-implementing policy (see Figure 1.2), and it was the bureaucratic actor's role to decide specific measures to control car exports to the EC, which excluded political leaders.

In contrast, in the liquor tax case, taxation is related to structural policy, while as a trade issue it fell into the individual-implementing policy category. While the bureaucratic actor was responsible for deciding the detail of the liquor tax reform, political leaders also assumed an important role in the decision-making, especially in encouraging domestic industrial groups to compromise with international organizations (GATT and WTO) as well as with the MOF on its budget/tax plan.

The Joint Declaration was a diplomatic issue handled exclusively by the MFA. The last case study is significant, however, in that the MFA avoided shifting the policy type to the structural level so that the decision-making actors would be limited to within the MFA, instead of involving other economic ministries or political leaders. Therefore, the correlation between policy type and decision-making structure can be seen in these cases: the stronger the individual-implementing feature of the policy, the more dominant role bureaucratic actors have.

Within the framework applied in the bureaucratic politics model, the difference in policy type determines the central decision-makers (the chief and partisans). In contrast to the original model based on the American case, the case studies showed that individual ministries in Japan are in the centre of decision-making of issues for which they are responsible. The automobile case was led by MITI, the liquor tax by the MOF, and the Joint Declaration by the MFA, rather than the Prime Minister taking the role of the chief. This weak presence of political leaders (except for the liquor tax case) was partly because all three issues were not in the structural or direction-giving level.

While the hypotheses were studied using the bureaucratic politics model, other points suggest important comparisons between Japanese decision-making and the model. In the first two cases, the MFA had a different priority from that of MITI or the MOF. The MFA demanded that any agreement made between Japan and the EC must be compatible with GATT rules and that the issues should be restrained so as not to exacerbate the overall relationship between the two. The MFA's attitude was particularly welcomed by the Europeans in the liquor tax case. Although the MFA's opinion did not greatly influence the decision that either MITI or the MOF chose to take, the MFA participated in the negotiation process between Japan and the EC, especially in the formal part. This indicates that in the Japanese policymaking process towards the EC, the government was not unitary to start with, and its decisions were made through intensive talks between governmental sub-units and industry. In the meantime the government was also subject to massive pressure from European industries. In the case of the Joint Declaration, the MFA was the sole Japanese decision-maker, but that situation was deliberately made by the MFA rather than given to them. Other ministries did not participate in decision-making not only because of MFA jurisdiction but also because the MFA set the agenda so that other ministries could not intervene. This fits the argument that decision-makers (players of 'pulling and hauling') are originally picked up by the central decision-maker (Krasner, 1973).

Throughout the case studies, a ministry division appears to be a unit of decision-making (*ohbeya-shugi*), within which there is no sign of divided opinions. In the case of the Joint Declaration, even though the two divisions responsible for the issue worked harmoniously, a clear demarcation defined the tasks of each division. As a result, one group could not talk about issues under the other's jurisdiction. On the other hand, the demarcation of jurisdiction was so clear in all issues that there was little direct intra- or inter-ministerial conflict.

INTERNATIONAL RELATIONS THEORY AND JAPAN–EU RELATIONS

The relationship of theoretical studies and empirical studies itself is a controversial and complicated matter of discussion.[6] This book attempted to see whether IR theories are useful in understanding and explaining Japan–EU relations. In practice, the book discussed to a large extent the domestic politics of Japan on the grounds that domestic politics is a significant factor in determining international relations, and vice versa (international relations determines domestic politics) (Gourevitch, 1978). Focusing on domestic politics in analysing events in international relations, it becomes clear that the distinction between domestic and foreign policy is barely important in examining the decision-making process and structure.

Studies on decision-making contribute significantly to understanding foreign policy. What is Japanese foreign economic policy towards the EU? The ad hoc nature of bureaucratic handling of trade issues suggests that the Japanese government lacks a comprehensive foreign economic policy. Therefore, the question is better changed to how is the policy made? Japanese bureaucracy is an indispensable element to be considered, and so are the interactions between the bureaucracy and other actors, including their European counterparts and Japanese and European industries. Depending on the individual case, it is also necessary to look into the role of political leaders in decision-making. The bureaucratic politics model was tested to examine Japanese decision-making towards the EC, and was most useful in the liquor tax case for distinguishing different actors within the domestic decision-making process.

On the other hand, the strict demarcation within Japanese bureaucracy limits the participating government agent in individual issues to only one responsible ministry, and it is necessary to adjust the model to perceive non-bureaucratic actors as partisans who participate in the decision-making. Moreover, the traditional models of decision-making, including the bureaucratic politics model, are based on a state-centric assumption, which is itself a traditional approach to international relations. The recent revival of the transnational approach includes transgovernmental relations, which 'could be regarded as the transnational equivalent of bureaucratic politics.' (Risse-Kappen, 1995b: 9.) This does not prevent consideration of non-governmental organizations as one of the main actors of 'bureaucratic' politics. In order to argue in favour of transnational relations, it is not necessary to be trapped in the dispute between state-centric realism versus society-oriented liberalism (Risse-Kappen, 1995c: 282).

The transnational approach has also been added in the understanding of Japan's decision-making. While many political scientists argue that the Japanese political system is pluralistic, they have not explained the impact of transnational actors, such as multinational enterprises, on Japanese decision-making. The influence of deepening economic transactions can be seen in the process of decision-making. European automobile makers, for example, managed to set a transitional period during which MITI monitored Japanese exports to the EU. In other words, MITI's policy of monitoring is directed to domestic carmakers, but the process that led to that particular policy was heavily influenced by international politics, including non-state actors. The question of whether transnational relations with the EU have changed Japanese decision-making *per se*, however, raises too much expectation to give a clear answer. After all, although the case studies are important issues in Japan's European policy, they are too partial to draw overall conclusions on Japanese foreign economic policy. In this sense, transnational relations do not provide an answer, but only cast more questions about cross-border interactions.

Unlike Japan–US relations, Japan–EU relations are still under-exploited in the area of theoretical and empirical studies of transnational relations. In the first and second case studies, there were several indications of growing transnational relations across state/non-state levels. These cases support the argument that there are areas in which the traditional framework of international relations is insufficient to explain the developing cross-border relationships. This is particularly obvious in Japan–EU relations in which state-to-state level contacts do not dominate, but rather transnational relations between Japanese firms and the European government, and European business and the Japanese government, are more frequent. In other words, there is an interesting twist in the phenomenon: while IR theory developed from state-centrism to add transnational relations, the development of Japan–EC/EU relations went in the other direction. There is a movement among the governments to promote political dialogue, which is inevitably state-level, in order to catch up with the transnational economic relations.

Japan–EU relations have not been regarded with great importance among Japanese political and bureaucratic leaders. In the meantime, the importance of foreign economic policy in international relations has increased, even compared to security matters, as reflected in the rise of international political economy (IPE). In order to analyse state decision-making on economic policies, some point out the importance of non-state actors, particularly multinational enterprises (Keohane, 1990; Stopford and Strange, 1991). While economists discuss economic policy and its decision-making, IPE emphasizes political motives more than economic 'rationality' for certain decisions, developing the argument in parallel with the expansion of world economic transactions since the 1950s. In IPE discussions, Japan–US relations – trade negotiations between them in particular – have had great significance, while an equivalent argument on Japan–EU relations cannot be found. As this book attempted, however, studies of Japan–EU relations can potentially contribute to improving existing models of IPE and other theoretical considerations. In particular, the transnational approach could develop further from careful study of Japan's decision-making towards the EC.

The analyses I have attempted in the case studies still focus on government actors as the central decision-makers, though at the same time the influence of non-state actors, including both domestic and foreign interest groups, is an indispensable determinant for the relationship between Japan and the EC. In addition, domestic structures are inevitably an important factor in the decision-making process and negotiations between Japan and the EC. Even if, in the context of Japan–US relations, domestic structure defines the transnational actors' strategies, how and to what extent transnational actors, such as multinational firms, influence domestic politics remains an important question (Katzenstein and Tsujinaka, 1995). Therefore, there is no reason to deny that the Japanese domestic structure should have the same effect in terms of Japanese–European relations. While Katzenstein and Tsujinaka categorized the style of transnational relations between Japan and the United States into three forms, 'bullying', 'buying' and 'binding', the case studies showed that the EU relied on similar means to those of the US: 'bullying', forcing the liberal trade ideology, and 'binding', trying to co-operate with the Japanese bureaucracy and trade associations (Katzenstein and Tsujinaka, 1995: 80).

In the liquor tax issue, Europe brought the case to the GATT and later to the WTO. While Scotch whisky makers threatened the Japanese government with such procedures, they also built business contacts with Japanese whisky makers to attain mild support. The implication of such deepening transnational relations between Japan and the EU is that IPE would benefit from the study of non-state actors between equally developed economies. While the role of multinational enterprises in developing countries is clearer (Stopford and Strange, 1991), the strategy of transnational actors between Japan and the EU may show a different aspect of the development of IPE.

In summary, the framework for this study is based on domestic politics decision-making, which transnational actors have increasingly influenced. On the one hand, the states remain central to the argument, particularly with bureaucratic actors as the central decision-makers. On the other hand, the states are not the sole focus of cross-border relations, but have to share important roles with non-state actors. Although this study did not extend to the area of non-governmental organizations, multinational firms actively participated in the process of decision-making.

The role of international organizations is another item beyond the scope of this book. As the time frame of the book excludes the WTO formed in 1995, a cursory study of the following years suggests an interesting development and possible shift. In a new multilateral trade framework, the bilateral relationship between Japan and the EU may experience a structural change. Such ideas and studies of the new trade regime and its impact are for future works.

As discussed above, Japan–EU relations could provide fertile ground for both theoretical and empirical studies, which have been under-exploited. Those serving in the government, such as politicians and bureaucrats, also have had little interest in relations between the two regions. Different priorities at the policy level between Japan and the EU add to the mutual indifference. While European issues – such as internal integration, application for joining the Union by former communist states in Eastern Europe, instability in Russia and the situation in former Yugoslavia – dominate the EU agenda, the main concerns of Japanese foreign policy are its changing relationship with the United States, the rapid development and recent stagnation in East Asia and the subsequent rise of regionalism in the area (Bridges, 1992: 18).

The limited nature of the relationship is reflected in that issues between Japan and the EU are mostly at the individual-implementing policy level, which would hardly involve political leaders. Nonetheless, the development of Japan–EU relations itself is not a negligible phenomenon for political and bureaucratic leaders or for academics. The first to realize and enhance the significance of the relationship were private economic actors. Their economic activities invited economic analyses, which gradually extended the research into the political impacts of such economic phenomena. There has not been, however, an attempt to link the transnational economic relations between Japan and the EU with frameworks built in international relations theory. This book tested the possibility of such a linkage. There is much to be explored on the subject. The reality of Japan–EU relations exhibits an alternative form to traditional international relations, providing a large pool for further scrutiny from transnational approaches.

Notes

INTRODUCTION

1 While the ratification of the Treaty on European Union in 1993 turned the European Community into the European Union, the economic pillar of the Union maintains the name of the European Community. Therefore, the following will refer to the EC in events prior to 1993, while EC and EU are used interchangeably for post-1993 when dealing with economic issues.

2 The GDP of the United States in 1995 was 6955 billion dollars, by far the largest among all national economies.

3 Interview with Mr Antonio Menezes, the Head of Press and Information Service of the European Delegation in Tokyo, 26 June 1992.

4 Also, for the distant relationship between Japan and the EC in the early 1980s, Wilkinson, 1980; Tsoukalis and White, 1982.

5 At around the same time, East and Southeast Asian economies grew dramatically and became a very important region for Japan's exports and outward investments. In terms of the level of maturity of the markets, however, the EC was more comparable with the US than with the upcoming Asian market. The following discussion, therefore, does not involve Asian countries and their region, but includes comparison with the Japan–US relations.

6 On the other hand, economic competition with Japan was a major factor that accelerated the integration of the European economies in the second half of the 1980s. Prior to the reinvigoration of integration movement, some member states took a 'national champion' industrial policy, by which they directly supported one or two big firms within an industrial sector so that they could gain international competitiveness without wasting their resources in domestic competition. This policy failed in global competitions with US and Japanese firms, consequently giving incentives to the European political and economic leaders to enhance cooperation among European industries.

7 Kunihiro Michihiko, Deputy Vice Minister of the Ministry of Foreign Affairs, Statement given at the Royal Institute of International Affairs, 'The external implications of the Single European Market: A view from Japan', 11 October 1988, London.

8 For example, Nester, 1991. As discussed later in Chapter 2, so-called revisionists also view Japanese political economy as heavily controlled by the central government.

9 Exceptional works that pay attention to political, environmental and other non-economic relations between Japan and the EC include: S. Strange, 1995:

21–2; Tanaka A., 1994. For the debate on security issues between Japan and Europe, S. Sato and Taylor, 1993; Maull, 1990.

10 So-called trade wars between the EC and the US were always averted at the last minute, for example, the case of Helms–Burton law and the case of banana dispute for EC imports.

11 The most distinctive example is the linkage between the issue of Okinawa reversion and the fibre trade concession in the late 1960s. Destler *et al.*, 1976; Destler, Fukui and Sato, 1979; Otake, 1979: 69–168.

12 Some criticized, however, that the US still refuses to make enough effort to understand Japan (Johnson and Keehn, 1994: 20–2).

13 For example, Obi, 1992; NHK reporters, 1990; Funabashi, 1987; Tanaka N., 1989. As for American non-academics, the most influential works include Prestowitz, 1988; Choate, 1990.

14 For example, Itoh and Ishiguro, 1993, although Ishiguro's background is international law; Akiyama, 1994; Bergsten and Cline, 1987; Maswood, 1989.

15 This work consists of case studies, including issues of textile, semiconductors, FSX and the Structural Impediment Initiative.

16 The next chapter examines the two-level approach more in detail, while it should be mentioned here that this approach was devised to describe the extent to which domestic politics determines the international negotiations (Krauss, 1993). Some political researchers in Japan have also attempted to apply IR/IPE approaches to trade issues between Japan and the United States; Nagao Satoru took the rice import dispute, while Oyane Satoshi discussed the Multinational Fibre Agreement in the framework of the two-level approach (Nagao, 1992; Oyane, 1992).

17 The transnational approach is further discussed in Chapter 1. As for its definition, I rely on Risse-Kappen's: 'regular interactions across national boundaries when at least one actor is a non-state agent or does not operate on behalf of a national government or an intergovernmental organization.' Risse-Kappen, 1995b: 3.

18 The major exception is Rothacher, 1983.

19 As for an exception, Bourke, 1996.

20 It refers to the system, established by the merger of two main conservative parties (the Liberal Party and the Democratic Party) in 1955 in which the conservatives were able to hold the power in such a stable manner to last 38 years.

21 The coalition between the LDP and the Liberal Party settled in January 1999 seems to have accelerated the political reform that would enhance the policymaking ability of party politicians, by way of preventing bureaucrats from substituting the ministers at the policy debate in the Diet.

CHAPTER 1: ANALYTICAL FRAMEWORKS – CONTRIBUTIONS FROM IR PERSPECTIVES

1 *Gaiatsu* refers to foreign pressure on Japan. See later section in this chapter.

2 The levels described above correspond to Waltz's third, second and

first image of international relations, respectively. Other categorizations discern different numbers of levels; J. David Singer distinguished two, the international-systemic level and national state level (Singer, 1961); Robert Jervis added a forth, the bureaucratic process level to Waltz's three levels (Jervis, 1976). In addition, F. H. Hinsley discussed the two different approaches towards the international relations (Hinsley, 1973). In his argument, nationalism and the international system clearly correspond to the second and the third levels of analysis by Waltz's definition.

3 For a list of works on this level of analysis, see Moravcsik, 1993: 5–6, 35–6.

4 As for a more recent argument that emphasizes the domestic sources of international relations, Zürn, 1993.

5 See Introduction.

6 Knopf, in his effort to develop the two-level model, sought to explain the negotiations between unfriendly blocs, i.e. the Western Alliance and the Soviet Union in the 1980s. As he distinguished three different forms of transnational interactions, he calls only the second type (between non-state actors) 'transnational relations'. This definition is narrower than the one I adopt here that is based on Risse-Kappen and others. See below.

7 Also, Risse-Kappen discussed the deficiencies of the state-centric view. Risse-Kappen, 1995b: 14–16.

8 Also, see Keohane and Nye, 1971: xii–xvi.

9 The term 'refract' is borrowed from Katzenstein and Tsujinaka, 1995: 81.

10 For criticism against the traditional approach, Ashley, 1986. In Japan, Kamo Takehiko criticized Robert Gilpin's counter-criticism against Ashley. Kamo, 1990: 97–116.

11 Strictly speaking, the GATT was not an organization, since the original attempt to establish the International Trade Organization based on the GATT agreement failed.

12 A case of the Japanese recording industry was a concrete example of the obscurity of national interest in economic and related fields; the industry supported the US attempt to expand intellectual property protection against the Japanese government's reluctance. *Financial Times*, 12 February, 1996, p. 4.

13 Steinbruner used the term 'analytic paradigm' to describe this type of decision-making model, questioning the degree of rationality of decisions in actual situations (Steinbruner, 1974).

14 Tsebelis's attempt is similar in the sense that he also focused seeming 'irrationality', which he explained are in fact optimal/rational (Tsebelis, 1990).

15 The idea of mutual adjustment of partisans was suggested earlier by Lindblom, 1965. He also suggested incrementalism to replace rational policymaking, which gave significant insights to Allison's bureaucratic politics model; Lindblom, 1965: 143–7; Braybrooke and Lindblom, 1963: 83–106. For the summary of the study of incrementalism, Tani, 1990.

16 Jervis gave abundant examples of misperceptions made by decision-makers.

Such misperceptions are categorized as: the tendency for actors to see others as more centralized and calculating than they are; the view that actors see other's actions as autonomous as opposed to being reactions to the actor's own behaviour; the tendency of wishful thinking; and cognitive dissonance (Jervis, 1976: 10). For each type of misperceptions, Jervis, 1976: Chapters 8 to 11. For introduction to cognitive approach, Sato H., 1989. Also see Jönsson, 1982; Holsti, 1962.

17 In the argument of cognitive theory, Steinbruner distinguishes three modes of thinking in organizational decision-making: what he called 'grooved' thinking, uncommitted thinking and theoretical thinking (Steinbruner, 1974: 125-36). 'Grooved' thinkers, in this definition, are those who tend to follow previous cases automatically, typically therefore to be found among bureaucrats. The organizational process model of decision-making (Allison's Model II) presumes this type of decision-makers, who loyally follow the organization's code of conduct. Secondly, many uncommitted thinkers appear at a higher level in an organizational hierarchy; they adopt generalized concepts rather than a narrow range of variants, since they are usually non-experts with regard to the issues in the process of decision-making. Therefore, this type of decision-maker is flexible enough to choose different belief patterns at different times for the same decision problem. At the same time, however, these uncommitted thinkers do not always compare different alternatives to choose the best among them, but tend to choose the last advice they have listened to. In contrast, the third type, the theoretical thinkers, maintain an abstract and strong belief system for a considerably long period, which is connected to concrete alternatives by a chain of inference; and their consistency and conviction in their views make it difficult to accept opposing views to reconsider their decisions.

The concept of an operational code was stylized by Alexander George (George, 1969). He criticized the term 'operational code' as misleading; 'it implies, incorrectly, a set of recipes or repertoires for political action that an elite applies mechanically in its decision-making.' Based on Nathan Leites' work, *A Study of Bolshevism*, George defined an operational code as 'a set of premises and beliefs about politics', and he divided these beliefs into two groups: 'beliefs about ends–means relationships in the context of political action' and 'the political actor's "philosophical" beliefs.'

Another explanation for defective decisions refers to groupthink: Irving Janis showed the danger of psychological distortions by group-thinking (Janis, 1972). He pointed out the tendency of decision-makers to reject outsiders' opinions and to take riskier courses of action, which derives from pressures from within the group to which they belong.

18 In Krasner's argument, when the President is interested in and pays much attention and energy to an issue, the bureaucracy has no other choice but to obey the President's instruction. Even when an issue does not attract the President's attention, the bureaucracy must be sensitive to his values. Krasner, 1973: 315.

19 In disciplines other than international relations, such as management studies or sociology, decision-making is often discussed and Japanese decision-making models in private companies drew much attention, especially in the 1980s. Ever since 1991, however, as the downturn of Japanese economy deepens, the Japanese corporations has lost its attractiveness as a model.

20 For example, Blaker, 1977b. In Japanese universities, diplomatic history is an established area of political studies, as is public administration.

21 There are a considerable amount of studies on decision-making in Japan's international relations; for example, Aruga *et al.*, 1989: vol 4; Hosoya and Watanuki, 1977. Nevertheless, when discussing decision-making, Japanese researchers tend to rely on American empirical studies in order to examine theoretical models. Moreover, Otake Hideo criticized that studies of Japanese political phenomenon remained merely applied foreign models (Otake, 1990: 3).

22 See Introduction.

23 Early post-WWII years saw a more dynamic role by socialists politicians. Establishing official diplomacy with People's Republic of China in the 1970s was the case in point. Since 1993, the possibility of changing the governing parties has raised the potential of opposition party politicians.

24 Although Robert Angel assessed the active leadership of the Prime Minister in Nakasone's tenure, the substance of his leadership is questionable in actual policymaking, as opposed to his style (Angel, 1989). Also, Hayao (1993) discussed the role Nakasone pursued as a Prime Minister, though the work indicates the severe limitations he had to face. For the lack of leadership by premier, Van Wolferen, 1989: 146–53, 297–8.

25 In the period of the LDP dominance until 1993, the ministerial positions were allocated according to the negotiations among factions within the LDP. Under the coalition government, similar negotiations have been carried out among government parties, but the situation that the Prime Minister does not have free choice of his cabinet members remains the same. Most recently, however, there is a reform plan under the alliance between the LDP and the Liberal Party to nurture policymaking ability among politicians in order to replace the seniority system within the party to produce ministers.

26 Otake, 1990: 39, 54; Allison, 1971: 176.

27 This article discussed the Japanese code of conduct in administration in comparison with Western tradition, showing differences between them without celebrating Japan's uniqueness.

28 For example, the case of opening diplomatic relations with People's Republic of China in the early 1970s (Fukui, 1977c). In this case, various politicians were deemed to have played a major role in deciding Japan's foreign policy towards China, whose actions were all under the understanding and directions of then Prime Minister Tanaka and Foreign Minister Ohira.

29 Schoppa concentrates more on domestic politics, and is very similar in terms of selection of cases and conclusion as Krauss, 1993. For the discussion of *gaiatsu* in the context of general transnational relations, Katzenstein and

Tsujinaka, 1995. In their words, 'bullying' corresponds to *gaiatsu* in a usual form. Among those, an exceptional work is T. J. Pempel's unpublished article that focuses on wider change in the global economy rather than *ad hoc* bilateral pressure on Japan from foreign partners (Pempel, 1998).

30 For example, Ishida, 1986; Fukui, 1977a.

CHAPTER 2: THE JAPANESE POLITICAL ECONOMY AND DECISION-MAKING STRUCTURE

1 This should not be confused with the 'bureaucratic politics model' originally based on the studies of American foreign policy, which Chapter 1 discussed. 'Bureaucratic dominance model' derives from the studies of Japanese public administration, not a subject of international relations.

2 There are more examples in the security issue area, in which political leaders showed their initiatives: Destler *et al.*, 1976; Fukui, 1977c.

3 For a comparison between Nakasone and Ozawa, see Watanabe, 1994.

4 Recent criticisms against the MOF and proposed reform also reflect the power the ministry has had. For example, *Financial Times*, 9 February 1996, p 5.

5 This practice of *amakudari* has been severely criticized, since various scandals in recent years involved many officials and former officials, suggesting the structural problem of abuse of power by bureaucrats.

6 'Tettei kensho: Kanryo no shinwa' (Probing the myth of bureaucracy), *Bungei shunju*, LXXII, 2 (February 1994), pp 154–219. This report consists of ten essays, some of which targeted their criticisms against particular ministries, such as the MOF, the Ministry of Agriculture, Forestry, and Fishery (MAFF) and the MFA. Also, ' "Sei to kan" no taiketsu: tokushu' (The confrontation between politics and bureaucracy: special report), *Bungei shunju*, LXXII, 14 (November, 1994), pp 112–43.

7 William Nester, for example, defines that Japan is as a neo-mercantilist state and has a very critical view towards Japan; (Nester, 1990; Nester, 1991). This neo-mercantilist interpretation is based on the neo-realist framework, which perceives that pursuit of power, in this case economic power in particular, as the central purpose of the states. So-called revisionists, as the later section discusses, also stress the power of the bureaucratic, political and economic elite.

8 The model is originated in an argument for the American political system (Mills, 1959). I refer to the elitist model in this book as a system in which those who are at the top level of administrative, political and economic groups monopolize the power in political economy.

9 Curtis criticized the 'Japan Inc.' model for its simplicity and lack of in-depth analysis.

10 Leon Hollerman, for example, used the term, 'the headquarters nation' to describe the view that Japan has a national strategic plan (Hollerman, 1991).

11 There are a number of variations of pluralism suggested by Japanese

researchers, sometimes with a coined adjective. For example, 'bureaucratic mass-inclusionary (*sic*) pluralism' by Inoguchi T., 1983; 'patterned pluralism' by Muramatsu and Krauss, 1987; and 'LDP-bureaucracy compound pluralism' or 'compartmentalized pluralism' by Sato S. and Matsuzaki, 1986: 153–72. Also, see Sone, 1986: 305–9.

12 They are *Keidanren* (the Federation of Economic Organizations), *Doyukai* (Japanese Committee for Economic Development), *Nikkeiren* (Japanese Federation of Employers' Association) and *Nissho* (Japanese Chamber of Commerce and Industry).

13 Comment by Suzuki Eiji, the Chairman of the Provisional Administrative Reform Promotion Council, quoted in Kishi, 1993: 18.

14 See the following argument on corporatism.

15 In terms of the political system, corporatism can mean several very different systems. Neo-corporatism, liberal corporatism and societal corporatism are terms used to describe the systems found in small and medium sized liberal democracies in Western Europe. On the other hand, corporatism is also associated with fascist and authoritarian states. See Williamson, 1985: 7–12; Schmitter, 1979a: 20; Panitch, 1979: 123.

16 Cawson, 1986: 83–125. The meso- and micro-level corporatisms can be found in Japan more easily than that on the macro-level. Decisions made at the meso- and micro-level, however, are mostly important in the fields of payment, management and production, and have very limited direct influence on foreign economic policies. Therefore, the following argument of corporatism concentrates on the macro-level.

17 For further discussion on corporatism versus pluralism, see Cawson, 1986: Chapter 1.

18 For example, Katzenstein, 1984.

19 A common comment by several officials who wish to be remain anonymous.

20 However, the concept of 'corporate pluralism' is criticized as its interpretation of pluralism is 'out-of-date' (Cawson, 1986: 30).

21 Also, Yamaguchi S., 1984.

22 This scandal originated from a company that was to expand its business opportunities in the information industry. In order to acquire favourable treatment by the Ministry of Education, Ministry of Labour and other related parties, it bribed politicians and high-rank officials with its shares before the company registered at the Tokyo Stock Market (Asahi Shimbun Shakai-bu, 1989).

23 The difference among the three views – bureaucratic dominance, pluralism and corporatism – is not necessarily clear, and there is a criticism that it is a futile argument what Japan's political–economic system should be called (Hiwatari, 1991: 3–4, 6).

24 The current economic downturn in Japan beginning in the early 1990s erased the fear of those revisionists that Japan might soon take over the United States.

25 Chalmers Johnson, counted as one of the main pillars of revisionists in the United States, denies being a Japan-basher. (Johnson, 1995: 11.)

26 Joseph Nye summarized the shared propositions among revisionists as: (1) Japan is different from other capitalist societies; (2) the differences between Japanese and American forms of capitalism are hurting the US economy; and (3) although Japan is changing, its speed is too slow to satisfy the US or the rest of the world (Nye, 1993: 102).

27 This article particularly focuses on the reactive nature of Japanese decision-making, although such a division itself is criticized as being too simplistic and of little use (Mikanagi, 1990).

28 For detailed process, see Omori, 1985.

29 See Chapter 1.

30 Also from a sociological perspective, see Befu, 1990.

31 Almost all textbooks in Japanese politics and public administration refer to this feature. Works by Masumi Junnosuke, Kyogoku Jun-ichi and Tsuji Kiyoaki are major authoritative textbooks. In addition, see Imamura, 1985.

32 Interview with a British official, 6 December 1995, London.

33 However, there are also some similarities between Japanese and EC decision-making in that, for example, Japanese decision-making is also dispersed among ministries.

34 There have been changes in the structure since the Maastricht Treaty; DG I was divided into divisions, one for political relations and the other for economic relations. However, the present structure has returned to the former form.

35 See Chapter 3, the automobile case. Before the Single European Act when the integration momentum staggered in Europe, trade policies were more dispersed among member states. The most famous examples include the case that in the early 1980s French customs made all Japanese VCRs imported go through Poitier where there was only one custom officer.

36 European Political Cooperation (EPC), until it was succeeded by the Common Foreign and Security Policy (CFSP) in 1993, was totally based on inter-governmental procedures among the member states (Nuttall, 1992). However, in the process of creating the CFSP, the Commission fiercely fought to secure its role in external relations and foreign policy against the intergovernmental decision-making body (Forster and W. Wallace, 1996: 423–4, 428–31.)

37 This corresponds to Lowi's immediate coercion against individual, as opposed to remote coercion against wider society (Lowi, 1972).

CHAPTER 3: CASE I – THE AUTOMOBILE AGREEMENT AND DOMESTIC FACTORS

1 Strictly speaking, automobiles include passenger cars and commercial vehicles (such as trucks). The following discussion, however, deals only with passenger cars, unless otherwise stated. This is mainly because commercial vehicles composed only a minor part of the total trade between Japan and the EC (1.8 per cent in 1990), while the passenger car sector symbolized the fiercest trade dispute.

2 However, Japanese-badged passenger cars made in Portugal and four-wheel-drive vehicles made in Spain, had fewer barriers so that the amount of import from these countries surpassed the permitted level of imports from Japan. Therefore, the figures in Figure 3.1 of Japanese cars in Italy indicate more than the official limits.

3 As for Germany, in particular, the situation has never been officially confirmed. Mark Mason gave two versions of the Japanese–German agreement: Mason, 1994: 417.

4 Interviews with an official of Toyota, and officials of Honda.

5 Deputy Vice Minister of MFA, Kunihiro Michihiko's statement given at the Royal Institute of International Affairs, 'The external implications of the Single European Market: A view from Japan', 11 October 1988, London. A number of publications in Japan since the late 1980s on the EC and its 1992 programme often focused on future European economic competitiveness and potential protectionism, including Kanamaru, 1987; Tanaka S., 1991. There were also special editions on the movement of EC integration in various journals, including *Shukan Toyo Keizai* (The Weekly Eastern Economy). See Imagawa, 1993, 1994. Within Europe, the economic potential was revealed in the enlargement of the Community, as those who were not members rushed to apply for membership, such as some EFTA countries and Eastern European countries.

6 *Nihon Keizai Shimbun* (*Nikkei*), 12 May, p 7 and 22 June 1989 (evening), p 3.

7 *Agence Europe*, 16 January 1991, p 9.

8 Interview with officials of Honda, Tokyo.

9 Although FDI includes service subsidies, such as distribution, which started earlier than manufacturing abroad, the discussion here is limited to the manufacturing FDI in order to concentrate on the 'transplants' issue. This was the most serious concern of Europe in this context.

10 As for the automobile industry, however, Thomsen and Nicolaides admitted that the FDI was to substitute rather than complement the exports (Thomsen and Nicolaides, 1991: 75).

11 The only exception is Mitsubishi Motors' affiliate in Portugal, which started production in 1973, though its production capacity remains as small as 1,500 per year. R. Strange, 1993: 178.

12 *Nikkei*, 4 March 1989, p 6.

13 *Nikkei*, 18 April 1989, p 1.

14 *Nikkei*, 3 May 1989, p 7. Japanese badged cars include both Japanese cars made in and outside Japan.

15 *Nikkei*, 19 April 1989, p. 9.

16 *Financial Times*, 10 April 1996, p. 23.

17 Interview with Mr Alasdair Morgan at the British Embassy in Tokyo. Also, see Togo, 1995.

18 *World Car Industry Forecast Report*, April 1995, and *Japanese Motor Business*, 4th quarter, 1994.

19 *Nikkei*, 16 August 1992, p 9.
20 *Financial Times*, 18 February and 11 March 1992; Nakamura, 1992.
21 *Nikkei*, 18 February 1992, p 5, reported Commissioner Brittan's comment.
22 *Financial Times*, 25 May 1995, p 4.
23 *Nikkei*, 30 June 1995, p 3.
24 This plan was to prescribe a 'people's car', small, cheap and mass-used by making auto manufacturers compete with one another. The aim was to establish mass production of this single type, so that it could be exported as well (Mutou, 1984: 285).
25 Lindbeck suggested that 'the most promising type of industrial policy is probably the one which improves the economic environment for decentralized decision-making' (p. 391), and that 'industrial policy in highly developed economies cannot rely either on economic analysis of the national economy or on imitation of national growth paths in other countries . . . (and that the) task of the government would . . . mainly be to try to create an economic, social and political environment.' (pp 395–6)
26 *Nikkei*, 2 August 1989, p 1.
27 However, the actual process of calculation by MITI was unknown to manufacturers. Interviews with officials of Honda and with an official of Toyota.
28 Interview with an official of Toyota, August 1994.
29 JETRO's jurisdiction is categorized into eight areas, defined as: (1) to research on the global economy; (2) to provide information acquired through such research to Japanese traders; (3) to promote public relations for the Japanese economy, trade, industry, economic policy, etc., with foreign countries; (4) to promote trade and industry in developing countries; (5) to promote imports and international industrial cooperation; (6) to promote trade in selected areas, including agricultural, fishery and forestry products, construction machinery, electronics, automobiles and shipbuilding; (7) to manage overseas offices for these purposes; and (8) to help middle- and small-scale enterprises adjust to international business. Tsusho sangyo-sho (MITI), 1994: 714–7.
30 This willingness to compromise on the MFA's part partly derived from the fact that it was (and still is) pursuing the seat of a permanent member of the Security Council of the UN for Japan.
31 In contrast, car parts manufacturers vary in size, though mostly small- and medium-scale companies.
32 When the consumption tax was introduced along with the overall tax reform in 1989, automobile taxation was also changed, one of a few occasions when automobile tribe politicians worked to represent automobile manufacturers in the process of taxation policymaking. One of the *jidosha-zoku* politicians, Shiozaki Jun, was once a Tax Bureau director of the Ministry of Finance, and naturally was a *zeisei-zoku* (tax tribe) member at the same time (Obi, 1992: 21). As a result of the tax reduction in automobiles, particularly

for large, luxury type cars, demand increased to the benefit of the industry.

33 Toyota, Nissan, Honda and Mazda set up in Brussels, whereas Mitsubishi had its office in Germany.

34 For example, when the LDP was ousted from the government in 1993, the new minister of international trade and industry from the Shinsei Party demanded the resignation of a director who was close to the LDP (Nippon Keizai Shimbun-sha, 1994: 38–51).

35 Interview with officials of Honda.

36 See Chapter 2.

37 *Nikkei*, 29 August 1989, p. 11.

38 JAMA, however, denied the contribution. *Asahi Shimbun*, 16 February 1990.

39 For a detailed description of the discussion among European industrialists and the Commission, see Mason, 1994; McLaughlin, 1994.

40 *Agence Europe*, 25, 26 February 1991, p. 6.

41 Interview with a former DTI official.

42 His argument is shown, for example, in an interview published in *European Affairs*. Calvet, 1991.

43 The Peugeot Group later joined the ACEA, and since the beginning of 1996, the chairman of the ACEA is Calvet.

44 However, this relationship was ended in 1994 by Rover's parent company, British Aerospace's decision to sell their share to BMW.

45 *Financial Times*, 28 December 1995, p 14.

46 The Automobile Committee of the European Business Community (EBC), established in Tokyo in 1989, also acted as a lobbying group for European car makers. Its activities included direct contact with MITI.

47 Bargaining over the control of Japanese automobile exports into the EC market coincided with the negotiation of the Joint Declaration between Japan and the EC. The negotiations were deliberately unlinked to each other. See Chapter 5.

48 *Nikkei*, 15 September 1989, p 11.

49 *Nikkei*, 7 December 1989, p 9.

50 *Mainichi Shimbun*, 3 February 1990, p 1. For the details of this European setback, see Mason, 1994.

51 *Nikkei*, 1 December 1990, p 5. Also, Story, 1994: 437; McLaughlin, 1994: 148–56.

52 *Nikkei*, 7 December 1989, evening issue, p 1; 9 January 1990, p 2; and 6 May 1990, p 3.

53 *Agence Europe*, 18 May 1991, p. 10.

54 'Elements of Consensus', 31 July 1991, para 14.

55 *Agence Europe*, 8 March 1991, p 6.

56 'Internal Declaration by the Commission concerning the Operation of the Monitoring System'

57 *Agence Europe*, 27 July 1991, p 5.

58 J. M. Lepeu, quoted in McLaughlin, 1994: 161.
59 'A review of the Japanese in Western Europe', *Japanese Motor Business*, 2nd quarter, 1994, p 61.
60 *Financial Times*, 31 January 1995, p 3.
61 Interview with an official of Toyota.
62 Interview with officials of Honda.
63 *Agence Europe*, 3,4 April 1995.
64 *Nikkei* reported the comment by the president of Fiat on 15 November 1991.
65 *Financial Times*, 28 March 1996, p 3.
66 COM(94) 49 final. Communication from the Commission to the Council and the European Parliament on the European Union automobile industry, p 9.

CHAPTER 4: CASE II – THE LIQUOR TAX DISPUTE, 1986–95

1 The tariff question was largely left to be handled multilaterally, i.e. the Uruguay Round of the GATT (1986–93). Thus it did not become the centre of this bilateral liquor trade issue.
2 United States Trade Representatives, *1993 National trade estimate report on foreign trade barriers*, 1993, translated in *Sekai Shuho*, 4 May 1993, pp 66–73.
3 *Nikkei*, 12 July 1995, p 5.
4 *Financial Times*, 21 November 1994, p 4.
5 Interview with Stephen Stacey and Ian Williams, London, 10 October 1994.
6 As for the interrelations among the MOF, LDP and interest groups in policy making, Campbell, 1977.
7 For the process of introducing indirect tax, see Kato, 1994: 110–220.
8 This trend seems to be changing again. Explaining the background of the 1993 liquor tax reform, the MOF emphasized the necessity of upwards revision of the liquor tax rate, as the liquor tax had been declining in proportion to the liquor price (Okura-sho, 1994: 336).
9 At this point, the LDP named the prospected mass indirect tax '*uriage-zei*' (sales tax). When the LDP together with the MOF challenged again in 1988 to introduce indirect tax, they decided to change the name because of the negative image attached to sales tax. '*Shouhi-zei*', consumption tax, was the name for the indirect tax this time, which was eventually introduced on 1 April 1989.
10 The initial proposal of the introduction of the mass indirect tax, then called *ippan shouhi-zei* (general consumption tax), was in 1979 under the Ohira cabinet, though the idea of mass indirect tax could go back as far as to the 1960s. Muramatsu and Mabuchi, 1994: 178–99; Kato, 1994; Kuribayashi, 1991: 26.
11 *Nikkei*, 16 December 1986, p 2.
12 An example of the composition of the price of Scotch whisky in Japan (pre-1989 tax reform):

168   *Japan and the European Union*

CIF	1,040 (yen)
Tariff	129.4
Liquor tax	1,754.1
Importer's profit	1,756.5
Advertisement	400
Gift box	280
Wholesaler's profit	800
Retailer's profit	1,600
Other cost	240
Total	8,000

Nikkei, 26 July 1987, p 21.

13 The Fair Trade Commission of Japan also included the marketing of Scotch whisky among areas in which the distribution was particularly inefficient and closed. H. Ishida, 1983: 325–6.

14 Keizai Kikaku-cho (Economic Planning Agency of Japan), 'A report of the enquiry to the Office of Trade and Investment Ombudsman', 5 August 1994.

15 Although Yamanaka was in the Nakasone faction in terms of intra-party politics, he did not get along with Nakasone personally.

16 Yamanaka was, however, said to be very strict in the sense that he never conformed to any interest groups on tax issues (Kuribayashi, 1991: 39).

17 Compared to other groups, *Nippon yoshu yunyu kyokai* was less influential, because it included major manufacturers of *sake* and *shochu* as well as the Japanese subsidiary of foreign manufacturers. As a result it was difficult for the group to co-ordinate the interests of its members.

18 *Zenkoku oroshiuri shuhan kumiai chuo-kai* (National Association of Liquor Wholesalers Union); *Biru oroshiuri shuhan kumiai chuo-kai* (National Association of Beer Wholesalers Union); and *Zenkoku kouri shuhan kumiai chuo-kai* (National Association of Liquor Retailers Union).

19 As later discussed in the chronology, such an attitude of the Japanese government increased European worry as to whether Japan was sincere enough in its effort to reduce the tax difference between *shochu* and other spirits.

20 In Takayanagi's case, he was not a so-called 'career' official, elite-track bureaucrat.

21 Interview with a former DTI official, London,, 5 January 1996.

22 Comment by Foreign Secretary, Geoffrey Howe, in a transcript of press conference given by Prime Minister Thatcher in Tokyo after the Summit conference, on Monday, 6 May 1986.

23 At the earlier stage of the issue, such as at the conclusion of GATT ruling in 1987, it was Willy De Clercq, a Belgian national, who was responsible for DG I. Between De Clercq and Brittan was Frans Andriessen, a Dutch national.

24 This does not, however, deny the organization's weakness in that it had

difficulty in co-ordinating the interests of its membership as a whole with the commercial advantage pursued by individual members, particularly large and powerful ones. As for analysis of the SWA, I owe much to the MGK's unpublished report.

25 In 1993, for example, Tim W. Jackson, the director of commercial affairs of the SWA, was at the same time the chairman of the Trade Committee of the CEPS.

26 Interview with Stephen Stacey and Ian Williams, London, 10 October 1994.

27 Correspondence from T. Jackson of the SWA, 28 October 1994.

28 There was also an international forum to combine North American producers with the Europeans: the International Federation of Wines and Spirits (FIVS). This interest group also directly lobbied the Japanese government, but with less frequency. Therefore, its impact was not as seriously felt in Japan as that of European based groups.

29 *Nikkei*, 12 July 1995, p 5.

30 Some Japanese domestic wine had labels that might mislead customers that the product was European origin.

31 As for the tariff question, the Japanese government lowered the tariff on alcoholic beverages in 1984. The European Commission did not much appreciate this decision, complaining that the tariff remained comparatively high, although at the same time admitting that the prior reduction in customs duties on alcoholic beverages positively affected European exports. *COM(85)574 final*. Communication from the Commission to the Council: analysis of the relations between the Community and Japan. 15 October 1985, p 21.

32 *COM(86)60 final*. Communication from the Commission to the Council: EC-Japan relations. 6 March 1986, p 8

33 EP working document (PE DOC) A2-86/86, Report drawn up on behalf of the Committee on External Economic Relations on trade and economic relations between the European Community and Japan, 10 July 1986, p 13.

34 In US dollar terms.

35 MGK 'Scotch Whisky Association', unpublished report.

36 This style of trade negotiation to open Japanese markets began with four areas in 1985, including automobiles. Itoh and Ishiguro, 1993: 13; Yamamoto T., 1989: 106; Miyasato, 1989: 37–46.

37 *Bulletin of the European Communities*, XIX, 7, 8 (1986) p 84: 'The Council meeting on foreign affairs on 21 July invited the Commission: (i) to pursue its efforts to reach a satisfactory solution regarding wines and spirits and, to this end, to request the immediate opening of consultations under Article XXII of the GATT; should a satisfactory outcome not be achieved by the autumn, the Community should not hesitate to invoke Article XXIII'.

38 The GATT, *Decisions and Reports*, Conciliation: Japan-customs duties, taxes and labelling practices on imported wines and alcoholic beverages: report of the Panel adopted on 10 November 1987, (L/6216).

39 While the tax issue remained the focus of disputes, the wine labelling issue was resolved before the GATT panel produced a concluding report. In response to the European claim that inaccurate wine labels might obscure product origin, the Japanese wine sector started 'voluntary' regulation rather than waiting for the government to build a legal framework. *Nikkei*, 5 January 1987, p 1.

40 *Keesing's Record of World Event*, 1987, p 35385.

41 *Nikkei*, 25 December 1986, p 7.

42 The panel was chaired by M. Tello from Mexico. Members included D. Bondad from the Philippines and C. Kauter from Switzerland.

43 *Nikkei*, 30 September 1987, p 1.

44 *Bulletin of European Communities*, XX, 10 (1987), p 57.

45 *Nikkei*, 2 June 1988 (evening), p 2.

46 *Bulletin of European Communities*, XXI, 4 (1988), pp 57–8.

47 *Nikkei*, 11 May 1988, p 3.

48 In addition to the claims from interest groups in the text, there was a claim from the Beer Brewers Association. It demanded more balanced taxation among different alcoholic beverages, on the grounds that in terms of the tax proportion of the retail price, the tax on beer was one of the highest. For the comparison of tax proportions, Okura-sho, 1989: 484.

49 *Nikkei*, 26 May 1988, p 3.

50 Interviews with an anonymous official of *joryushu kumiai*, and Takayanagi Akio, Tokyo, on 13 September 1994.

51 *Asahi Shimbun*, 1 October 1991, p 8.

52 Interview with an anonymous official of *joryushu kumiai*, 20 August 1994.

53 OJ C 42, 15 February 1993, Resolution on trade and economic relations between the European Community and Japan, pp 260, 270.

54 As for the role of the Prime Minister, John Major, see the section, *European actors*.

55 For example, the president of Guinness' Group visited Tokyo in September 1993 with the British Prime Minister. *Nikkei*, 6 October 1993, p 2.

56 The exact phrases by the GATT panel were: 'Japanese shochu (Group A) and vodka could be considered as "like" products in terms of Article III:2 because they were both white/clean spirits, made of similar raw materials, and their end-uses were virtually identical. . . . The panel concluded that the following alcoholic beverages could be considered to be "*directly competitive or substitutable products*" in terms of Article III: 2, second sentence: imported and Japanese-made distilled liquors, including all grades of whiskies/brandies, vodka and shochu Groups A and B, among each other.' GATT, *Decisions and reports* (L/6216), 5.7.

57 *Financial Times*, 18 May 1994, p 6.

58 *Financial Times*, 21 November 1994, p 4. The same demand to use the 1995/96 budget plan had been made by the vice president of the SWA in September. *Nikkei*, 20 September 1994, p 7.

59 Interview with Uchida Sadakichi, Tokyo, September 1994.

60 *Nikkei*, 20 September 1994, p 7.

61 *Financial Times*, 1 February 1995, p 4.

62 The EU had forewarned such action in April. *Financial Times*, 6 April 1995, p 7. The same warning was made by the SWA even earlier; *Financial Times*, 1 February 1995, p 4.

63 *Nikkei*, 23 June 1995, p 5.

64 *Nikkei*, 24 June 1995, p 9.

65 While the EU accepted the Japanese government's programme for tax reform, the United States demanded a speedier process. The WTO arbitrator found that Japan needed to end the discriminatory taxation on imported whiskies within 15 months.

66 A Japanese journalist criticized the United Distillers Group, a subsidiary of Guinness's spirits section, pointing out that the UDG kept the high price of its famous products while halting the export of less-known products. Consequently, consumers did not benefit from the tax reduction, since the producer would keep most of the price margin by sustaining the price. Hirasawa, 1989: 33. Also, the UDG built a subsidiary in Japan in order to terminate the sole agent contracts so that they could retain their profit from exclusive distribution. Kishi, 1992.

67 Interview with Uchida Sadakichi, Tokyo, on 8 September 1994. .

68 The GATT report stated that 'the European Communities claimed that the shochu category for tax purposes excluded spirits filtered with a birch charcoal filter, which prevented vodka from qualifying for the favourable shochu tax rates.' The GATT, *Decisions and Reports*, (L/6216), 3.2.

69 Takayanagi expressed resentment against abolishing the tariff even after the publication of Saji's article. Interview with Takayanagi Akio, Tokyo, on 13 September 1994.

70 Interview with Peter Wilkinson, Edinburgh, on 2 October 1994.

CHAPTER 5: CASE III – THE JOINT DECLARATION BETWEEN JAPAN AND THE EUROPEAN COMMUNITY

1 The first cancellation was in December 1987, because of the turbulence at the Budget Committee of the Japanese Diet. The second time was in June 1989, because the then Foreign Minister Uno had to hurry back to Tokyo to take office as Prime Minister, due to the sudden departure of Prime Minister Takeshita because of suspicions of bribery (the Recruit scandal).

2 There are numerous articles and books on American decline or non-decline, but the discussion here does not need to follow all of them. The arguments that gave the basis of the above understanding of the changing attitude of Japan and Europe towards the United States, include *Foreign Affairs*, LXX, 1 (1990/1), America and the World. See also Krauthammer, 1991; S. Sato and Taylor, 1993; Johnson, 1991; Spencer, 1990.

3 *Gaiko seisho* (Blue Paper of Japanese Foreign Policy) by the MFA in 1990 showed a significant difference from the previous year. The 1989

issue reiterated the importance of Japan–US relations as the main foreign policy, whereas the 1990 issue tried to cover a wider range of diplomatic purposes, a trend which has deepened in the following issues. Inoguchi K., 1987.

4 The automobile negotiations in the summer 1995, for example, showed a strain in political relations between Japan and the United States. 'Is "automobile" equivalent to the INF negotiation?' *Nikkei*, 18 June, 1995, p 11; *Nikkei*, 1 July 1995, p 5. On the other hand, the decline of the Japanese economy in the 1990s seems to have softened the US aggressiveness to Japan.

5 Interview with an official of the MFA, Jerusalem, 29 August 1995.

6 Sir Leon Brittan's comment, quoted in *Agence Europe*, 9 March 1995, p 5; also see Wilks, 1994.

7 In November 1990, the EC and its member states signed declarations with United States and Canada separately. However, the term 'Transatlantic Declaration' is used to describe the US–EC declaration only in the following argument, unless otherwise specified.

8 Also, see Tsoukalis, 1991: 3. On the other hand, however, trade wars between the US and the EU in the 1990s such as the cases of Helms–Burton Law, the Banana disputes and other agricultural trade issues, increased its bitterness and concerned many.

9 COM (95) 73 final.

10 For example, the textile trade dispute between Japan and the US in the late 1960s and early 1970s was a case of severe confrontation between the MFA and MITI. Destler *et al.*, 1979.

11 The system is to be changed so that all career officials including candidates for MFA diplomats must take the same examinations from 2002.

12 A major exception was the case of revising the US–Japan Security Treaty in 1960, when the Diet became the centre of the disputes. Recently, the same issue of security relations with the US, the Guideline Bills, has caused another significant policy debate, making the Diet a battlefield among political parties.

13 For example, at the time of the first oil crisis in 1973, the MFA had to rely on the information from trading companies (Rothacher, 1993: 70–1).

14 Also see Chapter 1.

15 Some anonymous officials from MITI and the Ministry of Post and Telecommunications mentioned similar opinions in informal conversations.

16 *Financial Times*, 4 April 1991, p 2.

17 Title III of the SEA was replaced by Title V of the Maastricht Treaty, which established Common Foreign and Security Policy in the framework of the European Union.

18 For the development of the EPC through the SEA, Nuttall, 1992. Also, Regelsberger, 1993; Forster and Wallace, 1996: 412–20.

19 For the summary of the Council's attitude towards Japan in the 1980s, Engering, 1989: 54.

20 However, an official said that informal talks within the MFA began earlier than the Transatlantic Declaration.
21 *Agence Europe*, 12 April 1991, p 9.
22 Interview with an MFA official on 12 October 1995.
23 *Agence Europe*, 12 April 1991, p 9.
24 *Agence Europe*, 17 April 1991, p 18.
25 *Agence Europe*, 17 April 1991, p 18.
26 *Agence Europe*, 18 May 1991, p 7.
27 Delors's report to the Commission after his visit to Japan, *Agence Europe*, 27, 28 May 1991, p 6.
28 *Agence Europe*, 24 May 1991, p 12.
29 *Agence Europe*, 7 June 1991, p 7.
30 Interview with an MFA official on 12 October 1995.
31 *Agence Europe*, 11 July 1991, p 7
32 Para 3. Objectives of Dialogue and Cooperation, Joint Declaration on Relations between the European Community and its Member States and Japan, The Hague, 18 July 1991.
33 Although only the foreign minister attended with the Prime Minister, at the ministerial level, there were bureau directors from major ministries, i.e. MOF, MITI, MAFF and the MFA. Interview with an MFA official on 12 October 1995.
34 The latter two types of meetings are the continuation of former arrangements.
35 *Financial Times*, 2 June 1992, p 20.
36 *Agence Europe*, 6, 7 July 1992, p 7.
37 Working Paper by the Council, Overview of EU–Japan relations, 25 March 1994.
38 For the meeting between Japanese Prime Minister Murayama and President Santer of the European Commission and French President Chirac, in June 1995, *Nikkei*, 20 June 1995. For the earlier meetings from 1991 to 1994, Tanaka, 1995: 438–41.
39 COM (95) 73 final.
40 As described in Chapter 1, transnational relations involve interactions between actors at least one of which is non-state actor. See Risse-Kappen, 1995: 3.

CONCLUSION
1 This expression was used in the press release for the agreements on motor vehicle standards and testing on 6 June 1995.
2 As for similar tendencies for different divisions within the MFA, Fukui, 1977a: 15–6; Fukui, 1981: 285.
3 One relatively recent example is that Peugeot attempted to block the sale of a French car parts manufacturer to a company related to GM. *Financial Times*, 14 May 1996, p 25.
4 *Financial Times*, 28 December 1995, p 14. See also Chapter 3.

5 Also, Mansbach and Vasquez discussed transnational approach, which referred to the bureaucratic politics model in order to criticize the traditional, realist view, particularly its state-centric view of international relations. Mansbach and Vasquez, 1981; Sullivan, 1989: 258–9.

6 For a recent discussion of the matter, Kohli *et al.*, 1995. For relations between case studies and their contribution to general theorizing, Zhao, 1993.

Bibliography

Agence Europe.
Asahi Shimbun.
Bungei shunju.
Chuo koron.
The Economist Intelligence Unit, *European Motor Business*, London.
The Economist Intelligence Unit, *International Motor Business*, London.
The Economist Intelligence Unit, *Japanese Motor Business*, London.
Financial Times.
Keesing's Record of World Event.
Mainichi Shimbun.
Nippon Keizai Shimbun (Nikkei).
Sekai Shuho.
Shukan Toyo Keizai.
World Car Industry Forecast Report, April 1995.

Akiyama, Kenji, 1994, *Nichi-bei tsusho masatsu no kenkyu* (The study of Japan–US trade friction), Tokyo.
Allinson, Gary D., 1987, 'Japan's *Keidanren* and its new leadership', *Pacific Affairs*, LX, 3, 385–407.
Allison, Graham T., 1971, *Essence of decision: explaining the Cuban Missile Crisis*, Boston.
Allison, Graham T. and Halperin, Morton H., 1972, 'Bureaucratic politics: a paradigm and some policy implications', Tanter, Raymond and Ullman, Richard H., eds, *Theory and policy in international relations*, Princeton, 40–79.
Angel, Robert C., 1989, 'Prime ministerial leadership in Japan: recent changes in personal style and administrative organization', *Pacific Affairs*, LXI, 4, 583–602.
The Anglo-Japanese Economic Institute, 1991, *Japan in a changing Europe*, London.
Anglo-Japanese Journal, 1993a, 'Action Programme to strengthen Euro-Japanese relations', *Anglo-Japanese Journal*, VI, 3, 6–9.
Anglo-Japanese Journal, 1993b, 'Euro-Japanese Action Programme – the British responses', *Anglo-Japanese Journal*, VII, 1, 7–10.
Art, Robert J., 1977, 'Bureaucratic politics and American foreign policy: a critique', Endicott, John E. and Strafford, Roy W., Jr, eds, *American foreign policy*. 4th edn, Baltimore, 240–52.

Aruga, Tadashi *et al.*, 1989, eds, *Koza Kokusai seiji* (International politics), 5 vols, Tokyo.

Asahi Shimbun Shakai-bu, 1989, *Document: Recruit Hodo* (Report), Tokyo.

Ashley, Richard K., 1986, 'The poverty of neorealism', Keohane, Robert O., ed, *Neorealism and its critics*, New York, 255–300.

Bacchus, William I., 1974, *Foreign policy and the bureaucratic process: the State Department's country director system*, Princeton.

Baerwald, Hans H., 1977, 'The Diet and foreign policy', Scalapino, *The foreign policy of modern Japan*, 37–54.

Balasubramanyam, V.N. and Greenaway, David, 1992, 'Economic Integration and Foreign Direct Investment: Japanese Investment in the EC', *Journal of Common Market Studies*, XXX, 2, 175–93.

Befu, Harumi, 1990, 'Conflict and non-Weberian bureaucracy in Japan', Eisenstadt, S. N. and Ben-Ari, Eyal, eds, *Japanese models of conflict resolution*, London, 162–91.

Berger, Suzanne, 1981a, ed., *Organizing interests in Western Europe: pluralism, corporatism, and the transformation of politics*, Cambridge.

Berger, Suzanne, 1981b, 'Introduction', *Organizing interests in Western Europe*, 1–23.

Bergsten, C. Fred and Cline, William, 1987, *The US–Japan economic problem*, Washington, DC.

Blaker, Michael, 1977, 'Probe, push, and panic', Scalapino, *The foreign policy of modern Japan*, 55–101.

Bourke, Thomas, 1996, *Japan and the globalisation of European integration*, Aldershot; Brookfield, VA.

Braybrooke, David and Lindblom, Charles E., 1963, *A strategy of decision: policy evaluation as a social process*, New York.

Bridges, Brian, 1992, *EC–Japanese relations: in search of a partnership*, London.

Buckley, Roger, 1990, *Japan today*, Cambridge.

Buigues, Pierre and Jacquemin, Alexis, 1994, 'Foreign direct investment and exports to the European Community', Mason, Mark and Encarnation, Dennis, eds, *Does ownership matter? Japanese multinationals in Europe*, Oxford, 163–99.

Calder, Kent E., 1988, 'Japanese foreign economic policy formation: explaining the reactive state', *World Politics*, XL, 4, 517–41.

Calder, Kent E, 1993, *Strategic capitalism: private business and public purpose in Japanese industrial finance*, Princeton.

Calvet, Jacques, 1991, 'Thank God for quotas', *European Affairs*, V, 6, 68–72.

Campbell, John Creighton, 1977, *Contemporary Japanese budget politics*, Berkeley.

Cavanagh, John and Clairmonte, Frederick F., 1985, *Alcoholic beverages: dimensions of corporate power*, Bechenham.

Cawson, Allan, 1986, *Corporatism and political theory*, Oxford.

Choate, Pat, 1990, *Agents of influence: how Japanese lobbyists are manipulating western political and economic systems*, London.

Commission of the European Communities, COM(85)574 final. Communication from the Commission to the Council: analysis of the relations between the Community and Japan, 15 October 1985.

Commission of the European Communities, COM(86)60 final. Communication from the Commission to the Council: EC–Japan relations, 6 March 1986.

Commission of the European Communities, OJ C 42. Resolution on trade and economic relations between the European Community and Japan, 15 February 1993.

Commission of the European Communities, Directorate General I, External Economic Relations, Unit for Relations with Japan, 'Market access problems in Japan', 25 January 1994, Brussels.

Commission of the European Communities, COM(94) 49 final. Communication from the Commission to the Council and the European Parliament on the European Union automobile industry, 23 February 1994.

Commission of the European Communities, COM(95)73 final. Communication from the Commission to the Council: Europe and Japan: the next steps, 8 March 1995.

Council of Ministers of the European Union, Working Paper, Overview of EU–Japan relations, 25 March 1994.

Cox, Robert, W., 1989, 'Middlepowermanship, Japan, and future world order,' *International Journal*, XLIV, 4, 823–62.

Curtis, Gerald L., 1975, 'Big business and political influence', Vogel, Ezra, ed., *Modern Japanese organization and decision-making*, Berkeley, 33–70.

Curzon, Gerard and Curzon, Victoria, 1987, 'Follies in European trade relations with Japan', *The World Economy*, X, 2, 155–76.

Cusumano, Michael A., 1985, *The Japanese automobile industry*, Cambridge, MA.

Daniels, Gordon and Gow, Ian, 1983, 'EC and Japan', Lodge, Juliet, ed., *The European Community: bibliographical excursions*, London, 225–35.

Daniels, Gordon and Drifte, Reinhard, 1986, eds, *Europe and Japan: changing relationships since 1945*, Ashford.

Daniels, Gordon, 1989, 'EC–Japan: past, present and future', Lodge, Juliet, ed., *The European Community and the challenge of the future*, London, 279–84.

Dassbach, Carl H., 1994, 'The social organization of production, competitive advantage and foreign investment: American automobile companies in the 1920s and Japanese automobile companies in the 1980s', *Review of International Political Economy*, I, 3, 489–517.

De La Croix, Guy Féaux, 1989, 'The Europe–Japan-initiative and the European year in Japan', *European Affairs*, III, 2, 96–103.

Destler, I. M. and Nacht, Michael, 1991, 'Beyond mutual recrimination: building a solid U.S.-Japan relationship in the 1990s', *International Security*,

XV, 3, 92–119.

Destler, I. M., Clapp, Priscilla, Fukui, Haruhiro and Sato, Hideo, 1976, *Managing an alliance: the politics of U.S.–Japanese relations*, Washington, DC.

Destler, I. M., Fukui, Haruhiro and Sato, Hideo, 1979, *The textile wrangle: conflict in Japanese American relations, 1969–71*, Ithaca.

Dodwell Marketing Consultants, 1989, *A study of opportunities for British companies in the Japanese market for speciality foods and drinks*, London.

Drifte, Reinhard, 1983a, 'The European Community and Japan', Lodge, Juliet, ed., *Institutions and policies of the European Community*, London, 217–26.

Drifte, Reinhard, 1983b, 'The European Community and Japan: beyond the economic dimension', *Journal of International Affairs*, XXXVII, 1, 147–61.

Engering, Frans, 1989, 'The future of economic relations between the EC and Japan', *European Affairs*, III, 1, 51–6.

The European Communities, *Bulletin of European Communities*.

European Parliament, EP working document (PE DOC) A2-86/86, Report drawn up on behalf of the Committee on External Economic Relations on trade and economic relations between the European Community and Japan, 10 July 1986.

Evangelista, Matthew, 1989, 'Issue-area and foreign policy revisited', *International Organization*, XLIII, 1, 147–71.

Evans, Peter B., Jacobson, Harold K. and Putnam, Robert D., 1993, eds, *Double-edged diplomacy: international bargaining and domestic politics*, Berkeley.

Featherstone, Kevin and Ginsberg, Roy H., 1993, *The United States and the European Community in the 1990s: partners in transition*, New York.

Forster, Anthony and Wallace, William, 1996, 'Common foreign and security policy: a new policy or just a new name?', Wallace and Wallace, *Policy-making in the European Union*, 411–35.

Frankel, Joseph, 1963, *The making of foreign policy: an analysis of decision-making*, London.

Fukui, Haruhiro, 1977a, 'Policy-making in the Japanese foreign ministry', Scalapino, *The foreign policy of modern Japan*, 3–35.

Fukui, Haruhiro, 1977b, 'Studies in policymaking: a review of the literature', Pempel, T. J., ed., *Policymaking in contemporary Japan*, Ithaca, 22–35.

Fukui, Haruhiro, 1977c, 'Tanaka goes to Peking: a case study in foreign policymaking', Pempel, *Policymaking in contemporary Japan*, 60–102.

Fukui, Haruhiro, 1981, 'Bureaucratic power in Japan', Drysdale, Peter and Kitaoji, Hironobu, eds, *Japan and Australia: two societies and their interaction*, London, 275–303.

Funabashi, Yoichi, 1987, *Nichi-bei keizai masatsu* (Japan–US economic friction), Tokyo.

Garrahan, Philip and Stewart, Paul, 1992, *The Nissan enigma: flexibility at work in a local economy*, London.

George, Alexander L., 1969, 'The "operational code": a neglected approach to the study of political leaders and decision-making', *International Studies Quarterly*, XIII, 2, 190–222.

Gilpin, Robert, 1990, 'Where does Japan fit in?', Newland, *The international relations of Japan*, 5–22.

Glasser, Harold A., 1988, *'Kokunaiho ni yoru tsusho no seigen'* (Limiting trade through domestic legislation), translated by Someya, Masayuki, *Jurisuto*, CMXXI, 49–54.

Gourevitch, Peter, 1978, 'The second image reversed: the international sources of domestic politics', *International Organization*, XXXII, 4, 881–912.

Greenwald, Joseph, 1990, 'Negotiating strategy', Hufbauer, Gary Clyde, ed., *Europe 1992: an American perspective*, Washington DC, 345–88.

Hanabusa, Masamichi, 1979, *Trade problems between Japan and Western Europe*, Basingstoke.

Hanrieder, Wolfram F., 1967, 'Compatibility and consensus: a proposal for the conceptual linkage of external and internal dimensions of foreign policy', *American Political Science Review*, LXI, 4, 971–82.

Hayao, Kenji, 1993, *The Japanese Prime Minister and public policy*, Pittsburgh.

Heitger, Bernhard and Stehn, Jürgen, 1990, 'Japanese direct investment in the EC: response to the Internal Market 1993?', *Journal of Common Market Studies*, XXIX, 1, 1–15.

Hindley, Brian, 1985, 'Motor cars from Japan', Greenaway, David and Hindley, *What Britain pays for voluntary export restraints*, London, 64–93.

Hinsley, F. H., 1963, *Power and the pursuit of peace*, London.

Hinsley, F. H., 1973, *Nationalism and the international system*, London.

Hirasawa, Masao, 1989, *'Naze kokyu sukocchi ha yasuku naranaika'* (Why doesn't the first class whisky become cheaper?), *Ekonomisuto*, LXVII, 14, 28–33.

Hiwatari, Nobuhiro, 1991, *Sengo Nippon no shijo to seiji* (Market and politics of postwar Japan), Tokyo.

Hollerman, Leon, 1991, 'The headquarter nation', *The National Interest*, XXV, 16–25.

Holsti, Ole, 1962, 'The belief system and national images: a case study', *Journal of Conflict Resolution*, VI, 3, 244–52.

Holsti, Ole, 1976, 'Foreign policy formation viewed cognitively', Axelrod, Robert, ed., *Structure of decision*, Princeton, 18–54.

Hosoya, Chihiro, 1977, *'Taigai seisaku kettei katei ni okeru Nichibei no tokushitsu'* (The characteristics of Japanese and American foreign policy decision making), Hosoya and Watanuki, *Taigai seisaku*, 1–20.

Hosoya, Chihiro and Watanuki, Joji, 1977, eds, *Taigai seisaku kettei katei no Nichibei hikaku* (Comparative studies of foreign policy making between Japan and the US), Tokyo.

Imagawa, Ken, 1993, *'Nippon–EC kankei Bunken tenbou'* (Bibliography of the

Japan–EC relations), *Keizaigaku ronsan*, XXXIV, 3–4, 267–83.

Imagawa, Ken, 1994, '*Nippon–EC kankei Bunken tenbou*' (Bibliography of the Japan–EC relations), *Keizaigaku ronsan*, XXXIV, 5–6, 267–83.

Imamura, Tsunao, 1985, '*Shocho-kan no seiji tetsuzuki*' (The political procedures among government ministries), *Nennpo Seijigaku, Gendai nihon no seiji tetsuzuki*, (The Annuals of Japanese Political Science Association; The political procedures in contemporary Japan), 117–46.

Inoguchi, Kuniko, 1987, *Posuto haken shisutemu to Nippon no sentaku* (Post-hegemonic system and Japan's alternatives), Tokyo.

Inoguchi, Takashi, 1983, *Gendai nihon seiji keizai no kozu* (The structure of political economy of contemporary Japan), Tokyo.

Inoguchi, Takashi and Iwai, Tomoaki, 1987, *Zoku-giin no kenkyu* (Study of tribe-politicians), Tokyo.

Ishi, Hiromitsu, 1993, *The Japanese tax system*, 2nd edn, Oxford.

Ishida, Hideto, 1983, 'Anticompetitive practices in the distribution of goods and services in Japan: the problem of distribution *keiretsu*', *Journal of Japanese Studies*, IX, 2, 319–34.

Ishida, Takeshi, 1986, 'Political development, decision-making and foreign policy in modern Japan', Daniels and Drifte, *Europe and Japan*, 23–9.

Ishikawa, Kenjiro, 1990a, *Japan and the challenge of Europe 1992*, London.

Ishikawa, Kenjiro, 1990b, '*EC ha tainichi sabetsu shugi ni keisha shite iku*' (The EC inclines to discriminate Japan), *Chuo koron*, CV, 8, 140–9.

Itoh, Daiichi, 1967, '*Keizai kanryo no kodo yoshiki*' (Behaviour of economic bureaucrats), *Nennpo Seijigaku, Gendai Nippon no seito to kanryo* (The parities and bureaucracy in contemporary Japan – since the Conservative fusion in 1955), 78–104.

Itoh, Motoshige and Ishiguro, Kazunori, 1993, *Teigen – Tsusho masatsu* (Supposition to the trade friction), Tokyo.

Jackson, Tim, 1993, *Turning Japanese: the fight for industrial control of the new Europe*, London.

Janis, Irving L., 1972, *Victims of groupthink: a psychological study of foreign-policy decisions and fiascoes*, Boston.

Jervis, Robert, 1976, *Perception and misperception in international politics*, Princeton.

JETRO, 1994, *Zaiou nikkei seizougyou keiei no jittai* (The report on Japanese manufacturers in Europe), Tokyo.

Johnson, Chalmers, 1982, *MITI and the Japanese miracle: the growth of industrial policy, 1925–1975*, Stanford.

Johnson, Chalmers, 1991, 'The end of American hegemony and the future of US–Japan relations', Schmergel, Greg, ed., *US foreign policy in the 1990s*, Basingstoke, 243–53.

Johnson, Chalmers, 1992a, '*Nippon no kenryoku kiban to sono tankyu*' (Inquiry into the bases of Japanese power: three approaches), *Leviathan*, XI, 145–64.

Johnson, Chalmers, 1992b 'Japan in search of a "normal" role', *Daedalus*, CXXI, 4, 1–33.

Johnson, Chalmers, 1995, *Japan: who governs? – The rise of the developmental state*, New York.

Johnson, Chalmers and Keehn, E. B., 1994, 'A disaster in the making: rational choice and Asian studies', *The National Interest*, XXXVI, 14–22.

Jokai Times, 1993, ed., *Zenkoku shurui seizo meikan* (The yearbook of liquor production in Japan), Osaka.

Jönsson, Christer, 1982, 'Introduction: cognitive approaches to international politics', Jönsson, ed., *Cognitive dynamics and international politics*, London, 1–18

Kamo, Takehiko, 1990, *Kokusai anzen hosho no koso* (The conception of international security). Tokyo.

Kanamaru, Teruo, 1987, ed., *EC–Ohshu togo no genzai* (European integration at present). Osaka.

Kaneko, Hiroshi, 1984, '*Shuzei-ho no mondaiten*' (The problems in the Liquor Tax Law), *Jurisuto*, DCCCIX, 31–7.

Kato, Junko, 1994, *The problem of bureaucratic rationality: tax politics in Japan*, Princeton.

Katzenstein, Peter J., 1978, ed., *Between power and plenty: foreign economic policies of advanced industrial states*, Madison.

Katzenstein, Peter J., 1984, *Corporatism and change: Austria, Switzerland, and the politics of industry*, Ithaca.

Katzenstein, Peter J. and Tsujinaka, Yutaka, 1995, ' "Bullying," "buying," and "binding": US–Japanese transnational relations and domestic structures', Risse-Kappen, *Bringing transnational relations back in*, 79–111.

Keizai Kikaku-cho (Economic Planning Agency of Japan), 'A report of the enquiry to the Office of Trade and Investment Ombudsman', 5 August 1994.

Keohane, Robert O., 1990, 'Multilateralism: an agenda for research', *International Journal*, XLV, 4, 731–64.

Keohane, Robert O. and Nye, Joseph S., Jr, 1971, eds, *Transnational relations and world politics*, Cambridge, MA.

Keohane, Robert O. and Nye, Joseph S., Jr, 1974, 'Transgovernmental relations and international organizations', *World Politics*, XXVII, 1, 39–62.

Keohane, Robert O., Nye, Joseph S. and Hoffmann, Stanley, 1993, eds, *After the Cold War*, Cambridge, MA.

Kishi, Nagami, 1992, 'United Distillers Japan: growing share of liquor market', *Journal of Japanese trade and industry*, XI, 2, 42–4.

Kishi, Nobuhito, 1993, *Okurasho wo ugokasu otoko-tachi* (The men controlling the Ministry of Finance), Tokyo.

Knopf, Jeffrey W., 1993, 'Beyond two-level games: domestic-international interaction in the intermediate-range nuclear forces negotiation', *International Organization*, XLVII, 4, 599–628.

Kohli, Atul, Evans, Peter and Katzenstein, Peter J., 1995, 'The role of theory in comparative politics: a symposium', *World Politics*, XLVIII, 1–15.

Krasner, Stephen D., 1973, 'Are bureaucracies important? (or Allison wonderland)', Head, Richard G. and Rokke, Ervin J., eds, *American defence policy*, 3rd edn, Baltimore, 311–20.

Krauss, Ellis S., 1993, 'U.S.–Japan negotiations on construction and semiconductors, 1985–1988: building friction and relation-chips', Evans, Jacobson and Putnam, *Double-edged diplomacy*, 265–99.

Krauthammer, Charles, 1991, 'The unipolar moment', *Foreign Affairs*, LXX, 1, 23–33.

Kume, Gorota and Totsuka, Keisuke, 1991, 'Japanese manufacturing investment in the EC: motives and locations', Yoshitomi, *Japanese direct investment in Europe*, 26–56.

Kuribayashi, Yoshimitsu, 1991, *Okura-sho shuzei-kyoku* (MOF Tax Bureau, Ministry of Finance), Tokyo.

Kuriyama, Takakazu, 1991, 'Japan's foreign policy: my two-year experience at a crossroads', *Japan Review of International Affairs*, V, 2, 109–33.

Kuroda, Makoto, 1990, *'Nippon no sangyo seisaku'* (Industrial policy of Japan), *Nippon keizai seisaku gakkai nennpo* (The Annual of Japan Economic Policy Association), XXXVIII, 28–37.

Kusano, Atsushi, 1989, *'Taigai seisaku kettei no kikou to katei'* (The organization and process of foreign policy making), Aruga *et al.*, *Koza Kokusai seiji, Nippon no gaiko* (Japanese diplomacy), IV, 53–92.

Lehmann, Jean-Pierre, 1982, 'Mutual images', Tsoukalis and White, *Japanese and Western Europe*, 14–30.

Lehmann, Jean-Pierre, 1984, 'Agenda for action on issues in Euro-Japanese relations', *The World Economy*, VII, 3, 257–76.

Lehmann, Jean-Pierre, 1989, 'Japan and a new world order: implications and an agenda for Europe', *European Affairs*, III, 1, 41–9.

Lehmann, Jean-Pierre, 1993, 'Japan and Europe in global perspective', Story, Jonathan, ed., *The new Europe: politics, government and economy since 1945*, Oxford, 115–39.

Lindbeck, Assar, 1981, 'Industrial policy as an issue in the economic environment', *World Economy*, IV, 4, 391–405.

Lindblom, Charles E., 1965, *Intelligence of democracy: decision making through mutual adjustment*, New York.

The Long-Term Credit Bank of Japan, 1990, *1992 and Euro-Japanese Economic Relations: the international competitiveness of European industries and Euro-Japanese economic friction*, Tokyo.

Lowi, Theodore J., 1972, 'Four systems of policy, politics, and choice', *Public Administration Review*, XXXII, 4, 298–310.

Ludlow, Peter, 1991, 'The European Commission', Keohane, Robert O. and Hoffmann, Stanley, eds, *The new European Community: decisionmaking*

Bibliography 183

and institutional change, Boulder, 85–132.

MGK, 'Scotch Whisky Association', unpublished report, London.

McLaughlin, Andrew M., 1994, 'ACEA and the EU–Japan car dispute', Pedler, R. H. and Van Scendelen, M. P. C. M., eds, Lobbying the European Union: companies, trade associations and issue groups, Aldershot, 149–65.

Maier, Charles S., 1981, ' "Fictious bonds . . . of wealth and law": on the theory and practice of interest representation', Berger, Organizing interests, 27–61.

Mansbach, Richard W. and Vasquez, John A., 1981, In search of theory: a new paradigm for global politics, New York.

March, James G. and Simon, Herbert A., 1958, Organizations, New York.

Mason, Mark, 1994, 'The political economy of Japanese automobile investment in Europe', Mason and Encarnation, Does ownership matter? Oxford, 411–34.

Mastanduno, Michael, Lake, David A. and Ikenberry, G. John, 1989, 'Toward a realist theory of state action', International Studies Quarterly, XXXIII, 4, 457–74.

Maswood, Syed Javed, 1989, Japan and protection: the growth of protectionist sentiment and the Japanese response, London.

Maull, Hans W., 1990, 'The unfinished triangle: European–Japanese relations in the 1980s', Contemporary European Affairs, III, 1/2, 51–71.

Mendl, Wolf, 1984, Western Europe and Japan between the Super Powers, Kent.

Mendl, Wolf, 1986, 'Regional policies in Europe and East Asia', Daniels and Drifte, Europe and Japan, 79–90.

Michalski, Anna and Wallace, Helen, 1992, The European Community: the challenge of enlargement, London.

Micossi, Stefano and Viesti, Gianfranco, 1991, 'Japanese direct manufacturing investment in Europe', Winters, L. Allan and Venables, Anthony, eds, European integration: trade and industry, Cambridge, 200–31.

Mikanagi, Yumiko, 1990, 'Sekai seiji keizai hendo no naka no Nippon' (Japan in a changing World Political Economy: an analytical framework for shifting foreign policies), Kokusai Seiji (International Relations), XCIII, 71–81.

Mills, C. Wright, 1959, The power elite, Oxford.

Ministry of International Trade and Industry (Japan), White Paper on International Trade of Japan, Tokyo, 1981–95.

Misawa, Shigeo, 1977, 'Taigai seisaku to Nippon "zaikai"' (Foreign policy and Japanese 'zaikai'), Hosoya and Watanuki, Taigai seisaku. 179–211.

Miyasato, Seigen, 1989, 'Beikoku no seiji katei' (Policy Process in the United States), NIRA (National Institute for Research Advancement), Nichi-bei-oh no keizai masatsu wo meguru seiji katei (Political process of economic friction between Japan and the United States and Western Europe), Tokyo, 37–61.

Miyasato, Seigen and Usui, Hisakazu, 1992, eds, Shin kokusai seiji keizai chitsujo to Nichi-bei kankei (New international political economic order and Japan–US relations), Tokyo.

Mizuguchi, Kenji, 1992, 'Small retailers disappearing', *Journal of Japanese Trade and Industry*, XI, 3, 34–5.

Moravcsik, Andrew, 1993, 'Introduction: integrating international and domestic theories of international bargaining', Evans, Jacobson and Putnam, *Double-edged diplomacy*, 3–42.

Muramatsu, Michio, 1981, *Sengo Nippon no kanryo-sei* (Japanese bureaucracy of postwar era), Tokyo.

Muramatsu, Michio and Krauss, Ellis S., 1984, 'Bureaucrats and politicians in policy making: the case of Japan', *American Political Science Review*, LXXVIII, 1, 126–46.

Muramatsu, Michio, and Krauss, Ellis S., 1987, 'The Conservative policy line and the development of patterned pluralism', Yamamura and Yasuba, *The political economy of Japan*, vol 1, 516–54.

Muramatsu, Michio and Mabuchi, Masaru, 1994, *'Zeisei kaikaku no seiji'* (Introducing a new tax in Japan), *Leviathan*, Supplementary issue: the decline of dominant parties, 178–99.

Muramatsu, Takeshi and Takubo, Chuei, 1990, *'Taidan: Shazai kancho Gaimu-sho muyo-ron'* (Discussion: Ministry of Apologies – unnecessary MFA), *Shokun*, XXII, 8, 26–39.

Mutou, Hiromichi, 1984, *'Jidosha sangyo'* (Automobile industry), Komiya, Ryutaro, Okuno, Masahiro and Suzumura, Kotaro, eds, *Nippon no sangyo seisaku* (Japanese industrial policy), Tokyo, 277–96.

NHK reporters, 1990, *NHK Special: Nichibei no shototsu* (Japan–US collision), Tokyo.

Nagao, Satoru, 1990, *'Nippon keizai gaiko no henyo: "kokusai seisaku" katei to Nichibei gyuniku orenji kosho'* (The transformation of Japanese economic diplomacy: 'international policy' making and the US–Japan beef and orange trade negotiations), *Kokusai Seiji*, XLIII, 82–97.

Nagao, Satoru, 1992, *'Nichibei kome mondai wo meguru kokusai kosho to kokunai seiji'* (International negotiations and domestic politics in the Japan-US rice issue), Miyasato and Usui, *Shin-kokusai seiji keizai chitsujo*, Tokyo, 211–38.

Nakamura, Takafusa, 1993, *Showa-shi* (The history of Showa), 2 vols, Tokyo.

Nakamura, Tsuneo, 1992, *'Nichio jidosha masatsu ga hi wo fuku hi ha chikai'* (The deteriorating automobile friction between Japan and Europe), *Sekai Shuho* (25 February), 56–60.

Nakano, Minoru, 1986, *'Koudo seicho igo no seisaku katei'* (The policy process after the rapid growth period), Nakano, Minoru, ed., *Nippon-gata seisaku kettei katei no henyo* (The transformation of Japanese decision making), Tokyo, 1–11.

Namiki, Nobuyoshi, 1989, *Tsusan-sho no shuen* (The end of MITI), Tokyo.

National Consumer Council, 1993, *Trade restrictions in the market for cars in the European Community: the impact of the EC–Japan agreement*, London.

Nester, William, 1990, *Japan's growing power over East Asia and the world economy*, Basingstoke.

Nester, William, 1991, *Japanese industrial targeting: the neomercantilist path to economic superpower*, Basingstoke.

Newland, Kathleen, 1990, ed., *The international relations of Japan*, Basingstoke.

Nippon Keizai Shimbun-sha, 1994, ed., *Kanryo* (The bureaucrats). Tokyo.

Nippon yoshu shuzo kumiai (the Association of Wine and Spirits Producers of Japan), *Shuzeiho-tou ni kansuru youbousho* (Request Paper on the Liquor Tax Law and others), (not published) Tokyo, September 1992, 1993.

Nishio, Kanji, 1985, '*Obei-jin ga egaku nihon-zo no okusoko ni arumono*' (What is underneath the image of Japan held by Westerners), *Chuo koron*, C, 2, 116–34.

Nishio, Kanji, 1986, '*Seio no jihei, Nippon no muryoku*' (Western Europe's indifference and Japan's non-influence), *Chuo koron*, CI, 12, 98–111.

Nuttall, Simon J., 1992, *European Political Cooperation*, Oxford.

Nye, Joseph S., Jr, 1993, 'Coping with Japan', *Foreign Policy*, LXXXIX, 96–115.

Obi, Toshio, 1992, *Nichibei kanryo masatsu* (Bureaucrats' friction between Japan and the US), Tokyo.

Ogata, Sadako, 1977, '*Nippon no taigai seisaku kettei katei to zaikai*' (Japan's foreign policy making process and the business circle), Hosoya and Watanuki, *Taigai seisaku*, 213–41.

Okimoto, Daniel I., 1989, *Between MITI and the market: Japanese industrial policy for high technology*, Stanford.

Okura-sho, 1989, *Kaisei zeiho no subete* (Comprehension of the reformed tax laws), Tokyo.

Okura-sho, 1994, *Kaisei zeiho no subete* (Comprehension of the reformed tax laws), Tokyo.

Omori, Wataru, 1985, '*Nippon kanryosei no jian kettei tetsuzuki*' (The policy formulation procedures in Japan's bureaucracy), *Nennpo Seijigaku, Gendai nihon no seiji tetsuzuki*, 87–116.

Osabe, Shigeyasu, 1987, '*Amerika no kage to shite no Nichio masatsu* (Euro-Japanese conflict in the shadow of the United States)', *Chuo koron*, CII, 1, 120–7.

Otake, Hideo, 1979, *Gendai Nippon no seiji kenryoku keizai kenryoku* (The political power and economic power in contemporary Japan), Tokyo.

Otake, Hideo, 1990, *Seisaku katei* (Policy process), Tokyo.

Oyane, Satoshi, 1992, '"MFA regime" *teppai no seisaku katei*' (Policy process of abolition of MFA regime), Miyasato and Usui, *Shin-kokusai seiji keizai chitsujo*, 239–67.

Panitch, Leo, 1979, 'The development of corporatism in liberal democracies', Schmitter, Philippe C. and Lehmbruch, Gerhard, eds, *Trends toward corporatist intermediation*, London, 119–46.

Pempel, T. J., 1978, 'Japanese foreign economic policy: the domestic bases for international behavior', Katzenstein, *Between power and plenty*, 139–90.

Pempel, T. J., 1998, 'Structural *gaiatsu*: international finance and political change in Japan', Unpublished paper prepared for the annual meeting of the American Political Science Association, Boston, 2–6 September.

Pempel, T. J. and Tsunekawa, Keiichi, 1979, 'Corporatism without Labor? The Japanese anomaly', Schmitter and Lehmbruch, *Trends towards corporatist intermediation*, 231–70.

Pizzorno, Alessandro, 1981, 'Interests and parties in pluralism', Berger, *Organizing interests*, 247–84.

Powell, Robert, 1994, 'Anarchy in international relations theory: the neorealist-neoliberal debate', *International Organization*, XLVIII, 2, 313–44.

Prestowitz, Clyde V., 1988, *Trading places: how we allowed Japan to take the lead*, New York.

Putnam, Robert D., 1988, 'Diplomacy and domestic politics: the logic of two-level games', *International Organization*, XLII, 3, 427–60.

Putnam, Robert D. and Bayne, Nicholas, 1987, *Hanging together: cooperation and conflict in the seven-power summits*, revised edn, London.

Ramseyer, J. Mark and Rosenbluth, Frances McCall, 1993, *Japan's political marketplace*, Cambridge, MA.

Regelsberger, Elfriede, 1993, 'European Political Cooperation', Story, *The new Europe*, 270–91.

Risse-Kappen, Thomas, 1995a, ed., *Bringing transnational relations back in: Non-state actors, domestic structures and international institutions*, Cambridge.

Risse-Kappen, Thomas, 1995b, 'Bringing transnational relations back in: Introduction', *Bringing transnational relations back in*, 3–33.

Risse-Kappen, Thomas, 1995c, 'Structures of governance and transnational relations: what have we learned?', *Bringing transnational relations back in*, 280–313.

Rix, Alan, 1988, 'Bureaucracy and political change in Japan', Stockwin, J. A. A. et al., *Dynamic and immobilist politics in Japan*, 54–76.

Rosecrance, Richard and Taw, Jennifer, 1990, 'Japan and the theory of international leadership', *World Politics*, XLII, 184–209.

Rosenau, James N., 1966, 'Pre-theories and theories of foreign policy', R. Barry Farrell, ed., *Approaches to comparative and international politics*. 27–92, reprinted in Rosenau, *The scientific study of foreign policy*, New York, 1971, 95–149.

Rosenau, James N., 1969, ed., *Linkage politics: essays on the convergence of national and international systems*, New York.

Rosenau, James N., 1971, *The scientific study of foreign policy*, New York, 1971.

Rothacher, Albrecht, 1983, *Economic diplomacy between the European Community and Japan, 1959–1981*, Aldershot.

Rothacher, Albrecht, 1993, *The Japanese power elite*, Basingstoke.

Saito, Shiro, 1990, *Japan at the summit: its role in the Western Alliance and Asian Pacific co-operation*, London.

Saji, Keizo, 1994, 'The status of Japan's liquor industry', *Japan*, XXI, 72–3.

Sakaiya, Taichi, 1994, '*Sengo Nippon no mittsu no shinwa*' (The three myths of postwar Japan), *Bungei shunju*, LXXII, 2, 155–8.

Samuels, Richard J., 1987, *The business of the Japanese state: energy markets in comparative and historical perspective*, Ithaca.

Sargent, Jane A., 1985, 'Corporatism and the European Community', Grant, Wyn, ed., *The political economy of corporatism*, Basingstoke, 229–53.

Sato, Hideo, 1989, '*Seisaku kettei-ron*' (Policymaking), Aruga *et al.*, *Koza Kokusai seiji, Gaiko seisaku* (Foreign policy), II, 9–63.

Sato, Hideo, 1991, *Nichi-bei keizai masatsu, 1945–1990*, Tokyo.

Sato, Seizaburo and Matsuzaki, Tetsuhisa, 1986, *Jiminto seiken* (LDP government), Tokyo.

Sato, Seizaburo and Taylor, Trevor, 1993, eds, *Security challenges for Japan and Europe in a post-cold war world*, Prospects for global order, vol 2, London.

Scalapino, Robert A., 1977, ed., *The foreign policy of modern Japan*, London.

Schmitter, Philippe C., 1979a, 'Still the century of corporatism?', Schmitter, Philippe C. and Lehmbruch, Gerhard, eds, *Trends toward corporatist intermediation*, London, 7–52.

Schmitter, Philippe C., 1979b, 'Modes of interest intermediation and models of societal change in Western Europe', Schmitter and Lehmbruch, eds, *Trends toward corporatist intermediation*, 63–94.

Schoppa, Leonard J., 1993, 'Two-level games and bargaining outcomes: why *gaiatsu* succeeds in Japan in some cases but not others', *International Organization*, XLVII, 3, 353–86.

Shigehara, Kumiharu, 1991, 'External dimension of Europe 1992: its effects on the relationship between Europe, the United States and Japan', *BOJ Monetary and Economic Studies*, IX, 1, 87–102.

Shindo, Eiichi, 1973, '*Kanryo seiji moderu*' (A critique of bureaucratic politics model), *Kokusai Seiji*, L, 46–64.

Shindo, Muneyuki, 1992, *Gyosei shido: kancho to gyokai no aida* (Administrative guidance: an interval between bureaucracy and private sectors), Tokyo.

Simon, Herbert A., 1976, *Administrative behavior: a study of decision-making processes in administrative organization*, 3rd edn, New York.

Singer, J. David, 'The level-of-analysis problem in international relations', *World Politics*, XIV, 1 (1961), 77–92.

Smith, Alastair and Venables, Anthony, 1991, 'Counting the cost of voluntary export restraints in the European car market', Helpman, Elhanan and Razin, Assaf, eds, *International trade and trade policy*, Cambridge, MA, 187–220.

Smith, Michael, 1992, 'The United States and 1992: responses to a changing European Community', Redmond, John, ed., *The external relations of* the European Community: the international response to 1992, Basing-stoke, 31–54.

Smith, Steve, 1980, 'Allison and the Cuban missile crisis: a review of the bureaucratic politics model of foreign policy decision-making', *Millennium: Journal of International Studies*, IX, 1, 21–40.

Smith, Steve, 1989, 'Perspectives on the foreign policy system: bureaucratic politics approaches', Clarke, Michael and White, Brian, eds, *Understanding foreign policy: the foreign policy system approach*, Aldershot, 109–34.

Snyder, Glenn and Diesing, Paul, 1977, *Conflict among nations: bargaining, decision making, and system structure in international crises*, Princeton.

Snyder, Richard, Bruck, H. W. and Sapin, Barton, 1962, *Foreign policy decision-making: an approach to the study of international politics*, New York.

Sone, Yasunori, 1986, '*Nippon no seisaku keisei-ron no henka*' (The change in the debate on Japanese policy making), Nakano, *Nippon-gata seisaku kettei no henyo*, 301–19.

Spencer, Edson W., 1990, 'Japan as competitor', *Foreign Policy*, LXXVIII, 153–71.

Steinbruner, John, 1974, *The cybernetic theory of decision*, Princeton.

Steiner, Miriam, 1977, 'The elusive essence of decision: a critical comparison of Allison's and Snyder's decision-making approaches', *International Studies Quarterly*, XXI, 2, 389–422.

Steinert, Marlis G., 1985, 'Japan and the European Community: an uneasy relationship', Ozaki, Robert S. and Arnold, Walter, eds, *Japan's foreign relations: a global search for economic security*, Essex, 33–46.

Stockwin, J. A. A., 1988, 'Dynamic and immobilist aspects of Japanese politics', Stockwin *et al.*, *Dynamic and immobilist politics in Japan*, Basingstoke, 1–21.

Stopford, John and Strange, Susan, 1991, *Rival states, rival firms: competition for world market shares*, Cambridge.

Story, Jonathan, 1994, 'Comment', Mason and Encarnation, *Does ownership matter?*, 435–9.

Strange, Roger, 1993, *Japanese manufacturing investment in Europe: its impact on the UK economy*, London.

Strange, Susan, 1995, 'European business in Japan: A policy crossroad?', *Journal of Common Market Studies*, XXXIII, 1, 1–25.

Strange, Susan, 1996, *The retreat of nation state*, Cambridge.

Sullivan, Michael P., 1989, 'Transnationalism, power politics, and the realities of the present system', Williams, Marc, ed., *International relations in the twentieth century: a reader*, Basingstoke, 255–74.

Suzuki, Yukio, 1994, '*Hosokawa-shiki "Okura-Tsusan izon taisei" no kozai*' (The merits and disadvantages of Hosokawa cabinet's dependence on Ministries of Finance and International Trade and Industry), *Chuo koron*, CIX, 3, 92–103.

Takayanagi, Akio, 1993, '*Zasetsu no kiseki*' (The orbit of defeat), *Nikkei*

Business, 13 September, 81–4.

Takayanagi, Sakio, 1971, '*Kokusai seiji to kokunai seiji no renkei model*' (Toward the formation of national-international linkage model: about J. N. Rosenau and W. F. Hanrieder), *Kokusai Seiji*, XLVI, 112–31.

Tanaka, Akihiko, 1994, '*Sekai no naka no Nippon-Seio kankei*' (Japan–European relations in the world context), *Kokusai mondai* (International Affairs), CDIX, 39–45.

Tanaka, Naoki, 1989, *Nichibei keizai masatsu*, Tokyo.

Tanaka, Sokou, 1991, *EC togo no sintenkai to Ohshu saihensei* (The new development of the EC and the restructuring of Europe), Tokyo.

Tanaka, Toshiro, 1995, 'EPC in World Society: the picture from Japan', *Hogaku kenkyu*, LXVIII, 2, 428–48.

Tani, Satomi, 1990, 'Incrementalism', Shiratori, Rei, ed., *Seisaku kettei no riron* (Theories of policy making), Tokyo, 38–64.

Thomsen, Stephen and Nicolaides, Phedon, 1991, *The evolution of Japanese direct investment in Europe: death of a transistor salesman*, London.

Togo, Fumihiko, Amaya, Naohiro and Sato, Seizaburo, 1983, '*Fushicho Amerika to Nippon no sentaku*' (Alternatives of the US and Japan), *Chuo koron*, XCVIII, 10, 84–97.

Togo, Shigehiko, 1995, '*Nichibei jidosha sensou boppatsu su*' (The US–Japan automobile war broke), *Bungei shunju*, LXXIII, 7, 292–9.

Tokito, Hideto, 1985, '*Seisaku keisei-ron no yuyo-sei to genkai*' (The merits and limits of decision making theories), *Seiji Keizai Shigaku* (The Politico-Economic History), CCXXIII, CCXXV, CCXXVI, 1–27, 32–47, 72–91.

Tsebelis, George, 1990, *Nested games: rational choice in comparative politics*, Berkeley.

Tsoukalis, Loukas, 1991, *The new European economy: the politics and economics of integration*, Oxford.

Tsoukalis, Loukas and White, Maureen, 1982, eds, *Japan and Western Europe: conflict and cooperation*, London.

Tsuji, Kiyoaki, 1958, '*Kanryo kikou no onzon to kyoka*', Oka, Yoshitake, ed., *Gendai Nippon no seiji katei* (Political process of contemporary Japan), Tokyo, 109–25.

Tsuji, Kiyoaki, 1969, *Shimpan, Nippon kanyosei no kenkyu* (Studies of Japanese bureaucracy – New Edition), Tokyo.

Tsujinaka, Yutaka, 1986a, '*Gendai Nippon seiji no koporatizumu-ka*' (Corporatist change in contemporary Japanese politics), Uchida, Mitsuru, ed., *Koza Seijigaku: seiji katei* (Political Science: political process), vol 3, Tokyo, 223–62.

Tsujinaka, Yutaka, 1986b, '*Roudou dantai – kyuchi ni tatsu roudou no seisaku kettei*' (Labour group – Labour's policy making in trouble), Nakano, *Nippon-gata seisaku kettei*, 267–300.

Tsujinaka, Yutaka, 1988, *Rieki Shudan* (Interest groups), Tokyo.

Tsukada, Norifumi, 1992, '*Kiseigai nerai de genchi seisan ni sattou*', *Shukan Toyo Keizai*, (11 January), 68–73.

Tsukui, Shigemitsu, 1993, *Commenter GATT*, Tokyo.

Tsusho sangyo-sho (MITI), *Tsusho hakusho* (White Paper on International Trade of Japan), Tokyo, 1981–1996.

Tsusho sangyo-sho and Tsusho seisaku kyoku (Bureau of Trade Policy and Ministry of International Trade and Industry), 1992, ed., *Fukosei boueki houkokusho: GATT to shuyo-koku no bouiki seisaku – Sangyo kouzou shingikai repoto* (Report on unfair trade: trade policy of GATT and major economies – report by Industrial Structure Deliberation Committee), Tokyo.

Turner, Charlie G., 1991, *Japan's dynamic efficiency in the global market: trade, investment, and economic growth*, Westport, CT.

United Nations, *United Nations Statistical Yearbook*, New York, 1997.

Van Agt, Andreas, 1993, 'Europe–Japan: conflict or cooperation?', Andersson, Thomas, ed., *Japan: a European perspective*, Basingstoke, 3–10.

Van Wolferen, Karel, 1989, *The enigma of Japanese power: people and politics in a stateless nation*, London.

Van Wolferen, Karel, 1991, 'No brakes, no compass', *The National Interest*, XXV, 26–35.

Vogel, Ezra F., 1992, 'Japanese–American relations after the Cold War', *Daedalus*, CXXI, 4, 35–60.

Wallace, Helen, 1990, 'Making multilateral negotiations work', Wallace, William, ed., *The dynamics of European integration*, London, 213–28.

Wallace, Helen, 1996, 'The institutions of the EU: experience and experiments', Wallace, Helen and Wallace, William, eds, *Policy-making in the European Union*, Oxford, 37–68.

Wallace, William, 1978, 'Old states and new circumstances: the international predicament of Britain, France and Germany', Wallace, W. and Paterson, W. E., eds, *Foreign policy making in Western Europe: a comparative approach*, Farnborough.

Waltz, Kenneth N., 1959, *Man, the state, and war: a theoretical analysis*, New York.

Watanabe, Osamu, 1994, *Seiji kaikaku to kempo kaisei* (Political reform and constitutional revision), Tokyo.

Wilkinson, Endymion, 1980, *Gokai: Europe vs. Japan* (Misunderstanding), Japanese edn, Tokyo.

Wilks, Stephen, 1994, *The revival of Japanese competition policy and its importance for EU–Japan relations*, London.

Williamson, Peter J., 1985, *Varieties of corporatism: a conceptual discussion*, Cambridge.

Womack, James P., Jones, Daniel T. and Roos, Daniel, 1990, *The machine that changed the world*, New York.

Yabunaka, Mitoji, 1991, *Taibei keizai kosho: masatsu no jitsuzo* (In search of new Japan–US economic relations: views from the negotiation table),

Tokyo.

Yamaguchi, Jiro, 1987, *Okura kanryo shihai no shuen* (The end of the dominance of the MOF bureaucrats), Tokyo.

Yamaguchi, Jiro, 1989, *Ittou shihai taisei no houkai* (The collapse of the one party control system), Tokyo.

Yamaguchi, Jiro, 1993, '*Seiji to gyosei: zeisei seisaku ni okeru sogo shinto wo megutte*' (Politics and administration: interpenetration in the fiscal policy making', *Shiso*, DCCCXXVI, 68–89.

Yamaguchi, S., 1984, '*Neo-corporatism to seisaku keisei*' (Neo-corporatism as a pattern of policy formation: a comparative analysis), *Nennpo Seijigaku; Seisaku kagaku to seijigaku* (Problems of policy science), 157–81.

Yamakage, Susumu, 1989, '*Sogo izon-ron*' (Interdependence theories), Aruga *et al.*, *Koza Kokusai seiji, Kokusai seiji no riron* (Theories of International Relations), I, 209–35.

Yamamoto, Takehiko, 1989, '*Keizai gaiko*' (Economic diplomacy), Aruga *et al.*, *Koza Kokusai seiji*, IV, *Nippon no gaiko* (Japan's diplomacy), 155–82.

Yamamoto, Yoshinobu, 1990, '*Seisaku kettei-ron no keifu*' (Genealogy of decision making theories), Shiratori, *Seisaku kettei no riron*, 1–36.

Yamamura, Kozo and Yasuba, Yashukichi, 1987, eds, *The political economy of Japan*, vol 1, The domestic transformation, Stanford.

Yanaga, Chitoshi, 1968, *Big business in Japanese politics*, New Haven.

Yokoyama, Sanshiro, 1993, '*EC no Nippon tsuigeki ga hajimatta*' (EC has begun to catch up with Japan), *Chuo-koron*, CVIII, 7, 44–55.

Yoshida, Nobuyoshi, 1990, *EC Jidosha daisensou* (Automobile War in the EC), Tokyo.

Yoshitomi, Masaru, 1991, ed., *Japanese direct investment in Europe: motives, impact and policy implications*, Aldershot.

Zaimis, Nicholas and Chance, Clifford, 1992, *EC rules of origin*, London.

Zeigler, Harmon, 1988, *Pluralism, corporatism and Confucianism: political association and conflict regulations in the United States, Europe, and Taiwan*, Philadelphia.

Zhao, Quansheng, 1993, *Japanese policymaking – the politics behind politics: informal mechanisms and the making of China policy*, Oxford.

Zimmerman, William, 1973, 'Issue area and foreign-policy process: a research note in search of a general theory', *American Political Science Review*, LXVII, 4, 1204–12.

Zürn, Michael, 1993, 'Bringing the second image (back) in: about the domestic sources of regime formation', Rittberger, Volder, ed., *Regime theory and international relations*, Oxford, 282–311.

Transcripts

Kunihiro, Michihiko, Deputy Vice Minister of the Ministry of Foreign Affairs, Statement given at the Royal Institute of International Affairs, 'The external implications of the Single European Market: A view from Japan', 11 October 1988, London.

Transcript of press conference given by the prime minister Mrs Thatcher, in Tokyo, after the Summit conference, on Monday, 6 May 1986.

Personal interviews

Iwamoto, Toshio, Manager, Europe Division (Automobile), Honda Motor Co. Ltd, Tokyo, 20 June 1995.

Johnson, Michael, former Head of the General International Trade Policy Branch, Department of Trade and Industry, London, 5 January 1996.

Kumada, Kazumitsu, Manager, Purchase Division, Toyota, Tokyo, 19 August 1994.

Menezes, Antonio, The Head of Press and Information Service of the European Delegation, Tokyo, 26 June 1992.

Morgan, Alastair, First Secretary (Economic), British Embassy, Tokyo, 6, 12 September 1994, and 13 June 1995.

Nuttall, Simon, a former official in the Directorate General I, the European Commission, 16 October 1995.

Stacey, Stephen and Williams, Ian, MGK, London, 10 October 1994.

Sumiyoshi, Isao, Executive Director, *Nippon yoshu yunyu kyokai* (Japan Wines and Spirits Importers Association), Tokyo, 7 September 1994.

Takayanagi, Akio, Director, *Nippon yoshu shuzo kumiai*, Tokyo, 13 September 1994.

Takiguchi, Haruo, General Manager, Europe Division (Automobile), Honda Motor Co. Ltd, Tokyo, 20 June 1995.

Uchida, Sadakichi, Director, *Nippon shuzo kumiai chuo-kai*, Tokyo, 8 September 1994.

Wilkinson, Peter, Scotch Whisky Association, Edinburgh, 2 October 1994.

Personal interview with an official who was in the British Embassy in Tokyo in the late 1980s, 6 December 1995, London.

Personal interview with an official of *joryushu kumiai*, 20 August 1994, Tokyo.

Personal interview with an official of the Ministry of Foreign Affairs, 29 August 1995, Jerusalem.

Personal interview with an official of the Ministry of Foreign Affairs, 12 October 1995.

Personal interview with an official of the Ministry of International Trade and Industry, 14 June 1993, Cambridge.

Personal interview with an official in the Tariff Bureau of the Ministry of Finance, 9 September 1994, Tokyo.

Correspondence with T. Jackson, Director of Scotch Whisky Association, 28 October 1994, Edinburgh.

Index